FUGITIVE ESSAYS

BY

JOSIAH ROYCE

Josiah Royce

FUGITIVE ESSAYS
BY JOSIAH ROYCE

WITH AN INTRODUCTION BY

DR. J. LOEWENBERG

Essay Index Reprint Series

BOOKS FOR LIBRARIES PRESS, INC.
FREEPORT, NEW YORK

First Published 1920
Reprinted 1968

46,296

LIBRARY OF CONGRESS CATALOG NUMBER:
68-16974

CONTENTS

EDITOR'S INTRODUCTION

THE essays which comprise the present volume are the occasional and, with the exception of the last three, the early fruits of Professor Royce's philosophic genius. The title "Fugitive Essays" was chosen not to emphasize the editor's judgment of them. However excellent in themselves, in the total body of Professor Royce's works these early achievements of his must needs occupy a subordinate place. This is said not to detract from their intrinsic and enduring worth but rather to testify to the greatness of their author. For such was his philosophic fecundity that products of a high order must, when one considers the wealth of his other contributions, be characterized as fugitive. There is also a more obvious reason for so designating them. They are fugitive in a literal sense. Most of them are now virtually inaccessible, buried as they are in the pages of local periodicals which have long since ceased to appear. Some were never published and others found their way to journals more or less ephemeral. Published here for the first time are the following: "The Practical Significance of Pessimism" (1879), "Tests of Right and Wrong" (1880), "On Purpose in Thought" (1880), and "Natural Rights and Spinoza's Essay on Liberty" (1880). The rest of the essays appeared in the following publications: "Schiller's Ethical Studies" in *The Journal of Speculative Philosophy* (1878); "Shelley and the Revolution," "George Eliot as a Religious Teacher," "The Decay of Earnestness," "Doubting and Working," "How Beliefs are Made" in *The Californian* (1880–1882); "The Nature of Voluntary Progress," "Pessimism and Modern Thought" in *The Berkeley*

Quarterly (1880–1881); "A Neglected Study" in *The Harvard Monthly* (1890); "The Problem of Paracelsus" in the publications of the Boston Browning Society (1893); and "Pope Leo's Philosophical Movement and its Relation to Modern Thought" in *The Boston Evening Transcript* (July 29, 1903).

To appreciate the biographical value of the early essays it must be borne in mind that an account of Professor Royce's life will probably never be written. Mrs. Royce has declared that it was her husband's wish that his personal history should not be published. He appeared to have had no taste for those biographies in which private fortunes and external circumstances form the chief theme. Did he not, as a young author, say of the poet Shelley that "the reality and the coloring of . . . [his] character we must seek in his works. And in his works, too, we must find the inspiring ideas concerning which he was permitted to speak, and speak grandly to his fellowmen"? Royce's distaste for conventional biographies was not strange. It had its roots in his philosophical conception of the self. The life of a man was for him the life not of his external fortune but of his moral achievement. The self he identified, for reasons at once practical and metaphysical, with loyal endeavor and choice and with active purposes and ideals. Thus man is reflected in his works. It behooves us, therefore, to seek Josiah Royce's own personality in his works, to an understanding of which his early essays may contribute not a little. For in them are mirrored his interests and his problems, his temperament and his character. The careful reader of the "Fugitive Essays" will soon recognize in the young author Royce's distinctive personality. His was a personality that exhibited continual growth and development without radical change or deviation from certain well-marked traits. The qualities which we have come to associate with the mature thinker—universality of mind, imaginative insight, wide range of interests, skill in subtle analysis, independence and originality of thought — predominate in these early essays. Here, too, are present the dignity, the earnestness, the sincerity, the humility, the reverence, so characteristic of all his thinking and writing. And here also his perennial sense of humor finds expression. It is these qualities which give to Royce's style unity and distinction. This style is indeed far from being uniform. And concerning its literary excellence there may be differences of opinion. In moral beauty, however, his style is everywhere uniform because he was always himself. He simply could not be trivial. On whatever topic he chose to write — on logic or history, on metaphysics or psychology, on religion or science — he at once raised his subject to a moral height, to an intellectual eminence. The only word perhaps which is adequate to describe his style is the word *nobility*. Of this style the "Fugitive Essays" are the early and the eloquent witnesses.

Not his printed works alone but his unpublished writings as well — of which a bibliography will be found in *The Philosophical Review* for September, 1917 — manifest the same qualities of his noble style. We should like particularly to direct attention to a Diary which Royce kept during the years 1879 and 1880, when most of the "Fugitive Essays" were written or conceived. It is a valuable document, revealing some characteristic traits of his personality, not the least important being an absence of introspective analysis. For the most part the Diary is a record of intellectual problems, an inner conversation, as it were, carried on with sincere passion, about ideas and about books and about plans for literary and philosophic ventures. There is among other meditations one which was intended as a sort of Preface to a contemplated work on metaphysics. It is the only one that may perhaps be called "subjective." It is dated February 12, 1879, and is here inserted, with the kind permission of Mrs. Royce, to disclose the temperament and the character of the author of the "Fugitive Essays." And the mood and the spirit which it reflects, are they not equally characteristic of the mature Royce?

"MEDITATION BEFORE THE GATE"

I am a Californian, and day after day, by the order of the World Spirit (whose commands we all do ever obey, whether we will it or no), I am accustomed to be found at my tasks in a certain place that looks down upon the Bay of San Francisco and over the same out into the water of the Western Ocean. The place is not without beauty, and the prospect is far-reaching. Here as I do my work I often find time for contemplation. . . .

That one realizes the greatness of the world better when he rises a little above the level of the lowlands, and looks upon the large landscape beneath, this we all know; and all of us, too, must have wondered that a few feet of elevation should tend so greatly to change our feeling toward the universe. Moreover the place of which I speak is such as to make one regret when he considers its loveliness that there are not far better eyes beholding it than his own. For could a truly noble soul be nourished by the continual sight of the nature that is here, such a soul would be not a little enviable. Yet for most of us Nature is but a poor teacher.

Still even to me, she teaches something. The high dark hills on the western shore of the Bay, the water at their feet, the Golden Gate that breaks through them and opens up to one the view of the sea beyond, the smoke-obscured city at the south of the Gate, and the barren ranges yet farther to the left, these are the permanent background whereon many passing shapes of light and shadow, of cloud and storm, of mist and of sunset glow are projected as I watch all from my station on the hillside. The seasons go by quietly, and without many great changes. The darkest days of what we here call winter seem always to leave not wholly without brightness one part of the sky, that just above the Gate. When the rain storms are broken by the fresh breezes from the far-off northern Sierras, one sees the departing clouds gather in threatening masses about the hilltops, while the Bay spreads out at one's feet, calm and restful after its little hour of tempest. When the time of great rains gives place to the showers of early spring one scarcely knows which to delight in the more, whether in the fair green fields, that slope down gently to the water, or in the sky of the west, continually filled with fantastic shapes of light and cloud — nor does even our long dry summer, with its parched meadows and its daily sea winds leave this spot without beauty. The ocean and the Bay are yet there; the high hills beyond change not at all for any season; but are ever rugged and cold and stern; and the long lines of fog, borne in through the Gate or through the depressions of the range, stretch out over many miles of country like columns of an invading host, now shining in innocent whiteness as if their mission were but one of love, now becoming dark and dreadful, as when they smother the sun at evening. So, while the year goes by, one is never without the companionship of Nature. And there are heroic deeds done in cloud-land, if one will but look forth and see them.

But I have here . . . to speak not so much of Nature as of Life. And I shall undertake to deal with a few problems such as are often thought to be metaphysical (whereby one means that they are worthless), and are also often quite rightly called philosophical (whereby one means that it were the part of wisdom to solve them if we could). With these problems I shall seek to busy myself earnestly, because that is each one's duty; independently, because I am a Californian, as little bound to follow mere tradition as I am liable to find an audience by preaching in this wilderness; reverently, because I am thinking and writing face to face with a mighty and lovely Nature, by the side of whose greatness I am but as a worm.

This meditation supplies a background not unsuited for the early "Fugitive Essays." It fixes our attention upon Royce the Californian. It reminds us of his early environment. If one were to write the "forbidden" biography of Josiah Royce, a narrative of his California period would form one of its most interesting chapters. For it was in California that he was born, and there he was bred. Surrounded by pioneers and explorers he imbibed their spirit and became himself a pioneer and explorer in regions deeper and more fascinating than those of gold mines. In philosophy Royce was essentially self-taught. There were no regular and systematic courses laid out for him at the University of California. His autobiographical sketch, the only one we have of him, now printed in *The Hope of the Great Community*, tells us how he was forced to find his own way through the mazes of philosophic doctrine and theory. This independence which the meditation from his Diary singles out as a California trait informs the "Fugitive Essays." They are the fruits of lonely and ardent exploration; they are the independent labors of a self-conscious Californian.

From the year 1878 to 1882, when these California essays were written, Royce taught English at the university of his native state. His pedagogical activities, it would seem, coincided thus very little with his speculative problems. Yet it was not his nature to keep the two long asunder. At the outset of his professional career his academic interests fused as they later always did with his technical speculations. He could not regard the teaching of English composition and literature as something divorced from the deepest and gravest issues of life and of thought. The subject of English appeared to him as one possessing definiteness and profundity — both of which it frequently lacks — for which he sought a solid foundation. This he found in the study of logic. And with the inventiveness and the independence so characteristic of him he wrote and published his *Primer of Logical Analysis for the Use of Composition Students* (San Francisco, 1881), employing it as text in his classes, we know not with what success. Logical thinking, *i. e.*, orderly thinking, in a severe and rigid sense, seemed to him the most natural basis for the writing of English. Thus fundamental was his mode of dealing with English composition. No less fundamental was his attitude towards English literature. It was neither pedantic nor impressionistic. His ideas on Literary Criticism, voiced casually in "A Neglected Study," the essay of a later period included in the present volume, are already embodied in his early literary studies. In the paper in question he deprecates the view of literature as the exclusive domain of "scholarly" philological "research." But for the "whimsical" critic, the "purely literary man," with his "light" and "prophetic" and "phosphorescent literary glowing" Royce has nothing but scorn. "Is life so very light an affair?" he asks. His California essays on literature exemplify a different type of Literary Criticism. They are profoundly philosophical. They are expressions of that reflective insight which he later came to associate with the activity of "interpretation," a process of knowledge differing alike from "perception" and "conception," to which we shall presently recur. But aside from this, from his earliest utterances Royce appears as the champion of the dignity of poetry and as the discerner of its deeper worth. Poetry for him is an articulate response to the problems of passion and of will. In an unfinished revision of "The Decay of Earnestness" we find this significant passage: "Literature often bears to philosophy in general, and yet oftener to Ethical Philosophy, the relation of fountain to stream.

What the poet suggests about the meaning and the obscurity of life, the ethical philosopher makes the subject of a formal study. The poet sees a tragedy of destiny; and the philosopher makes of it a problem in dialectics, where words war instead of souls. Certainly the stream in this case rises no higher than the source. No ethical system, unless it be the work of a philosopher who is himself a poet, will be found to have in it more insight into life than poetry has already suggested." To this view of poetry Royce was always faithful. Literary values could not for him be severed from ethical significance. His essays on literature are concerned with nothing less than with an evaluation of the "tragedies of destiny" as seen and felt by the poets. And this interest in the wills and the passions of men — and of what else does genuine poetry consist? — is thoroughly consonant with the spirit of his philosophy. In truth, it is one of the deepest and most abiding motives of his "Voluntarism."

Truly remarkable is the distinctness with which the later personality of Josiah Royce speaks to us through his early casual essays. And more remarkable still is the explicitness with which some of his mature and systematic views are there anticipated. The substance of his later teaching seems to have become crystallized at a comparatively early stage of his development. It is amazing how clearly certain ideas which are characteristic of all his later writings are already formulated in the "Fugitive Essays." The outline-form of his technical system may be traced back to his earliest utterances. In what follows the attempt is made to suggest the intimate relation of his early views to his later works. A systematic and minute exposition of Royce's entire philosophy would indeed be required to do this adequately. But only a summary statement can here be essayed.

Speaking most generally, his system as embodied in *The World and the Individual* and in *The Problem of Christianity* — his *magna opera* — is a theme with variations. The theme is a theory of knowledge and of reality which in its essence is activistic and social. The definition of an idea as a "plan of action" is, in his earlier work, the basis of both his epistemology and his metaphysics. To know is not to copy a so-called external reality. Knowledge is a mode of action; it is an active search for the fulfillment of purpose. Without purpose as basis, the meaning of knowledge, he contends, can be made articulate only with the aid of unwarranted assumptions and glaring contradictions. The alternative to a copy-theory is, for Royce, an activistic doctrine of knowledge. Reality is indeed external to the knower's *momentary* purpose. Externality, however, is not alien to purpose. It is embedded in its very nature. The purpose which seeks fulfillment seeks what *as yet* is other than or external to itself. The relation between knowledge and its object is for Royce, in *The World and the Individual*, a relation between purpose and fulfillment. This results in a definition of reality which is both objective and spiritual. For the real world is simply the absolute and complete embodiment of purpose. And the proof that an "infinite multitude" results from the expression of a "single purpose," contained in the "Supplementary Essay" to *The World and the Individual*, enables Royce to define the real universe as both single and plural. The very unity of the universe, as the expression of a single purpose, demands its multiplicity and complexity. Royce's Absolute is preëminently a *social* concept. It is this social character of Royce's Absolute—often overlooked—which distinguishes it from the simple and undifferentiated and unutterable One of the mystic. The Absolute is defined by Royce as "in its form inclusive of an infinity of various, but interwoven and so of intercommunicating Selves."[1] "Simple unity," he emphatically declares, "is a mere impossibility."[2] Unity and multiplicity are for him interdependent concepts. The Absolute has the unity of a social organism; it is the complete integration of a complexity and variety of purposes, wills, and ideals. It is but natural that in his later formulation the concept *Universal Community* tends to replace the term Absolute. The union of One and Many — the heart of Royce's metaphysics — is denoted more explicitly by the term "Community" than by the term "Absolute." A community, Royce states, is "both one and many; and unless it is both one and many, it is no community at all."[3] The community, as defined in *The Problem of Christianity*, is the one individual life of its many individual members precisely in the sense in which the Absolute in *The World and the Individual* is interpreted as an "Individual Whole of Individual Elements."[4]

A detailed study of both these major works would unquestionably reveal differences as well as similarities. But not to regard the "Absolute" of *The World and the Individual* as identical with the "Universal Community" of *The Problem of Christianity*, and *vice versa*, is seriously to misunderstand the main thesis of both works. "This essentially social universe," says Royce himself, "this Community . . . we have now declared to be real, and to

[1] *The World and the Individual*, second series, p. 298.
[2] *Ibid.*, p. 331.
[3] *The Problem of Christianity*, vol. ii, p. 17.
[4] *The World and the Individual*, first series, p. 538.

be, in fact, the sole and supreme reality, . . . the Absolute." [1] Again: "The universe, if my thesis is right, is a realm which is through and through dominated by social categories. . . . The system of metaphysics which is needed to define the constitution of this world . . . must be the generalized theory of an ideal society. *Not the Self, not the Logos, not the One, and not the Many, but the Community will be the ruling category of such a philosophy.*" [2] "The universe is a community of interpretation whose life comprises and unifies all the social varieties and all the social communities . . . . The history of the universe, the whole order of time, is the history and the order and the expression of this Universal Community." [3] That Royce himself viewed his "metaphysics of the community" as no radical departure from his previous doctrine but rather as a novel formulation of it, is borne out by this quotation: ". . . I still hold by all the essential features of . . . [my] former attempts to state the case for idealism. But at present I am dealing with the World of Interpretation, and with the Metaphysics of the Community. This I believe to be simply a new mode of approach to the very problems which I have formerly discussed." [4] But of this important topic we reserve for the future a more elaborate discussion.

The more explicit recognition in his later work of the "social" constitution of reality leads Royce to a theory of knowledge more explicitly "activistic." He calls it by the name "interpretation." And it is of course more than a new name for the former epistemology based upon the definition of an idea as a "plan of action." In essence, however, the epistemology defended in *The*

[1] *The Problem of Christianity*, vol. ii, p. 296.
[2] *Ibid.*, p. 281 (italics mine).
[3] *Ibid.*, p. 273.   [4] *Ibid.*, p. 295.

Problem of Christianity is identical with that formulated in *The World and the Individual*. Just as, in the earlier treatise, an idea seeking embodiment or fulfillment can find it completely but in an Absolute conceived as a *social* being, so, in his later work, the interpretation of a "sign" must generate by virtue of its own nature a *Community of Interpretation*. Details of the doctrine of Interpretation — one of Royce's most original contributions to philosophy — can not be touched upon here. Its activistic and social aspects alone are now pertinent. Interpretation is the expression of a "creative intelligence" — to use a current phrase — and the goal of interpretation is a Universal Community whose reality is presupposed in every interpretative act.[1] Thus, the same theory of knowledge and of reality, activistic and social in its very core, is the outcome of both *The World and the Individual* and *The Problem of Christianity*.

This inadequate sketch of the main theme of Royce's two great works must suffice for an appreciation of his early writings. Central in these writings is the same theory of knowledge and of reality. And central it is not alone in the technical but also in the general essays. The doctrine of the "creative intelligence" now so ardently proclaimed is no unique product of its recent exponents. In the philosophical efforts of the young Royce one will find the essential and the enduring truths of this doctrine, but linked with ideas strangely at variance with those of modern pragmatism. But a few pregnant statements can here be cited. "Thoughts are not dead and finished mind-products," argues the young author in "Shelley and the Revolution," "that you can lay away on a shelf, so as to take them down entire, dry, and sound, when you want to use them. Thoughts are liv-

[1] *The Problem of Christianity*, vol. ii, pp. 253 ff.

ing, and each thought lives in the most literal sense, but a moment. You must create your thought afresh whenever you want it .... The essence of thinking is originality.... Men's affairs, in so far as they are matters of thought at all, are solely what men make them." The same idea is voiced in "How Beliefs are Made." "No knowledge," Royce there contends, "... without hospitality in the minds that receive the knowledge. But as soon as we recognize in mental life this our power to modify our knowledge by means of our activity, just so soon do all the old comparisons of the mind to a wax tablet, to a sheet of paper, or to other like passive subjects of impression lose for us their meaning. ... *All knowing is, in a very deep sense, acting; it is, in fact, reacting and creation.*[1] The most insignificant knowledge is in some sense an original product of the man who knows." "Thoughts are always transformed reality, never mere copies of reality." And in "The Nature of Voluntary Progress" we read: "Beliefs are always the satisfaction of individual wants. No belief can be said to be forced upon anyone in any other sense than that it is accepted because it satisfies a conscious want. ... The adjective 'true' is applied to a belief by the one whose intellectual wants it satisfies, at the time when it satisfies them."

Many more passages might be quoted, from the general essays alone, to show Royce's early "Voluntarism." But it is significant to note how the "activistic" element of knowledge is intimately bound up with the "social." The notion of truth as *individual* satisfaction — the essence of a crude pragmatism — is explicitly rejected by Royce. As he says in "How Beliefs are Made": "... in discussing the nature of knowledge, we are tres-

[1] Italics mine.

passing on the borderland of ethics." Thinking is indeed
"creation," creation for the satisfaction of needs, but
the needs are viewed neither as momentary nor as personal. The satisfaction sought is permanent and socially
significant. "What would be the abiding and satisfactory truth?" — this is the problem with which the
young Royce is concerned in "Doubting and Working."
The aim in seeking for truth, so he there states, is "to
harmonize the conflicting opinions of men, to substitute
for the narrowness and instability of personal views . . .
broadness of view." "You dare not," he exclaims,
"you dare not accept a faith simply for the satisfaction
it gives you. You dare not, I say, because as a thinker
your true aim is not to please yourself, but to work for
the harmonizing views of mankind. . . . You ought to
work not to increase the variety of human opinions, to
render closer the limits of personal experience, but to
extend the field of harmony and to unite men, so that
they may cease their endless warfare and have a common experience . . . . What is acceptable to my intellectual needs . . . [is not] the truth. My needs are
narrow and changing. It is humanity in its highest development to which the truth will be acceptable. I must
give up my desires that the unity of all human spirits
may be sooner attained."

Vague indeed is the language in which a superpersonal
and social standard of truth is here couched. But in the
phrases "a common experience," "humanity in its
highest development," "the unity of all human spirits"
we have in embryo the later social Absolute or the Universal Community. The necessity of a superpersonal
center of reference, essentially social in character, is
emphasized throughout these essays. "No man liveth
to himself" is the constant refrain. Personal satisfac-

tion is nothing, the common social life everything. "The
world is more than the men in it," Royce says in "Shelley and the Revolution." "The total life is something
more than the sum of its parts." And in "The Nature
of Voluntary Progress" the later doctrine of the community is distinctly foreshadowed in this passage: "...A
concert of individual action produces a resultant greater
than the numerical sum of the individual contributions,
or else different in kind from this sum. Thus by discussion and by the aid of tradition, the united effort of men
produces thoughts which no individual thinking, however acute and continued, could ever have evolved. The
resultant of united political activity is again the state,
an institution different in kind from the contributions
brought by any one member of society, whose power is,
therefore, not the mere arithmetical sum of the powers
of its subjects, but an organic product of all of them."
This anticipates with remarkable lucidity the later
teaching that a community is a "human being" on a
higher level.[1] In "Pessimism and Modern Thought" the
theory of the community is again suggested. Thus:
"The one goal is the rendering as full and as definite as
possible all the conscious life that at any one moment
comes within the circle of our influence. Devotion, then,
to universal conscious life, is the goal of conscious life
itself; or *the goal is the self-reference or self-surrender of
each conscious moment to the great whole of life . . . . Separation from other conscious life means failure. Conscious
union with other conscious life means for every conscious
being success.*"[2]   Individual life is evil. Life for Self
must of necessity end in pessimism. And the moral of
pessimism is simply this: "Expect . . . nothing from Self

---

[1] Cf. *The Problem of Christianity*, vol. i, pp. 165 ff.
[2] Italics mine.

or for Self. Labor to cast Self aside, and to live in the universal life . . . . Tell [men] that they can find happiness only when they cease to seek it for themselves. Talk no more of golden ages. Talk of golden deeds."

The significance of these quotations is too obvious to require extended comment. They show so clearly the trend of Royce's early thinking. The theoretical and the practical interests of man are interpreted in terms of principles which indeed only later become definite and articulate. In outline, however, these principles are here already present. Thinking is an activity devoted to universal ends. Life is a task whose meaning consists in loyalty to superpersonal ideals. The goal alike of thought and of conduct is rooted in a world conceived as essentially social. Moral salvation — escape from evil — lies in the direction of conscious devotion to the universal social order. And through such devotion alone does the individual attain dignity and stability. We see thus in these general essays distinct indications of Royce's later systematic ideas.

But the two technical papers included in this volume — "On Purpose in Thought" and "Tests of Right and Wrong" — contain more than a mere indication of Royce's later ideas. In these remarkably finished products of philosophical reasoning the student of Royce will find much more than can here be suggested. But central in them are the voluntaristic and social ideas. The paper "On Purpose in Thought" deals with the question of the final end of purely theoretic thought. Psychological and logical analyses fail to reveal an adequate aim which thinking may be said to pursue. Another mode of approach must be invoked — the "teleological." Various principles, such as uniformity, identity, postulated as the "ends" of thought, are analyzed and their axiomatic character disputed. Only one axiom — the "time-axiom" — is found to be indispensable to thought, the axiom that "*facta* cannot become *infecta*, that the past can never be undone. This asserts something of the whole future. In all coming time the inviolability of every moment will be secured as soon as the moment is past." And the validity of this "time-axiom" is demonstrated by the method which Royce later regarded as securing absoluteness. It is the method of finding that a true proposition is presupposed by its own denial.[1] This later method is explicitly employed in proving that the act of conceiving a future, and in conceiving it in terms of an irrevocable past, is an absolutely valid act. "The denying," so Royce says, "of the validity of this fundamental act is the assumption of its validity," for "try to assume a condition of things in which time has ceased, and you introduce a time-element into your assumed condition. Try to conceive an end of experience, and you conceive of your experience as continuing after it has ceased." But the notions of past and future derived from an analysis of the "time-axiom," and acknowledged to be indispensable to thought, are nothing but "constructions" of the activity of the present moment. "We always find ourselves dealing with a present thought," Royce asserts, "we can never directly know anything but a present thought. Past and future, as past and future, are never immediately given. . . . At this moment we project our world-picture into an ideal past and an ideal future. The present moment is the builder of both the branches of the conceived time stream." By the notions of past and

---

[1] Cf. *The World and the Individual,* first series, p. 11; cf. also "The Principles of Logic" in the volume entitled, *The Encyclopedia of the Philosophical Sciences: Logic,* 1913, p. 122.

future thus conceived as the product of the present activity of thought, "working upon the data given in the
present moment of consciousness," experience is rendered coherent and significant. "Then experience,"
continues Royce, "will not appear as an indifferent flux
of phenomena, which thought follows without any true
power to anticipate the content of the flux; but, on the
contrary, whatever notions we have of past and future
experience will be seen to be the construction of our own
thought, working upon data immediately given in the
present." And the *end* or the *purpose* of thought? It is
simply this: Past and future should be conceived as
wholes, as standing for one world. Our conception of
past and future is assumed in order that "the thought of
the present may have breadth, fullness, and unity, and
in order that present acts may appear not as sufficient
unto themselves, but as having an immeasurable import
in their relation to a whole universe." "The present
and immediately given content of consciousness should
be found to be . . . but a moment in a world of life."

Here, in technical form, we have the characteristic
tenor of Royce's thinking. The present moment assumed as alone real reveals itself, once its implications
are analyzed, as "creative" and "social." Self-reference
to a past and a future *not* given but actively "acknowledged" as real confers meaning upon the "present"
moment, which must be conceived as standing in relation to "a whole universe," to "a world of life." In the
essay of the same year, in "Tests of Right and Wrong,"
we have a more cogent analysis and application of this
theory of "the present moment." Here the creative and
the social aspects of the "present" are more clearly
recognized. And here also is emphasized the union of
theoretical and practical problems. The problem con-

cerning tests of right and wrong is for Royce no mere
ethical problem, for "the nature of knowledge in general," as he says, "determines the particular nature of
ethical knowledge." And knowledge in general is here
interpreted in Kantian terms. Without data there can
indeed be no knowledge, but "the datum itself as datum
cannot carry with it a certificate of objective validity."
Objectivity and validity and significance without which
there can be no real knowledge are products of some
mental activity. "Knowing," Royce here reiterates,
"is . . . itself activity . . . but if knowledge is activity,
nobody would call simple knowledge a species of conduct." Conduct is distinguished as activity directed
towards an end. When we determine to act for an end
we conceive of possible experiences. The conception of
possible experience, however, is bound up with the conception of time. The ethical significance of time upon
which, in his later works, Royce laid so much stress is
here already made prominent. "The complexity of our
conduct," he says, "is determined by the extent of time
we take into account. The present moment is given.
To act with reference to it alone, is not conduct at all. . .
Conduct increases in complexity and definiteness according as we act with reference to a more extended
time, posit a greater past time as real, expect a greater
future time as yet to come." What, then, is the test of
right conduct? Right conduct is determined at each
moment by explicit reference to the remotest future and
to the welfare of all conscious life. Consistent conduct
must at the moment of action theoretically take into
account *all* future time and *all* conscious beings. This
"chronosynoptic" and superpersonal standard is derived by Royce from the very nature of the "present"
moment. For conduct is an activity directed towards an

end "projected" in the future, and since the future is
not given but "expected," no particular future moment
may be logically singled out for preference. "No conscious moment," Royce argues, "is a datum for any
previous moment, but can only be expected in that moment. All future consciousness then, as equally to be
expected, as equally real when it comes, as equally unreal until it comes, is equally an object of present striving. Every present act should therefore be ordered for
the welfare of all future conscious life, in case it should
be ordered for the welfare of any conscious life at all."
Thus the rule for right conduct is found. Moral activity
being essentially one which transcends the *real* present
and being employed in the service of an *ideal* time, must
avoid what Royce calls the "illusion of time-perspective," and must regard no particular moment in the
future as more real than another, since "all future is
alike not given but only expected, and all is alike real
when it comes." Hence, our conduct must if it be directed to *any* future take into account *all* future. On the
same principle, my moral activity cannot single out *my*
future as the goal of its endeavor, since the Ego, as
Royce declares, "is not more a datum than is the Alter.
My future is as much a mere expectation as is your future at this moment. The reality of the one is the reality
of the other. Work for one must become work for both,
or else be indefensible." Active extension of my future
until it embraces the future of all conscious beings is,
then, the goal of my moral striving. The result is a theoretical solution of the problems of conduct in superpersonal and social terms. The practical solution, Royce
himself significantly adds, "belongs perhaps to far-off
centuries."

Irresistible is a comparison between the main trend of

this essay and the later doctrine of the community. In the early paper the solution of the moral problem is accomplished through a twofold "extension" on the part of the moral agent: *temporal* and *social*. The logical necessity for such extension is derived from the analysis of the "present moment." If the present *alone* is given, then what is *not* present is always a "construction" of the present. And since the very essence of conduct, as activity for an end, consists in transcending the present no limits can logically be assigned to the realm of the non-present to be constructed. Whatever is not present is ideal. Equally ideal, then, are all past moments and all future moments. Equally ideal are Ego and Alter. It is the equal "ideality" of past and future, of Ego and Alter which logically forbids conduct to act with reference to a limited portion of time or to a limited being or group of beings. Such limitation would be arbitrary. Consistent and defensible conduct, therefore, transcending as it must the present, requires reference to *all* time and to *all* beings in time. This is the reasoning in "Tests of Right and Wrong." Similar is the reasoning in *The Problem of Christianity*. The solution of the moral problem consists for the later Royce also in the twofold "extension," temporal and social, of the individual. That the individual self is not a "present datum" but an "ideal," the product of an active "construction" or, in his later terminology, "interpretation," is one of Royce's cardinal teachings. It is emphasized over and over again. Our idea of the individual self, he says, "is no mere present datum, or collection of data." [1] Again: "Nobody's self is either a mere datum or an abstract conception." [2] "Never in the present life," so he insists

[1] *The Problem of Christianity*, vol. ii, p. 43.
[2] *Ibid.*, p. 111.

in *The World and the Individual,* "do we find the self as a given and realized fact. It is for us an ideal." [1] Once more: "The true self of any individual man is not a datum but an ideal." [2] The self of the moment without temporal extension has for Royce little meaning. "The present self," he remarks, "the fleeting individual of to-day, is a mere gesticulation of a self. The genuine person lives in the far-off past and future as well as in the present." [3] "Considered simply in this passing moment of my life," so he declares, "I am hardly a self at all." [4] The same idea is voiced with greater directness in an unpublished Lecture written in 1915 for a Boston Extension course in Ethics. Thus: "There is a most excellent reason why you cannot get coherent or satisfactory knowledge of the self through any intuition, through any direct acquaintance, through any mere hiding away in the 'interior' of your personality, through any direct perception. Your own true self simply does not just now exist to be known. It belongs to the past as well as to the present; and your whole life is needed to embody and to live out what it means." [5] What, then, is the self? It is for Royce a life "whose unity and connectedness depend upon . . . interpretation of plans, of memories, of hopes, and of deeds." [6] It is a being which never exists as a *finished* product; it is a process which extends forward as well as backward. And no limit, Royce holds,

---

[1] *The World and the Individual,* second series, p. 290.
[2] *Ibid.,* p. 287.
[3] *The Problem of Christianity,* vol. ii, p. 67.
[4] *Ibid.,* p. 41.
[5] Cf. also article "Mind" in *Encyclopedia of Religion and Ethics,* edited by James Hastings, vol. viii, pp. 649–657; *Outlines in Psychology,* p. 294; *The Philosophy of Loyalty,* pp. 168 ff.
[6] *The Problem of Christianity,* vol. ii, p. 111.

can be placed upon the ideal extension of the self in time.[1] The very life of the self is a process, of extension. The activity which achieves such self-extension is called by Royce "interpretation." This for him is a cognitive process distinct from perception and conception. Data are objects of perception; universals objects of conception. Objects of a different order, however, called by Charles Peirce "signs," *i. e.*, signs of meaning, address themselves to the third cognitive mode of interpretation. Such "signs," for instance, are the past and the future. "The time-order," says Royce, "in its sense and interconnection, is known to us through interpretation, and is neither a conceptual nor yet a perceptual order."[2] Again, "Our very conception of our temporal experience, as of all happenings, is neither a conception nor a perception, but an interpretation."[3] Interpretation, as here used, is indeed not identical in detail with the act of "acknowledging" the past and "anticipating" the future as employed in "Tests of Right and Wrong." The fundamental idea, however, is the same.[4] In the early essays as well as in the later works a definite time-order is recognized as the basis for the self and his moral activity, a time-order, moreover, which is not "given" but which is "constructed" or "interpreted." Common to the early and to the later Royce is the explicit thesis that the self if he is not to shrink into a meaningless

[1] *The Problem of Christianity*, vol. ii, p. 66. [2] *Ibid.*, p. 155.
[3] *Ibid.*, p. 157; cf. also article "Mind," *op. cit.*
[4] Cf. the extract from Royce's Diary on p. 32, where this process of regarding each moment or event or fact in reference to a postulated class of facts or to a time-stream is characterized as a "form of apperception" distinct from "comparison or association." Royce calls it "the form." It seems as if the process of interpretation, in its cognitive aspect, as a distinct "form of apperception" were here foreshadowed.

time-point must actively relate himself to an ideal, *i. e.*, non-given, time-series. That the ideal time-series to which the individual must necessarily be related can have no personal boundaries is already emphasized in "Tests of Right and Wrong." The self in his extension must include all conscious beings. "All future conscious life"; "The whole world of future experience"; "All the world of being" — are some of the expressions which there occur denoting the self's social extension. Of this fundamental thought, so persistently held by the young Royce, the doctrine of the Community, as formulated in *The Problem of Christianity*, is the mature expression. The very essence of the community depends upon the power of individual selves to extend their lives without any definable limit.[1] Many selves form one community when all are ideally extended so as to include the same past and the same future.[2] The community is made possible when each member includes in his own ideally extended self the deeds of coöperation accomplished by the other members.[3] But men do not form a community, Royce holds, merely in so far as they coöperate. They form a community "when they not only coöperate, but accompany this coöperation with that ideal extension of the lives of individuals whereby each coöperating member says: 'This activity which we perform together, this work of ours, its past, its future, its sequence, its order, its sense — all these enter into my own life, and are the life of my own self writ large.'" [4] Here we have Royce's later solution of the moral problem. The test of right and wrong is defined in terms of "extension." The final result which temporal and social extension is to accomplish is nothing less than the identification of the indi-

[1] *The Problem of Christianity*, vol. ii, p. 61.
[2] *Ibid.*, p. 64.   [3] *Ibid.*, p. 90.   [4] *Ibid.*, pp. 85, 86.

vidual self with the life of the community. This is the
goal of our loyal deeds. And this is the aim of our cognitive endeavors.

Thus the twofold extension of the individual, temporal and social, introduced for the first time in "Tests
of Right and Wrong" is at the root of the later notion of
the community. Not moral "salvation" alone is the
fruit of ideal extension. Religious and metaphysical
problems as well find for Royce in such ideal extension
their solution. And through all his works this solution
runs like a continuous thread. Of this, however, no more
can here be said. Yet to one aspect of Royce's method
by which such solution is achieved we cannot in this connection refrain from alluding. It is common to all his
works, and is already employed with skill in "Tests of
Right and Wrong." For want of a better name it may
be characterized as *constructive analysis*. Paradoxical
though it may sound it is logical analysis which produces syntheses. Rigid analysis of any idea finds it embedded in a system of ideas. Philosophical analysis in
Royce's use does not tear asunder. It builds. This is
clearly seen in "Tests of Right and Wrong." The analysis of the "present moment" assumed as alone real
yields a time-order as an ideal construction. Because it
does transcend the present, and because no theoretical
justification exists for conferring upon a particular moment in the future more reality than upon another,
moral conduct must choose all future as its standard of
reference. It must, similarly, take into account all future beings, since no particular being in the future can
lay claim to more reality than another. The goal of
moral endeavor becomes thus as a result of progressive
analysis a *whole* world of conscious beings in an *endless*
time-order. We have seen that this is the Universal

Community in embryo. What should now be noted, however, is the fact that in *The Problem of Christianity* the notion of an Infinite Community is reached by the same mode of creative analysis applied to the process of interpretation. When once initiated interpretation, the cognitive mode dealing with "signs" or meanings, generates by virtue of an analysis of its own nature a community having the structure of a determinate infinite.[1] Both the social complexity and the infinity of interpretation are analytical constructions. The *triadic* form of interpretation, depending as it does upon three terms — sign, interpreter, and interpretee — and thus differing from perception and conception which are dyadic, defines for Royce the logical structure of a community. It is this triadic structure which constitutes the social basis of knowledge. An interpretative act at its very inception creates a "community of interpretation."[2] An interpretation once begun, however, leads to an endless wealth of new interpretations. "By itself," so Royce declares, "the process of interpretation calls, in ideal, for an infinite sequence of interpretations."[3] And this is no mere assumption. The infinite character of interpretation is derived from an analysis of its very nature. Interpretation being itself a "sign" calls for a fresh interpretative act, the result of which is in turn a new object for still further interpretation, and so on *ad infinitum*. A Universal Community "whose processes are infinite in their temporal varieties"[4] is the ideal *goal* of every interpretation. And this goal is not merely postu-

[1] Cf. note on "Interpretation as a Self-Representative Process," in *The Philosophical Review* for May, 1916, pp. 420–423.
[2] *The Problem of Christianity*, vol. ii, pp. 142, 204 ff.
[3] *Ibid.*, p. 150.   [4] *Ibid.*, p. 324.

lated but is real, Royce argues, in whatever sense any finite interpretation is real.[1] Aside from the epistemological and metaphysical issues which Royce's theory of interpretation is designed to meet, here we have the latest expression of the same method of creative analysis exemplified in "On Purpose in Thought" and in "Tests of Right and Wrong." The method by which we know is one which secures the progressive expansion of ideas through systematic analysis. The "twofold extension" of which we have spoken, the necessary self-transcending and time-transcending activity of every present idea, is rooted in the very cognitive process by which ideas are apprehended. To apprehend is to interpret. To interpret is to advance progressively through "problematic situations" in which contrasts and antitheses prevail to a state of mediation and consequent unity.[2] The task of interpretation is thus socially complex and temporally endless, demanding over increasing expansion and expression — a task for which Royce finds in the work of scientific and philosophic communities the most potent illustration.

Interpretation, then, is creative analysis. The method which in *The Problem of Christianity* is used in constructing the metaphysics of the community is essentially the one which in "Tests of Right and Wrong" leads to a whole world of conscious beings in an endless time-order as the moral goal of every "present" moment. And we may remark in passing that constructive analysis is the philosophical method which prevails in most of Royce's mature works. Thus in *The World and the Individual* the idealistic definition, or the Fourth Concept, of **Reality** is the result of an exhaustive analysis of what is meant by "idea." In the "Supplementary Essay" to the same

[1] *The Problem of Christianity*, vol. ii, p. 269. [2] *Ibid.*, pp. 264 ff.

work, an "infinite multitude" is analytically developed
out of "the internal meaning of a single purpose," [1] to
exemplify the social nature of the Absolute. Here with
the aid of examples drawn from modern mathematics
and logic we have perhaps the most technical and yet the
most lucid vindication of the analytical method as constructive. For the concept of a determinate infinite is
here viewed as the result of the self-development of
thought.[2] Earlier, in *The Conception of God*, the analysis of the nature of human ignorance leads to the notion
of an "absolutely organized experience," regarded by
Royce as identical with the philosophical conception of
God. Earlier still, in *The Religious Aspect of Philosophy*,
the rigid analysis of the "possibility of error" termi-
nates in the constructive conception of Absolute Truth
as known to an "Infinite Thought." In all these works
— whatever their result — the method of argument is
the same. It is the method of orderly and constructive
analysis of experience and of thought.[3]

We have given so much space to a discussion of the
essay on "Tests of Right and Wrong" because here, as
has been shown, we have in technical form the seeds of
Royce's mature teachings. The twofold extension of the
"present" we regard as the fundamental thesis alike of
the early and the later philosophical products. The
present as such is meaningless. The present — be it a
present moment, a present idea, a present thought, a
present self — derives its meaning from a constructive

---

[1] *The World and the Individual*, first series, pp. 502 ff.
[2] *Ibid.*, pp. 492–493.
[3] And it may here be also noted that Royce's method thus
suggested is the one which underlies his definition of logic as a
"Science of Order." Cf. his "Principles of Logic" in *The Encyclopedia of the Philosophical Sciences: Logic*, 1913.

process of self-extension. And the whole technique of Royce's thinking is dominated, as we have seen, by this process. It is important, therefore, to glance once more at the Diary which he kept during the years 1879 and 1880, and to observe the persistence with which he pondered over his theory of the "present moment." The Diary is full of speculations, theoretical and practical, all revolving around this theory. But a few extracts can here be included.

April 3, 1879.
"The New Phenomenology"; Would this title be sacrilegious? And this for an opening: "Every man lives in a present, and contemplates a past and future. In this consists his whole life. The future and past are shadows both, the present is the only real. Yet in the contemplation of the shadows is the real wholly occupied; and without the shadows the real has for us neither life nor value. No more universal fact of consciousness can be mentioned than this fact, which therefore deserves a more honorable place in philosophy than has been accorded to it. For it is in view of this that all men may be said to be in some sense Idealists."

October 21, 1879.
Succession in time is an unreality, if by succession is meant non-existence of past and future as implied in the existence of the present. The truth of succession is this: There exists eternally among the independent and enduring contents or truth certain series of relations known as time-relations.

The world of being is thus found to be made up of an infinity of simultaneous truths; and the way in which one escapes from the bondage of the present moment is this: Easy it is for the present moment to find itself as alone the real, and to look upon past and future as its own creations. They are so, viz., *its* past and *its* future. . . . But the present moment in thus singling itself out as the one real, fails in its claim for the reason that it must call itself *present*. By thus doing it opposes itself to a past and a future. Its own reality and truth depend upon theirs, as theirs upon itself. Of all the moments this holds true. All alike are real. All are simultaneous. It is the succession that is the true illusion.

There are no atomic beings, no monads in the world. The world is an aggregate of simultaneous truths.

July 25, 1880.

Very characteristic of human thought it is to regard each moment an event or fact in reference to a postulated class of facts. So the single event or fact loses its individual character. Thus in probabilities, the single event is judged by the type (Venn and C. S. Peirce). In all thought the single experience is localized in the postulated stream. In Ethics the one act is given a worth by the worth of the whole class. The duty of voting is a good example. I know that my vote will probably determine nothing yet my duty to vote is measured not by the probable effect of the act but solely by the importance of the issue. Here the individual is exalted far beyond its actual rank. Now this familiar process is more than comparison or association. It is a form of apperception. One might say, "the form."

August 20, 1880.

New in this essay ["Tests of Right and Wrong"] was the explicit statement of my present doctrine of the moral principle, a doctrine not very greatly altered from that of the Kant Lectures in 1877, but much elaborated, and set in new light by the addition of the present moment theory. New in stating the theory itself was the use of the terms acknowledgment and expectation as names for the attitude towards past and future. The names occurred to me as I was walking home from B. the other evening.

August 30, 1880.

I work on Kant in the evening. I reflect on the analogy between Kant's *"Ich denke"* and the doctrine of the active present moment to which I find myself driven in my efforts to understand more problems than one. Kant puts the case thus: There is the stream of *Vorstellungen.* This stream he seems tacitly to admit as phenomenally real, even though it were no subject of thought, though he does not lay stress upon it as an ultimate datum (Shadworth Hodgson does). Yet he seems to imply its assumption. In itself, to be sure, the stream is no steam; only the form of our *Anschauung* makes it seem a stream. But whatever it is itself, the stream is real (cf. *Kr. d. R. V.* 2 ed., pp. 53, 54). Now this stream as real is known first in the *Anschauung* for which it appears as a stream, and secondly in thought, through the unity of apperception. The second condition need not always be realized, but must always be capable of being realized. (*Das Ich denke muss alle meine Vorstellungen begleiten können.*) Otherwise the stream as it is in itself, or as it is simply intuited in the form of time, would not be my *Vorstellungen* at all. As thought or known, however, through the second condition, the stream becomes the basis of all knowledge.

Now I put the case thus: Given in every case of conscious knowledge is the content of a present moment, given as in synthesis, and as a whole. At the same time with this datum there is an active conception (acknowledgment or anticipation) of past and future contents, not given, but postulated as having been, or as yet to be, real. The act of postulating in a single moment of consciousness a not given manifold content, *i. e.*, the act of putting this manifold in relation to the one present moment, constitutes synthetic knowledge. To conceive of a not real knowledge as past or future or possible, *i. e.*, to conceive of another than the present act of knowledge, one must conceive a like activity with other content. To conceive of past or future consciousness in which there has been or will be no active knowledge, is to disregard the activity of the present moment, and to view only the content; postulating that in some other moment there was the content without the activity. But we cannot conceive the content without conceiving the activity as at least possibly present, unless we regard the supposed content as out of all relation to the present, *i. e.*, as out of time. Hence "*das Ich denke muss alle meine Vorstellungen begleiten können*": or, in other words, all past moments must have been possibly knowable as present moments and as in the same time-series as that in which the real present actually is. The *Ich denke* = Unity of Apperception = Activity of present moment.

September 4, 1880.

I see Kant as I never saw him before. But we must put our problem differently. Thus says Kant: What is the relation of knowledge to its object? Thus say we: What is the relation of every conscious moment to every other? Our question may be more fundamental, and can be made so only through study of him.

March 10, 1879.

Faust's contract with Mephisto is, in Goethe's view, no extraordinary act, no great crime, but simply the necessary fundament of an active life that strives for the Ideal. Here is the whole view as I just now conceive it to have been. *Im Anfang war die Tat, i. e.,* the essence of life and being is activity. This activity is not on the one hand simple blind force (*Kraft*), nor on the other hand pure subjective thought (*Sinn*) but the living union of both as seen in the work of the individual moment. The *Kraft* never is known but in the individual *Tat:* and in this individual *Tat* is contained also the only possible realization of the *Sinn.* And so the essence of life is found in the individual moments of accomplishment, and in those alone. But on the other hand, the individual moment is in its inmost nature unrestful, fleeting. The *Kraft* is represented in the individual moment, but not adequately. The *Sinn* is realized, but not wholly nor finally. The individual moment is the Real; but it is so only in so far forth as it denies itself, strives to pass out over itself, to plunge on into a future. Were it content with itself, it would be no longer *Tat.* It would become the dead *factum,* instead of the living Action. Such continual striving from one moment to another is the Universe itself. The works of creation are glorious because they are in eternal movement and action. They are incomprehensible, simply because the thought involved in them is never at rest in the permanent clearness of the *Sinn,* but is ever changing with all the life of the *Kraft.* To comprehend (*begreifen*) would be to hold fast. And the life of the individual moment may not be thus held fast; but flows eternally.

The place of man, of the individual consciousness in general, is secured, in the midst of this activity, only in and through compliance with the general law. The individual moments of our lives must be full of action, the fuller the better: but they must also be, for the very same reason, full of unrest. No content of the moment, however great, must lead us to wish to remain stationary in this moment. This content in the present moment is denial of activity; it is death.

The rest will follow easily; I can better set it forth another time. The Act as Act comprehends only itself. All other Acts are but phenomena, baseless visions to it. Yet in its discontent it seeks from the contemplation of them, higher development for itself. And the seeking is contracting with the devil, the spirit of deceit, of appearances. The contract with the devil is the eternal attendant of the striving of the present moment. Life is Action. Passivity, the negative aspect, must at every moment be set up and conquered Every moment we must enter into contract with the devil; every moment use his services for our own development. And when we say "*Verweile doch*"; at that moment the contest is over; the Passive has gained its end. We sink into nothing. But the universe, with its eternal activity remains. For the individual the passive element, whose conquest is his own destruction, appears as of its essence diabolical. For the universe this passive element, everywhere present as the reverse of the active, and so destructive not of the All but of the Individual, appears as *Das Ewig-Weibliche*.
Bold, isn't it?

These extracts show how central in Royce's mind was the theory of the "present moment." Others speak of his project to elaborate and to systematize it. Thus, on July 21, 1880, he writes: "Reflected further on the present state of the systematic development of philosophy I am undertaking. The opening and foundation thereof is surely the theory of the world of reality as a projection from the present moment." Various plans, some of them preserved among his unpublished writings, were actually carried out only to be finally rejected. On August 9, 1880, he records: "Spent the evening on my new beginning under changed title 'The Work of Thought.' When shall I come to the end of these everlasting beginnings? This one strikes me well. But so, alas, did they all." Yet not many days later, August 20, we read: "And now my plans have shifted once more, and I project for the first book a series of essays, say five, as thus: I Introductory, 'The Study of Philosophy,' II 'The Ideas in Themselves (a condensed statement of the logical theory),[1] III 'The Purposes of Human Thought,' IV 'Tests of Right and Wrong' (the present essay enlarged), V 'The Business of the Philosophy of Religion.' This work might be finished before long." But it was not. It shared the fate of its predecessors. Hardly begun, it was forced to yield to a new plan. Different projects following one another in rapid succession are thus found recorded. "I add another to the already numberless" — is a phrase used in the Diary introducing an elaborate sketch of a new plan.

These "numberless" plans, outlines, sketches, and fragments of a systematic book we should have to examine with care were it our purpose to reconstruct Royce's mental biography. But this is not the task of the present essay. They are here mentioned merely to disclose a method of work which was always characteristic of Royce, and of which the bibliography of his unpublished writings gives abundant evidence. The tentative attempts to formulate in a variety of ways the same thoughts constitute a vast portion of the unprinted material he left behind him. Between Royce's manner of work and his philosophical method of "constructive analysis" there is an interesting psychological connection. This, however, we have no room here to discuss. This essay, we fear, has already grown beyond the customary confines of an Introduction.

"I strongly feel," Royce said in an autobiographical mood, "that my deepest motives and problems have centered about the idea of the Community, although this idea has only come gradually to my clear conscious-

[1] Developed in his Doctor's Dissertation. — Ed.

ness."[1]   His entire system of philosophy is in a sense a
development of this ruling idea. It is certainly his most
characteristic and his most persistent theme. In the
idea of the Community, as he understood it, modern
thought has received one of its richest philosophic conceptions. With its aid Royce sought to interpret the
deepest issues of metaphysics, the profoundest problems of knowledge, the ultimate questions of religion.
And so focal is it in his ethics that, from his point of
view, the whole moral task of humanity finds in terms
of the community articulate expression. Thus supreme
for Royce was the category of the community. Herein
lies the significance of his "Fugitive Essays." They
show how early and how clearly his "deepest motives
and problems have centered about the idea of the community."

J. LOEWENBERG.

BERKELEY, CALIFORNIA,
    April, 1920.

[1] *The Hope of the Great Community*, p. 129.

FUGITIVE ESSAYS

SCHILLER'S ETHICAL STUDIES

[1878]

THE history of literature is full of philosophic problems; no period in it more so than that of the German classical literature. The philosophic problems concerned are, indeed, not those of the most purely theoretical interest; they are, on the contrary, the great practical problems of life. But their general interest is none the less for that reason, as one is easily convinced by a very superficial consideration. It is with the philosophic problems that engaged the attention of a great literary man, the second of the great leaders of the classical literature, the popular and much-loved Schiller, that the following essay treats. Not a contribution to philosophy but only an attempt to aid in the understanding of the poet, shall form the substance of our task. It is from an age full of outer and inner conflicts that our subject is taken. We shall seek to describe only one of the heroes, and him only in respect to one of his great adventures.

Schiller is profoundly an ethical poet. Not that he began life as a great ethical theorist. On the contrary, his early philosophic education was neglected, and until he was full thirty years old he knew of the great movements of thought of his day only superficially and by hearsay. But still, from the "Ode to Rousseau" down to "William Tell," you always find Schiller grappling with some problem as to the conduct of life. If he cannot speak the language of the school, he speaks his own language, and that is commonly much better. If he cannot give a final solution for his difficulties, as the schools always do for theirs, that only makes his expression more poetic, his development freer, and his ideas more life-like. And when at last he is brought to spend three or four years on abstract, ethical, and æsthetic studies, the consequence is a return with greater vigor than before to the work of poetic production, and a daring effort to put all the results of his thinking into poetic form, and so to make them of worth for real life. From first to last his motto seems to be that nothing is too earnest for the earnestness of life, and nothing relating to life too barren for the transforming hand of poetry.

Popular instinct has long since recognized this fact of the ethical tendency of Schiller. To his own nation he appears as the poet of freedom, of ideal aspiration, of active striving for the better. The history of literature contrasts him with Goethe by making him the representative of the element of restless progressive effort in the classical period, as Goethe is the representative of the element of repose, of trust in nature, of self-surrender to life as a process, instead of self-affirmation in life as a free construction. No reader can mistake this tendency in Schiller. It is the merit, as it is the weakness, of all his best work, that it is throughout determined by ideas that have relation to action. Whatsoever things are in his eyes pure, lovely, of good report — these, and no others, he seeks to realize in his poetry. And so, as his ethical conceptions develop, his poems develop with them. In short, when you study the principles that governed Schiller's thought on practical questions, you enter at once into the laboratory where his genius worked, and witness at least a part of the process, in so far as that can be made visible, by which his productions reached maturity. And this is the ground of the importance of Schiller's ethical studies in the history of his life and works.

These studies were, as we have indicated, not for the first the fruit of an intimate and systematic acquaintance with philosophy, or with the special branch of it concerned. It is much rather true that Schiller finally came to busy himself quite systematically with philosophy because he had first long been an independent student of ethical problems, and had been unable to solve them satisfactorily.

In fact, to give a complete account of Schiller's ethical studies one would have to write a running commentary on all his works from first to last. And, at the same time, to take notice only of those of his writings wherein his opinions are stated in technical language, as a result of his special studies undertaken at one particular period, would be to give a false impression, and substitute only a very small part for a whole. We may perhaps avoid both errors by briefly sketching Schiller's development up to the time when he felt himself led to a special study of philosophy in hope of solving his difficulties and clearing his ideas on ethical and æsthetic problems; by then giving some account of this period of theory and its results, and by finally indicating the consequences which all this had for the poet's last and greatest period of productive activity.

The general chronology of Schiller's life favors such a division of the subject. And as this chronology is of some importance for the formation of clear ideas as to his course of development, I take the liberty of pausing for a moment over it.

Schiller was born November 10, 1759, and died May 9, 1805. A glance at the dates of his works assures one that by far the greatest of them belong to the last ten years of his life, from the beginning of 1795 on. The philosophic lyrics, the mass of the ballads, the dramas from "Wallenstein" to "Tell," the correspondence with Goethe, would all have been lost to the world had Schiller's illness of the year 1792 and the following year proved fatal — a result which seemed at the time very imminent. The works between 1780 and 1795 may, in the next place, be considered as falling under three periods: that from 1780 to 1783, inclusive, in which his first dramas, "*Die Räuber*," "*Fiesco*," and "*Kabale und Liebe*," together with the "Odes to Laura," and a few minor lyrics, fall; that from 1784 to 1788, inclusive, a transition period in his poetic style, marked principally by "Don Carlos," the tale known as the "*Geisterseher*," and the "*Philosophische Briefe*"; and that from 1789 to 1794, the transition period in his mental development, in which he gives up poetic production almost altogether, and busies himself first with history, then with philosophy. Finally, in this last-mentioned period, we have, as the sub-period of special philosophic study, the years 1791 to 1794. In these, Schiller busied himself principally with the Kantian philosophy, and wrote the well-known series of æsthetic essays.

We have, accordingly, first to treat of Schiller's ethical studies, systematic or otherwise, as they find expression in his writings previous to the year 1791. We shall then be prepared to speak of Schiller the Kantian, from the year 1791 to the year 1795, and shall look ahead for a single moment at Schiller the classical poet, belonging to no school, and in fact to no nation, but to the history of the human mind as a whole, and to the literature of the world at large.

An unsolved theoretical problem may be, to a simple investigator, a source of pleasure. But an unsolved practical problem is to a poet only a cause of trouble. In so far as Schiller in his early views on ethical questions is uncertain, we may expect to find him unhappy. And, indeed, when we consider the problems that arouse his anxiety, we shall not be astonished. Let us mention some of these problems.

In the first place, then, we find Schiller deeply perplexed by the narrowness, the essential limitation, of all human character, knowledge, and attainment. That we have desires and powers in themselves perfectly justifiable, and yet in the nature of things incapable of finding in the actual world adequate objects — this impresses Schiller as containing a great and intensely practical problem in itself. What are we to do with these powers and desires? Are they illusions, through which nature makes use of us for unknown purposes? And must we therefore learn to rise above them, to despise them, to become cynics? Or are they not rather indications of a high and supernatural vocation of man, whose full realization is for the present hindered by powers of evil which we cannot understand? If this be the case, then do not these powers and desires open up to us the means of forming to our minds the ideal of a perfected and victorious humanity, an ideal that we may never see attained, although our business must be to strive for it unceasingly? This is the query of all Schiller's early poetry. As a poet he inclines to the latter solution. There is nothing cynical about his true nature. But how he shall arrive at such a solution he cannot see; and when he writes a confidential letter, or attempts an especially mournful or passionate love song, he often tries to convince other people that he is a cynic after all, that he does not believe in the true or in the good very seriously, and that he should not wonder if the whole turned out to be only a figure in the great dance of atoms. He quickly recovers in all cases, at least sufficiently to demand a way out of his difficulties from some one, or to dream out one for himself; but nothing can prevent the conflict from beginning all over again.

This difficulty is a very real one for Schiller, and not a mere subject for poetic fervor. The circumstances of his life have impressed it upon him, and given it a peculiar tinge. His youth was not one of freedom, but of bondage in a military school. Even his course of study for his profession was, with the profession itself, forced upon him. He had no choice. His culture had thus been neglected, notwithstanding that his education was in a sense quite broad, although not exactly liberal. Sympathy, too, was lacking. And thus in all directions he felt his freedom of movement walled in. To be a citizen of the world, to be free, to know no law but what a higher consciousness sets for itself — this is the wish that breathes everywhere from his early poetic efforts.

Often the wish is obscurely expressed; often it asks simply that indefinite fullness of consciousness, that unordered overflow of intense feeling, which every one at first is apt to conceive as the essential effect of the beautiful, and the essential content of higher life. But, unstable as this view of things is, the poet must pass through it on his way to better understanding of his task, and in passing he makes this personal problem a universal one, and finds unlimited food for thought in the continual strife in the world between the desire for independent activity on the part of the individuals and the iron necessity with which mother Nature surrounds all her children. As early as in his graduation essay (*Ueber den Zusammenh. d. thier. Nat. d. Mensch. mit seiner geistig*) he had given a provisional solution to the problem. In this essay the body of man is taken as a general representative of the necessity of nature, and the soul as the general representative of the desire for freedom. The soul is shut up in the body, he reasons, because otherwise it could not develop its powers. Hearing and seeing, moving and constructing — yes, even much of thinking — are all obviously determined by the body.

Suppose a newly-created soul set alone by itself, without any body. It cannot hear nor see, it cannot act, it will never find out how to think — in fact, it might as well not exist. In short, by this reasoning the young surgeon finds it so easy to prove the value of having a body that we are almost tempted to ask, What, on this basis, may be the use of having a soul? The essay is eminently proper, eminently tedious, perhaps not quite sincere, but at all events unmistakably materialistic in its consequences. Schiller was not conscious of this fact, and was, at all events, no materialist at any point of his career. The incompleteness and instability of the solution he here proposes merely serve to show how far Schiller was from the full attainment of his end — the end, in fact, he never attained until the day of his death. The necessity of nature, which is the unspiritual; the needs of the spirit, which seem in this world but accidental — these are the two members of Schiller's Antinomy; and Antinomy it always remained, through abstract thinking and poetical enthusiasm, down to the end of his career.

The essay we have just mentioned is the first extant prose work, if we except "The Robbers" (which, notwithstanding the form, must be reckoned as poetry), in the course of Schiller's life as an author. If in its somewhat dry way it attacks the poet's pet problems, we may accept the fact as a sign that when Schiller writes prose again he will not forget to discuss anew the same topics,

and, if he can, in better form. And, accordingly, we find
further on, in 1786, a series of philosophic letters, in
which, in the form of a correspondence between two
friends, the ethical problem is once more taken up and
its solution sought in an attempt at a poetic scheme of
the universe. Perhaps these letters may serve best to
introduce the few words we have to say of Schiller's
ethical studies as influencing his poetry in this first
general period; for the letters are themselves highly
poetical in their form, and are more systematic than
any one of the lyrics from near the same time. In fact,
no better commentary on the *"Lied an die Freude"*
could be found than just these letters.

The external motive for the writing of the letters was
the friendship of Schiller and Körner, and the intercourse and correspondence that grew out of it. Körner,
the father of the poet Theodor Körner, who died in the
Befreiungskrieg, was himself a man of no small talent,
but more a thinker than he was a writer. His place in
Schiller's early development is that of a quiet and kindly
opposition. When Schiller is in despair, Körner encourages him. When Schiller jumps at conclusions,
Körner invites him to study philosophy, and trust more
to his understanding. When Schiller plunges into hard
study, Körner reminds him of his vocation as a poet.
And so throughout — with a curious mingling of affection, criticism, reverence, advice — Körner gives his
great friend just the stay the perplexed soul needed.
The correspondence of the two has long been famous.
It was natural that Schiller should discourse of his difficulties concerning the problems of life with his thoughtful friend. Körner seems to have been a Kantian from
the first, and he was not slow in recommending Schiller
to search for a solution of his difficulties in that philoso-

phy. But only the theoretic part of the system had as yet appeared. It was hard reading; Schiller's philosophic preparation was imperfect, his interest in his art very great, his outward circumstances not entirely satisfying, and his future still doubtful. He felt only the need of appealing to some kind of philosophic doctrine to escape from the weight of his problems. His reading in this direction had been mainly confined to the popular philosophy of the *Aufklärungs-periode*. With wonderful intuition he had seized on just the points that were fitting for a general doctrine of nature such as he sought, and now he made use of this material as a basis on which he might build his own speculation. This is the way in which the "*Philosophische Briefe*" originated.

The "Letters" are, as said, supposed to pass between two friends. Julius and Raphael are the names — Julius representing Schiller himself; Raphael, Körner. In fact, Körner is in part the author of the letters of Raphael. The form is in itself significant. At this time Schiller hopes to find in friendship the concrete solution of the ethical problem. This problem was: How shall man, who aspires to something incomparably higher and nobler than nature, be able to exist and develop in a world where he is cramped everywhere by iron laws of necessity, laws that are totally indifferent to his aspirations? Schiller hopes to find this as the answer: Man must become happy by making himself a friend to a fellowman — by loving and being loved; for in friendship there is combined utter surrender of self to a foreign power — utter abandonment of self to a need of nature — and yet at the same time the highest freedom, the completest self-consciousness.

Julius finds himself full of doubts as to the nature and government of the world just at the point where he most needs assurance. For he is likewise in doubt as to the vocation of man; and how shall his doubts be put away if he cannot tell whence man came, nor whither he goes? Reason were a glorious treasure, he says, if it only might reveal to us something. But this god is put into a world of worms. The body with its needs is there; nature with its rigid regularity hems in the aspiring spirit. The vasty deeps of space are open to the mind; immeasurable spheres of activity seem offered — only that the mind may not think two ideas at once, nor have any certainty as to present, past, or future at any time. This is the most terrible of imprisonments; and that soul seems happier that never attains the knowledge of its imperfection, but remains for all life in the stolid indifference of ignorance.

This is the dark side of the picture. But Julius sees one hope of escape. What if this iron necessity of nature be itself but an illusion, and the free aspiration of the spirit be the reality? If there must be illusions somewhere, why not on the side of the party of evil? Perhaps, then, if we give free rein to fancy and construct for ourselves the picture of the best possible world, we may in the end be able to show that our real world does not differ so much from this picture after all.

Here is the starting point for Julius as Natur-philosoph, or, as he seems to prefer to be called, Theosoph. We cannot follow him into details. Suffice it to indicate the direction his thought takes. A world wherein the ordering of nature is to be in radical union with the aspirations of the spirit must be a world of love. Only by this means can the desire for individual freedom be reconciled with the bowing before external power, viz., when the individual feels himself united to the whole by the bonds of all-embracing affection. The feeling that links heart to heart in sympathy must be the principle that moves all things; otherwise, nature is a dead mass to us. God must, therefore, be the highest expression of this principle of love, and all the world must have been created by Him simply for the sake of realizing in all its infinite modifications the one idea of love. And in this world our duty, our highest vocation, must be the intensifying and increasing of the human affections with which we are endowed. Towards all mankind, brotherly love; towards our friends, the most perfect self-sacrifice; towards the ideal of love, worship — such is the whole duty of man.

Julius finds it easy enough to postulate this theory. He is sadly at loss for means to prove it. He can at best say only that the world ought to be at least as good as the thought of one poor mortal like himself. And Raphael offers no better consolation than that Julius should wait for more light, and study up "the limits of human reason"; by which, of course, our prosaic friend Körner means nothing more or less than the "*Kritik d. reinen Vernunft*."

Such is the main content of the "*Philosophische Briefe*," which remain after all only a fragment, but which are very suggestive of the inner life of our poet. It is obvious what must be the consequence as to his poetic productions in general during this period. If his ethical ideas govern his poetry, you must find, these ideas being what they are, a double tendency, producing two classes of poems. Is the poet chiefly occupied with the nobility of the higher affections, is he thinking of the worth of friendship and love for humanity — then the difficulties suggested by the dead mass of nature will be pushed into the background; the poet will see only the

bright side; he will extol duty as the mere natural outburst of affection; he will vivify nature itself, and see
love and harmony everywhere. Such a mood gives birth
actually to the early lyric, "*Die Freundschaft*," and later
to the "*An die Freude*." In the first occurs that famous
apotheosis of friendship, which is, no doubt, the finest
triumph of Schiller's genius to be found in the "*Anthol-
ogie*," or in the other productions of the same time. The
second needs no special reference. Critics may, indeed,
say that the "*An die Freude*" is not a perfect poem, and
that the effect is a little disordered. That, however, does
not touch the fact that it is a very great poem, and that
the effect is incomparable.

But is the poet more vividly conscious of the oppression of the order of nature, more attentive to the limits
of consciousness, then the ethical tragedy, in which
Schiller from first to last excelled, comes into the fore-
ground — the world becomes a prison, nature a mysterious and cruel divinity, duty an external and inimical
power; while love, the one saving feature of the whole,
sinks into an accidental subjective phenomenon, beautiful but powerless. Only the poet's earnestness and
manliness prevent him in these cases from becoming
sentimental and tiring the reader with weak complaints.
The examples of this style of poetry are, in this first
period, common enough. In so far as the play of "The
Robbers" has any plan at all, it rests on this idea. The
original design of "Don Carlos" was the representation
on the stage of poor, lonely love in a world of foes, rush-
ing through life in an agony of passion, and finding
destruction in the end — a sentimental design, indeed,
and altered to answer the needs of the poet himself, who
was in reality made of much better stuff than would be
indicated by such a picture. The lyric "Resignation" is

another variation of the same theme — the conscious spirit crushed before unconscious necessity, and only comforted by the thought that everybody else fares about as badly ("*Mit gleicher Liebe lieb' ich meine Kinder*"). The original form of the "*Götter Griechenlands*" contains a few especially fiery stanzas, wherein the poet expresses his opinion of the order of nature while pretending to believe that it was not always so bad, and praising a mythical antiquity. The most outspoken of these stanzas were afterwards omitted.

Here, then, is an inner contradiction — a stubborn, insoluble residuum, as it were — in all Schiller's early thinking and constructing. If his ethical postulates are to be satisfied, he must be permitted to idealize the doctrine of nature. But if nature is stubborn, if she refuses to reveal to him anything but eyeless law — necessity that swerves from its course for the sake of no aspiration or demand or need of the individual — then the ethical postulates remain unsatisfied, the moral law is a heavy load, poetic idealism is but idle fancy.

From this standpoint there remain for Schiller but two provinces free to a greater or less degree from the burden of this perplexity. The one province is that of simple action. Man may work with ideal purpose so long as he lives; this, at least, the iron necessity of nature permits. And so long as one is hard at work, he is excused from answering abstruse questions. This spirit, the *solvitur ambulando* of modern thought and life in general, is characteristic of Schiller's own laborious effort through his whole career. The other province where a partial reconciliation of necessity and freedom may be sought is that of political development. Man makes the State, thinks Schiller; therefore the State is, as a free construction, to a certain extent removed from the interference of dead nature. Here may be room for ideal energy, and here the ethical vocation of man may be in part realized. Schiller's thoughts on this subject are put into the mouth of the Marquis Posa, a character who is indeed, with all his nobility, a kind of filibuster, and whose advent in Schiller's brain during the composition of "Don Carlos" was the cause of a general revolution in the ordering of that drama — quite as great as the revolution caused in King Philip's court when the marquis appears on the scene. But he is an honest character, although fantastic; and his political idealism is the true expression of the attempt Schiller made to solve his ethical problem by considering the greater man of Plato's Republic, the State. It was the Schiller of the time we are now describing who hailed with hope the commencement of the French Revolution, just as it was Schiller the Kantian who lived to lament the bitter disappointment of these hopes.

The substance of all the foregoing is that the Schiller of the first period is not a nature-poet, and must not be judged as one. His sympathy with nature is, in fact, not developed; and if it were, he would not know what to do with it. He sees in nature a great display of forces, but does not pause much over the beauty or the significance of single features. He is too deeply troubled by unrest to be contemplative, too much in doubt to be submissive; and the reflective nature-poet could in modern times hardly succeed without one of these qualities. The Schiller of the "*Spaziergang*" is still far away, and years of progress come between. And yet, as we shall see, the Schiller of the "*Spaziergang*" himself was only half a nature-poet. The problems of this first period remained always in part unsolved.

The study of the antique classical models from 1788

on — a study which did so much to perfect Schiller's style — did not assist him in his ethical difficulties. The study of history only made the material of facts, on which his doubts were founded, greater. He appealed to the reigning philosophy for aid, and in 1791 commenced the study of Kant.

What Kant was to that age it is difficult for us fully to appreciate. His friends and foes came together into parties each of which combined many very heterogeneous elements. We find it thus very hard to say just what the early Kantians were in tendency — what they consciously meant as a body. Somewhat similar was this critical movement in its external character to that originating under the stimulus of Darwin's Origin of Species today — a similar combination, that is, of the most devotedly scientific and the most unfeignedly popular features of the thought of the time. But such a comparison is necessarily imperfect. Suffice it for our purpose that the *Critique of Pure Reason* was then read or read of by everybody who made any pretensions to keeping pace with the thought of the age, that every one had an opinion of its merits, that many were confident of great revolutions of thought to spring from it. Schiller had long heard of the book, had long been advised to read it, had often been frightened from it, and now determined to approach it. He approached it, however, carefully, by first reading the "*Kritik d. Urtheilskraft*," Kant's systematic treatise on æsthetics and connected subjects. A poet could not have chosen a better means of becoming acquainted with Kant, for the "*Kritik d. Urtheilskraft*" is truly as entertaining a book as the sage of Königsberg was capable of writing. Schiller followed this up by reading Kant's principal ethical treatises and essays, in so far as they had yet appeared. The results of his study in this province will interest us here.

Kant's philosophy is a glorification, not of self, but of Consciousness. In Consciousness is all knowledge rooted; through Consciousness is all truth known. This is the starting point. To conceive of the universe in part, or as a whole, is an act of Consciousness. To judge the truth or falsity of your conception is to judge Consciousness. But this consciousness is not the mere disordered mass of sensation — it is the result of formally ordered sensation, of organized experience; and this, in its completest phase, is called science. The rules by which experience is ordered are the special property of Consciousness; without them it would not be consciousness. The Experience is the raw material that is to be organized. This is, in a word, the Kantian Theory of Knowledge. His Ethical Theory has a like basis. Nothing can be a rule of conduct that does not commend itself as such to Consciousness. If such a rule does commend itself to Consciousness as the one right one, then it ought to be followed, and the *Ought* remains eternally binding, no matter whether the rule actually ever is followed or not. Kant's deduction of the principles of conduct does not here concern us. Our business is only with the application of this foundation-maxim to the doctrine of the Ideal and Real as subjects of practical interest.

Suppose the demands of your moral consciousness are not realized in the world. Suppose the *Ought* of your ethical postulate finds no actual fact to correspond with it. What refuge have you from endless perplexity at the course of events? You have, says the unshaken advocate of the rights of consciousness, you have even the Ethical Idea itself. Consciousness, as represented in the

Practical Reason, is the support for this Idea, which is for that very reason judged better than the actual world in which it fails to find its realization. Accept this Idea for its true worth; be free from the bondage that depends on the sense, instead of on the moral consciousness, for the fulfillment of the latter's demands; be an ethical, and not a sensual, being.

In this direction these seek for the solution of the problem of Ideal and Real. The Ideal is that which is in conformity with your highest moral demands. Does it lie within your own power to make this Ideal an actual fact — then work for this end. But, is the realization beyond your power, and is the Real of Nature opposed to your Ideal, then your duty lies in independence. The reason in that case judges, postulates, examines, but never departs from its confidence in its own fixed principles. In these it finds a satisfaction that is greater than the disappointment; for it recognizes its own incomparable superiority amid the confusion about it.

The interest that all this must have had for Schiller's problems is evident. Especially, however, must he have been struck by one feature of Kant's theory. The rights of the moral Reason are asserted as against the simply arbitrary play of fancy, as well as against the extravagant discontent of the disappointed senses. Not merely must you find a higher satisfaction in the possession of the ethical ideas, whether or not they be found realized in the actual world, but you must also not try to substitute for this higher satisfaction any mere appeal to the fancy to solve the world-problem by imagining a world behind the one we see, like it in being a world of sense, but unlike it in being a perfectly good and happy world. In other words, all such attempts as Schiller's own undertaking in the "*Philosophische Briefe*," to make the world more tolerable to a poet by fancying that it is all an illusion, covering up a goodly, poetic, fair, and free world behind the scenes, are, according to Kant, unsatisfactory. The poet's constructions are judged on æsthetic grounds; but the philosopher must be condemned if he has not held to reality, however unwelcome it be. The Reason needs no such support. It needs only confidence in itself. It does not ask to make a world out of mist, to correct this one that is made out of rock. No! The Reason is destined for a higher object. It is destined as the judge of all things.

The vocation of man is, therefore, the strictest obedience to the moral law, without regard to any hope he may have or not have of seeing all its precepts ideally realized. And the true equilibrium of life is attained when the Reason that supports the moral law has come fully to realize its own complete self-sufficiency, and to cease despairing of its own worth if it finds that it is not able to govern the course of outer Nature. So much, then, in general, for the inner contradictions of life which had so long oppressed Schiller's mind. If this treatment of them did not remove them, it at least opened a way towards rising above them. But, in particular, as to the content of these contradictions: Schiller had looked upon the iron necessity of nature as a power opposed to the desires and aspirations of the individual, and had found in this the ground of all the perplexities of life. What is the sense of Kant on this point? It is this: Instead of calling Nature, where it seems to oppose the realization of the moral needs of man, a non-ethical and inimical power, it were better to call it an obstacle, to all intents and purposes accidental in relation to the Reason. Reason does not see in Nature an enemy, but simply an unformed material that needs a transforming hand. That

Nature does not produce ready-made statues does not arise from the opposition in Nature to the realization of the beautiful. It is simply the result of the fact that any agreement of Nature's rock-forms with the demands of the sculptor is a pure accident for the sculptor himself. His duty is, not to go statue-hunting through the mountains, but to take suitable material and make statues. The vocation of man is not to be found in the world merely, but it is to be realized by labor.

Such is the character of the Kantian Ethical doctrines in so far as we here have to deal with them. Schiller could not fail to be deeply influenced by them. They transformed him, in fact, from the hesitating, uncertain, despondent poet of the first period to the great Idealist of the classical time. They did not ever entirely conquer his former difficulties, but they brought him to the stage at which difficulties become incentives to earnest labor — not insurmountable barriers that terrify. They never entirely reconciled him with Nature, but they caused him to come nearer to her, and learn more from her. They did not make him contented with life, but they rendered his discontent a healthy, and not a morbid, one.

To determine how much external influences had to do with this change in Schiller, to follow the interaction between the philosophical and the literary elements in the life of a man who was studying Kant and the antique at the same time, to calculate the effect of the historical studies on the author of the "Netherlands" and of the "Thirty Years' War" — all this, in itself an interesting task indeed, must be excluded from the present discussion. We can only, in conclusion, mention a few of the most prominent of the results of the study of the Kantian Ethics as these appear in Schiller's works themselves.

The conception of Nature and of its relation to the poet — this, we have said, is changed for Schiller from this time on. How changed? In the three principle æsthetic essays you find a view of Nature in many respects peculiar. This view is foreshadowed as early as 1789, in *"Die Künstler."* It is most fully expressed later, in the *"Spaziergang."* Its development belongs to the era of the Kant-studies. This view is briefly expressed thus: Nature is the idyllic state of *naïve* perfection from which man starts. It is the ideal state of conscious perfection to which man must finally return. The object of culture is to make man in the full exercise of free choice become that which nature in the simple necessity of her own methods originally produces. What has this view in common with the previous one — the view that found Nature an iron necessity that oppresses man? How comes one from the other? In answer to this question we must of course not hope to go too far beyond the fact itself of the change. The simple truth is that, be it because of happier circumstances, or because of the gradual growth of the intimacy with Goethe, or by means of the study of the Greek poets — be it from any or all of these causes, Schiller had come to appreciate and enjoy nature-beauty more. This we must accept as truth, and question no further as to means. But the ethical studies now united themselves with this change of mood. The restless fantasy had previously complained of nature as an enemy, where she did not satisfy poetic needs. The more carefully trained judgment now is willing to let nature pass wherever she does not agree with the moral demands, to avoid her instead of reproaching her. But where she does conform to the ethical postulates, where in her simplicity and necessity she finds time also for excellence, here the ripened receptivity, the newly-developed submissiveness of the poet, is now ready to accept and to rejoice; and in these particulars is nature set up as a model for man, that she may shame his bungling intelligence with her unconscious skill.

Had Schiller been able to rest here, he would have become a nature-poet, like Goethe; but he would have suffered by the comparison. He had not been at school under the great teacher very long — while Goethe was her well-beloved child. But the ethical earnestness does not suffer our poet to rest at this point. The worth of Nature is now understood; but the problem as to Man — what form shall he give that? Old questions are aroused afresh here, and the awakening love of nature is disturbed by elements that forever keep it from becoming entirely pure or completely independent. The old opposition between the conscious effort and the unconscious power that limits effort is transferred to the sphere of consciousness itself, under the Kantian influence; and now we hear of the strife between the ethical tendency, which seeks harmony of spiritual life under the moral law, and the tendency of the senses, which introduces distraction continually. The presence of this strife, which the poet never succeeds in stilling or in reconciling with higher demands, casts a melancholy shadow over the whole of the classical period, and is the feature in it that corresponds to the discontented murmuring of the first period.

Something of the influence of Fichte, with whom Schiller was for some time in companionship, is seen in the "*Briefe über die ästhetische Erziehung*," in which this matter is for the first time discussed at length. There is the same sharp contrast between the person and its rights and the distracting influence of the senses and desires, the same demand for a self-assertion which shall bring unity into the infinite diversity of life, the same despair of any final attainment of the harmony desired, the same heroic determination to enter the conflict, to work for the goal, though complete victory be infinitely removed, which are found in the works of the author of the "*Vorlesungen über die Bestimmung d. Gelehrten*" and of the "*Wissenschaftslehre*." But, as Schiller was a poet, and not always in the heroic mood, the joy of the warrior in the conflict is not always to be found in what he writes, and simple progress without hope of completion is often a wearisome enough prospect to his mind.

In one of the well-known lyrics he describes himself as a pilgrim who has been seeking for the place where "The earthly shall become heavenly, eternal"; long he has wandered from his father's house, night and day he has not stood still, but yet heaven ever remains far above — never touches earth; death is coming fast; he is past the age where he can hope for great changes; the stream bears him away; his Ideal can never be found — *das Dort ist niemals hier.* In the "*Ideale,*" written as early as 1795, he even represents himself as deserted by his enthusiasm for a better life, deserted by everything but memory and friendship and the power to work. And again and again you find the same complaint, all through the classical period. The individual limits are recognized as inherent to the individual life. Nature is not blamed for them as she once was; but none the less are they limits.

The enthusiastic spirit often returns. The hand that wrote the "*An die Freude*" in 1785, can in 1795 pen "*Das Reich der Schatten,*" or, as we know it now, "*Das Ideal und das Leben.*" Here the soul is to become a conquering Hercules; to forget its limits, and so to destroy them for consciousness; to rise in contempt above the incomplete actuality; to storm heaven, and find — what? Oh! the nectar of Jove, the Truth, the timeless and spaceless Eternal, and what not — in short, the Indescribable. Here the poet's strong inspiration fails; one moment of sublime enthusiasm, one glimpse of a most excellent glory, and he is on earth again; he has tried to transcend the limits inherent in all individual life, and he has attained something too much like death to be an object on which our thoughts can long dwell without a chill. The first breath of the night-wind of Romanticism has touched the classic fields, and the "Hymns to the Night," the "Fate-Tragedies," the "Epilogue in Heaven" of the Second Part of Faust must all follow in their due course. The Classical spirit might have endured longer could it have but answered its own questions as to the vocation of man.

But the field of actual striving life — here is hope for something, is there not? Yes, but not for any complete satisfaction. In the "*Spaziergang*" you have the whole story told in brief form. The best that man has done is worse than the fair nature he has departed from in doing it. Culture has given birth to luxury, to fraud, to anarchy. Against your will you must recognize the superiority of Nature, and look in her for the accidental realization of the good you so long to see freely realized in man. Human history seems like a bad dream, and the poet can only comfort himself by looking up to the rocky hills, untouched by builder's hand, and thinking: Here is, still, material. There is hope yet, for all is not behind us; something remains to be done. The same mingling of earnestness in labor and melancholy in reflection pervades the whole of the "Song of the Bell." Political life is, indeed, not a subject for hope, thinks our poet, in so far as relates to the near future. There is no Marquis

Posa for the French Revolution. But in the community, in the life among small bodies of men, there is interest and hope. For the great people, you must look far ahead. Let Reformation begin at home.

We have followed our poet as far as we proposed to do at the outset. And here we must take leave of him. To sum up in briefest form the results, we have found Schiller busied in his first period with the problem of the relation of man to nature; in the second, with the relation of the actual man to the ideal man. Both problems are ethical; both, in reality, but different aspects of the same problem — that of the vocation of man. All our author's poetic productions are more or less tinged with the ethical element — all, therefore, more or less conditioned by the understanding he may have of his problem. In the first period Schiller doubts the possibility of a reconciliation with nature; in the second, the possibility of attaining the harmony of life. The first doubt lost its significance when the poet became a follower of Kant; the second remained with him till death. The first was the stepping-stone to his classical poetry; the second gave the signal for the commencement of the romantic school in literature. "The Robbers," in which the first tendency received its expression, was the last great work of the *Sturm und Drang* period. "*Die Braut von Messina,*" wherein the second tendency dominates all, wherein it becomes the foundation for a vague terror in view of all life and all action, and seeks refuge in mysticism, is the first of the *Schicksals-tragödien*. With any general judgment of an æsthetic nature on Schiller's whole career we have not here to do, and it would be useless to discuss what time has already settled. But one cannot help expressing a genuine admiration for the equipoise, the personal power, of the man who could so deeply feel the force of the problematic side of human life, and yet never give way to *Weltschmerz;* who could endure so many conflicts, and yet win for himself the honors of a classical poet. All is not conquest in the great idealist's life history; all is not repose and perfection in his view of life. But is this so sad a failing? If it is, let him for whom life has no problems yet unsolved sound the first complaint.

SHELLEY AND THE REVOLUTION

[1880]

SHELLEY'S life is known to us as yet only in fragments. Motives of delicacy and of family pride
unite to keep the materials locked up, that, if published, would answer very important questions. Meanwhile the literature about the poet's fortunes and acts is
large and unsatisfactory. To go among his biographers,
who together fill a long library shelf, and to ask them for
help in understanding him, is to enter a company of cul-
tured and critical people who are all talking among
themselves in low whispers, and, withal, quarreling.
You may admire their enthusiasm, but they do not and
cannot put your mind at rest. Furthermore, you are a
little saddened to see how they hate one another. Each
abuses at least one of his fellows, and all mystify. "If,"
says each, "if I were permitted to state my source of information, I could show that the real meaning of this or
that event is quite other than the stupid and unworthy
soul of my colleague, A. B., has held it to be." "I am
informed by a person well qualified to judge, that," etc.
Or, "Certain indications, which it were not prudent to
explain at present, lead me to a grave suspicion just
here, a suspicion, however, that I will not more clearly
define, but only say that I have it. People of insight will
follow me. I care for no others." Such is the tone of your
true Shelley biographer. Exceptions to the rule there
doubtless are. Two later biographers, Mr. W. M. Rossetti and Mr. J. A. Symonds, are tolerably plain spoken
and satisfying, Mr. Symonds especially so. Yet they are
limited by their material. They can not alter the fact
that those who are best able to give us the truth about

Shelley at first hand have not seen fit to do so, and that the tea-pot ocean of anecdote concerning our poet is yet ever liable to convulsive tempests of angry argument, whenever any new investigator sees fit to hunt up for us some scrap of news, and another investigator to abuse the first for doing so or for failing to add something else. Of this the moral is that we can not from Shelley's biography gain very much aid in understanding him as a man. Important it is to know about his life what we do; yet, with the rude sketch in black and white that is thus furnished, no one can be for a moment content. The reality and the coloring of our Shelley's character we must seek in his works. And in his works, too, we must find the inspiring ideas concerning which he was permitted to speak, and speak grandly to his fellowmen. With these ideas, and not with the outward embodiment of them in the wondrous and obscure happenings of the poet's life on the earth, our business must chiefly be whenever we speak in earnest and with genuine purpose about the poet Shelley.

Shelley must be viewed from as many sides as any mountain peak. I choose for the present to consider his place in the great mountain chain or range of his age, an age as full of great and of small things, of beautiful and of terrible things, as ever were Ural Mountains or Sierra, Andes or Himalaya. Shelley is a poet of the age of the Revolution. To this age we still belong. Do or say or think what we will, the Revolution — political, social, moral, religious, philosophical, poetical — is all about us in the air we breathe. Escape from it we cannot. For a full hundred years the spirit of the Revolution has forced every one to take some position in reference to itself. One may be conservative, or progressive, or reactionary; one may content himself with his newspaper,

or spend all his days in studying the thought of his time
in its best expressions; one may think for himself, or be
able to buy his whole system at a bookstore for a few
dollars, and stow it away half read on a shelf, as is just
now the custom of very many who revere the name of
Herbert Spencer; one may publish continually all that
passes through his brain, and more, too; or one may preserve that enviable love of silent contemplation which is
no less creative than are the great life-giving forces of
springtime, when the little blades of grass fill their
places and do not advertise their beauty — yet, do
what one will, one is a unit in the great process of tremendous change which has gone on, now swift and now
seemingly regressive, now terrifying and now quiet, but
always intensely active, from the dawn of the French
Revolution itself.

As a great man of the age of Revolution, and as a most
characteristic man, one in whom the "passion for reforming the world" went side by side with the most
original perception of the forces that move the world,
Shelley is a form of life that we dare not leave out of
sight in any effort we may make to survey the most important tendencies in modern thought and feeling. As
undeveloped as he was many-sided and unfortunate, our
poet is an image of the modern spirit itself — ardent,
keen-sighted, aspiring, striving to be tolerant, yet often
angry with misunderstanding; studious of the past, yet
determined to create something new; anxious for practical reforms, yet conscious how weary the work of reform
must be; above all, uncertain of the end, often despondent, not knowing what the fates may have decreed as a
reward for all this strife, and incomplete, raw, or obscure, even in its most cherished and loftiest ideas. Of
such a nature, I say, is Shelley, like the spirit of the age

itself — not now, to be sure, strictly as poet, but as man, as moral teacher, as thinker. As poet, in the stricter sense, Shelley represents not so much the age as himself. For it pleases the World-Spirit at times to think highly original and peculiar thoughts; and these, embodied in living men, may make them incomparable with their fellows in some one respect, models and not things modeled after others; and such a distinct and lonely embodiment of ideas was Shelley the poet, who, as poet, might have been dropped down into any other age as well as into ours. Only as intellectual and as moral being may we claim him for our time, and find him one of the most striking representatives of the struggle with life problems which we ourselves carry on.

In studying, then, the relation of Shelley to the Revolution, one studies our poet, not in his most peculiar and most individual aspect, but without doubt, as I hold, in that aspect of his nature which means the most for the world at large. We always admire, to be sure, wonderful individuals. The "dæmoniac" power, whereby one soul conquers others with its fascination and leads them whithersoever it wills, is a power to which we delight to yield ourselves, with that love of the strongest which always guides us, even when we think ourselves most selfish. But the admiration for individuals is not the highest form of enthusiasm. The world is more than the men in it. The total of life is something more than the sum of the parts. The place of a man in the universe, in humanity, or in his age, is a more profitable subject for study than the remarkable skill, or beauty, or genius of this man himself. Shelley the moral man, the teacher, is higher in the scale of interest than Shelley the imaginative genius. And with Shelley the man we are now chiefly concerned.

When people speak of Shelley as preëminently a lyric poet, they commonly neglect to notice what profound consequences for his whole character, as a teacher of truth, are implied in this statement. Shelley is a lyric poet; but what is meant by the lyric power in poets? Is it not the power to view emotional experiences by themselves, to separate each of them from all others, to regard every grand moment of life as standing alone, as out of the chain of causes and effects, as a glorious or terrible accident? If this is the fact, and we shall find it true in Shelley's case, the peculiar fitness of our poet to embody and set forth the ideas of a period of revolution will at once be evident. When men break with past methods, the future seems to them a dark field full of strange adventures. What may come they know not; they are sure only of this: that the unexpected will happen, and nothing but the unexpected. The poet, who shall express their emotions, will then naturally be one to whom the world is less a finished system than a scene of grand actions, less a world of certainty than a world of magic. And such a poet will be lyric, rather than dramatic or epic. Let us trace some of the consequences of this general tendency in the case of our poet.

Born in the year 1792, just at the beginning of the most terrible days of the French Revolution, Percy Bysshe Shelley grew up in an atmosphere of unrest. That he was sensitive and misunderstood, inquiring and dissatisfied, we know. Many other boys in quieter times have been like him in these things. But his sensibility was fed with stimulating ideas that not all men hear of very early in life. Of these ideas the most commonplace, perhaps, were the ones that had to do with superstition and mysticism. The Revolution at the end of the last century began, as everybody knows, with not purely rationalistic tendencies. Rousseau was no rationalist, rather reactionary in these respects than otherwise. The whole revolutionary spirit rebelled not merely against the traditional social forms of Europe, not merely against the religious beliefs of ages, but also against the superficial philosophy of the eighteenth century itself. To explain the world by mere understanding was felt to be but a poor satisfaction for the many desires and hopes and fears and impulses that, in this time of restless activity, tinged men's notions of things. So, often in the early revolutionary period you find a vein of mysticism running side by side with the most stoutly radical tendencies. The greatest writers of the time have a mystical tinge in some part of their writings. Rousseau goes into raptures over the mysterious Being he feels everywhere in nature. Goethe, in his childhood, sets up an altar to worship the Eternal after his own fashion, in his early youth studies alchemy and speculates on the Trinity, in his early manhood writes the first part of *Faust*, in his old age the mystical choruses of the *Epilogue*. Schiller, less given to free contemplation of the world, is, by so much the more, a prey to reflective speculation on the hidden soul of things, and the *Ghostseer* and the philosophic lyrics testify to a sense of the mysterious, and an insight into the problematic side of life, which rationalism would wholly fail to comprehend. I need not speak at length of the German Romantic School proper, which sold its birthright to the succession of poetical empire for the poor boon of speculating on the realm beyond experience. England did not escape the contagion. To be sure, much of the nonsensical in this mystical reaction against rationalism was imported from Germany. "Monk" Lewis and many translators familiarized the public with what were little more than vulgar ghost stories, detestable even of their kind. But the genuine spirit, that was willing to see and express the mysterious in the strange destinies, emotions, and fears of a period of change, this natural and justifiable spirit of wonder, found in Coleridge's early poems, in Scott's healthy love of the marvelous, and, later on, in the early stages of the so-called Transcendental movement, a place on English, and, finally, on American ground. We must not despise even vagaries, in so far as they were honest vagaries, of this modern mysticism. Men felt, in the beginning of the Revolution, that the ground was insecure under their feet, that the future held great possibilities, that the world concealed the most weighty secrets. In all this, surely, they were right. To feel in view of the changes a superstitious terror, to picture in the realm of the possible all kinds of fantastic shapes, to interpret the world-secrets in terms of human emotions — all this was doubtless wrong; yet certainly it was natural. Shelley was early a mystic. While yet a boy he read tales of wonder, and wrote them; he dabbled in such occult sciences as common acids and primitive electrical apparatus make possible, and believed he was treading on the verge of nature's deepest and most awful secrets; he conjured the devil with solemn earnestness, and hunted about in the dark for ghosts. Always a sceptic, he never ceased to be a mystic, and, if faith can be found among the followers of a revolution, Shelley held firmly to the end by this one faith, that, be this world what it may, it is at all events wonderful.

More important than his love of the mysterious was his love of freedom. This emotion Shelley breathed in the air about him, and found it intensified by his own heart. Few men have had the love of freedom in a purer form than he. Most men would like to be free themselves, and are willing that others should be what fortune makes them, so long as their lot be not all too hard. Shelley was absolutely universal, perfectly unselfish in his desire that men should be free. Freedom meant for him the same as the universal good of mankind. The slightest shadow of revenge he considered unworthy of the philanthropic soul; and so he would not deprive of liberty even the man who by wrong-doing had seemingly forfeited the right to it. In this one idea of liberty he bound up all his beliefs as to the rules of practical life. To study Shelley's theory of freedom is to study his poetry and prose, once for all, in its whole practical aspect. Most thoroughly an expression of the Revolution was our poet in this direction of his thought.

But yet another set of ideas went to the making of Shelley's world. Early he developed and enduringly he held by a sense of the worth of emotional experiences. In this sense of the significance of feeling Shelley is at one with the best spirits of the early revolutionary age. The rationalism of the first half of the eighteenth century had reduced everything to a mere affair of the understanding. The outburst of poetry which is contemporary with the outbreak of the political revolution is based on the recognition of the importance of feeling. Such a recognition the Storm and Stress poets forced on the German mind, and afterward the Lake school upon the English public, and again, years later, the French Romanticists on the thought of their own country. And one of the most dramatic histories that could be related of this century would be the history of the war of the intenser human feelings to gain and hold a place in esteem and influence beside the higher forms of human intellect. Our modern life is full of this conflict. Literature and daily experience furnish us numberless cases of the struggle, fought out on the grandest and on the humblest fields. An age full of change and of great thoughts is naturally an age of such tragedies.

Shelley never *came* to possess the sense of the worth of emotion; he always possessed it. In a sense in which few men have been uniformly and marvelously impressible, he was so. The power of vision never forsook him. We find him, to be sure, lamenting over his own weakness and poverty of experience:

O world! O life! O time!
On whose last steps I climb,
Trembling at that where I had stood before,
When will return the glory of your prime ?
No more — oh, never more!

Out of the day and night
A joy has taken flight;
Fresh Spring, and Summer, and Winter hoar,
Move my faint heart with grief — but with delight
No more, oh, never more!

But we know that all this divine sadness belongs to a world into whose lowest sphere we ascend but once in a long time. We know that the high visions the poet mourns are such as our eyes see not at all, while his monotony would be to us the most stirring emotional life. The poet moves us to sorrow; we lament with him, but these tears, this cry of anguish, these sobbing measures, we understand their true cause as little as if we were present at the funeral of a god, whom the other gods of high heaven were loudly mourning. What know we of climbing the last steps of life and time, or of the poet's joys that thus took wing? I speak of us as we are in general, single glimpses aside.

Thus far, then, we have noted certain tendencies in Shelley that seem directly expressive of the revolutionary spirit. Like all the general statements about poets, ours must have been found tedious and vague enough. We shall, in the sequel, do what we can to correct our fault by more special references to the poet's works themselves. Yet, before we go farther in this direction, a great question meets us face to face and demands answer, a question very general indeed, but very important. We have been speaking of the age and spirit of the Revolution. What do we mean by the revolutionary spirit? What by the Revolution itself? What is the true significance for human progress of the great movement in which Shelley is but a unit, in which, as we saw in the beginning, we ourselves must play our part, whether we will or not? I conceive it to be a necessary portion of the work planned at the outset that we should give some space to a brief summary of one view at least concerning this great problem.

To state, then, once more, our query: What is the revolutionary spirit? What is in general a revolution of human affairs and of human life? To answer the question neither too vaguely nor too hastily requires that we should revert for a little to first principles.

Our ideas of the world, of the society about us, of life, of ourselves, exhibit, when we look at them somewhat closely, this wonderful characteristic: namely, that we are ever forming them afresh, ever reconstructing them out of their elements, ever creating, as it were, the very products we are supposed most permanently to possess. When we speak the word Humanity, or the word Universe, or Life, or Time, or Being, we can do no real thinking with these words, unless, be it never so quickly and vaguely, we build up, put together, make syntheses of simpler ideas into the form of the great and complex idea suggested by the word used. Thoughts are not dead and finished mind-products that you can lay away on a shelf, so as to take them down entire, dry, and sound, when you want to use them. Thoughts are living, and each thought lives, in the most literal sense, but a moment. You must create your thought afresh whenever you want it. You create it, it flashes into active life for a moment, and then it is forever past. That thought cannot be recalled. You may make another like unto it. You may build ever afresh airy castles, and let time tear them down as soon as they are made. But retain the same thought more than an instant you cannot. Whatever treasures your mind possesses belong to it only in so far as you recreate them, reconquer them again and again, your whole life long. Activity, and ceaseless activity, is the price of the possession of even the humblest kind of knowledge. Give up acting, and all your past labors go for nothing. Even the most plodding soul is thus in so far original in its thoughts as that these result always from its own efforts exerted anew on every impulse. If one ceases entirely to be original, he ceases to think altogether. The essence of thinking is originality.

Our thoughts are thus always the products of momentary, immediately exerted activity. And so, of course, is our practical behavior in so far as it runs parallel to our ideas. We do this or that because Society approves of it, or because Law sanctions it, or because Humanity is benefited by it, or because the world appears to us such and such in nature and ordering, so that in it just this course of action is good. So, at least, we commonly account for our deliberate and most worthy acts. But to behave in this wise presupposes ideas of the world, of humanity, of law, of society — ideas complex and far-reaching, which must, as shown, be formed anew whenever we have reason to form them.

So, then, in order to act at all well and deliberately in the greater affairs of life, men must be able easily and accurately to build up for themselves, just when they want them, clear notions of the great powers and facts that are concerned in human life. They must and do have well formed, if not quite finished, if often quite erroneous, ideas about the universe and about destiny in order to live well the humblest lives.

I lay stress on this great fact, because to understand it is necessary if you want to understand what is revolution. Men's ideas and practices are in so far changing and changing ever, as men active and men thoughtful are alike ever building up anew for themselves their world of ideas, of traditions, and of aims. The whole thought-fabric of human life is there, because human beings will at each and every moment that it should be there. The most cruel wrong, the most painful superstition, the most worthless prejudice, is what it is, because mankind please at this instant to suffer it or to conform to it. The highest aims, the most enduring truths, the most comfortable persuasions, are what they are, because at each and every moment human consciousness creates them again out of chaos. The same mind-power that originated still sustains all that is great or contemptible, morally good or morally evil, in human life. Men's affairs, in so far as they are matters of thought at all, are solely what men make them. Only our sensations escape our control. Our thoughts are our own.

But there is another and a very different aspect to this same truth. Changing, renewing themselves, are all our thoughts and principles ever, but the new thoughts are commonly like the old thoughts, the new acts follow the track of their predecessors. If it is true that our lives at any moment are the products of that moment,

it is none the less true that the product is formed with
the least possible effort, and that the least possible effort
means conformity to previous acts. Hence, along with
the fact of ceaseless activity in human thought and life
goes the no less far-reaching fact of ceaseless economy
of energy, of perennial laziness, in human thought and
life. The world of thought for men is at each moment
what men choose to find it; but let men alone, and they
will choose to find or construct it at each moment just
like the world of the previous moment. Without stimulus, without definite ends in view, men will indeed go on
rebuilding their ideas every instant, but the rebuilding
will not be a reformation, in the ordinary sense, but a
building after the old models. This is what we mean by
conservatism. The conservative spirit creates, indeed;
it must do so. But it creates after the plan of its former
creations. It originates, but by copying. All of us, however, left to ourselves, are conservatives. We need stimulus to make us otherwise. Wants that the old fashions
by constructing our ideas will not satisfy, experiences
that demand new forms of effort to bring them into harmony with older experiences, forces in the world beyond
that call forth new answering strivings in our own hearts
— these are the motives that lead us to be aggressive
and revolutionary, to build our ideas after new fashions,
to originate in a double sense, to will and purpose new
things, to dwell as it were in a new world. Eating and
drinking and sleeping are strictly conservative activities;
they have to be performed ever afresh, but each new
effort is like the former ones. Let us alone, entirely
without disturbance, and conforming our lives to the
rule of least waste of effort, we should inevitably do
nothing but eat and drink and sleep. Disturbances
arouse us, our fellowmen interfere with us, the struggle

for life claims us, experience urges us with its scourge of
many knotted problems, we cease to be purely conservative for a time, and rush on to some new stage of equilibrium. Our methods once formed and conformed to
our circumstances, we act again in peace and with regularity, build our ideas according to our methods, and
remain conservative till new impulses forbid us to continue longer in the same system and away we fly again
in new revolution. Whence it follows that every revolutionary soul is seeking for nothing so much as an opportunity to become once more conservative, while every
conservative differs not at all in his final aim from the
upholder of revolution; for both desire to do with the
least waste of effort what they must do as long as they
live. Each seeks the easiest methods of forming his
ideas and ordering his action. Only the thoughts of the
revolutionary soul are more confused, and so harder to
bring into clearness, than are those of the conservative;
while the ideas of the conservative are less complex, less
evolved, and so less lively and rebellious, than those of
his brother. The innovator is higher in the scale of being, but he is imperfectly developed on his plane. The
supporter of the old is a completer creature on the earth,
but he is farther from Heaven. The restlessness of the
revolutionary spirit is contagious, and reminds the conservative what he ought to be seeking — namely, something higher. The regularity of conservative methods
that have grown to be a second nature is instructive, and
admonishes the rebellious preacher of progress as to
what he is seeking through all changes — namely, rest
and stability.

A revolution, then, in life or in society, is, on its intellectual side, a great change in the methods whereby
men form their notions of the things of life and the

world — a change arising from this, that new material in experience or emotion refuses to be conquered by the old methods, or to conform itself to ideas of the old pattern. But as men are accustomed to conceive of new things after old fashions so long as it is possible to do so, the old fashions of forming ideas will remain unchanged so long as there are not formed great masses of experience that rebel against the old methods. Then, at length, when the impossibility appears of thinking of the world and of life, of the government or of custom, of one's fellows or of nature, in the old way, then suddenly, with anguish and strife, the old methods are abandoned, the entire mode of forming ideas is changed, the fountains of the great deep are broken up, chaos seems imminent, and the struggle for new modes of living and thinking begins.

Of the great practical changes that go side by side with these theoretical changes, we need not speak at length. The alteration in ideas concerns us the more. And one or two especially noticeable things come just here in our way. The ideas, namely, and the ways of forming ideas, that were accounted useful and permanent before the revolution, become upon the approach of the revolution itself objects of unbounded contempt. A holy zeal to destroy takes possession of men. In the service of the Highest, they think, must they tear down and root out. Forgetting that the old methods were adequate for the old problems, that the old way of building ideas mastered the old material, and was in so far forth a true way, leading to relatively true ideas, men denounce the old age as an age of shams and errors, and speak of their present work as a work of regenerating or of creating the truth. Men do not bethink them that the old age, too, was creative, only in a conservative sense. The old ideas they call lies. For "lie" is a name quite often applied to an unserviceable truth, whether its uselessness arises from old age or from extreme novelty. Nor does the imperfection stop here. The revolution, like everything else in life, must have its own ways of forming ideas. Even provisionally, in all the confusion, notions about the world and about destiny must ever anew be created. The revolution throws away the old methods. Its system is not yet completed. It must furnish off-hand new methods. It resorts to high-sounding commonplaces, and wearies us with shallow truisms. The innovator talks of Liberty, of Nature, of Equality, as if with these barren ideas the whole complexity of life could be measured. Forgetting the negative character of the notions he recommends, forgetting that Nature means only the absence of voluntary interference, Liberty the absence of restraint, Equality the absence of definite moral relations, he calls upon all to solve the world-problem with him by repeating these abstractions, and he leaves us as unsatisfied and restless with it all as even his most unbounded revolutionary zeal could have desired to see us.

Such then is revolution, a conflict undertaken in the service of peace, a vast toil accepted in the interest of indolence; or, again, a destruction of numberless ideas and faiths, with the purpose of building up both knowledge and persuasion. No one understands the revolutionary spirit, I think, who does not see the deep-lying identity with it of the conservative spirit. As human nature is eternally active, the innovator is but the conservative with more perplexing facts before him, and the conservative only the upholder of revolution who has now, at length, no more worlds to conquer.

Thus, then, we have sought to give a clear, if very inadequate, idea of what revolution is. And, returning once more to our poet, we shall now understand better the meaning of the facts stated about him, and how he reflects in his own nature the spirit of a revolutionary time. We see how the unrest of the age finds expression in his mingling of the sceptical and mystical in his thought, how the gospel of the Revolution itself is embodied in his practical creed, and how the emotional strivings of the age receive in him a most wonderful representative. It remains for us to examine how these results of the Revolution, as embodied in the poet Shelley, are found to bear fruit in his works, and what lesson is thence to be drawn concerning the value of the tendencies of our time.

Shelley, the practical reformer, is the inspirer of such conceptions as the *Prometheus*, or as the *Revolt of Islam*. Shelley, the poet of great experiences, sparkles in a multitude of rare gems of lyric poetry. Shelley, not only as lyric poet, but as seer and mystic, produces such marvels as the *Triumph of Life*, the *Epipsychidion*, or the *Adonais*, and adorns the *Prometheus* itself. In all these three directions of activity Shelley is the child of the Revolution in so far forth as his aims, his problems, and his beliefs are framed by the revolutionary spirit.

Let us consider briefly the " Prometheus Unbound." A poem in the form of a drama, all of whose characters are supernatural beings, and withal abstractions, might be supposed lacking in human interest. It is not so, however. The keenest sense of the real problems of life pervades every line. The imagery is sometimes colossal, and sometimes subtle and delicate in the extreme, but never cold. A certain tendency to declamation one feels now and then in the first act; but, on the whole, a greater triumph over stubborn material cannot easily be found. The intensest sympathy with human sufferings and hopes could alone have made such triumph possible.

Prometheus is the representative of the soul of man. Personified as he is and given a real body and a real love, he loses something of his perfect character as representative, but gains in human interest. As we know him in Shelley he is a kind of divine man, strong, wise, good, deathless, sleepless. His fortitude in suffering claims our worship at first, his joy and dignity our sympathy at the end.

Forget for a moment, however, the personification. We are not enjoying the poem now, but thinking of its meaning. Let us see through the allegory to the truth beneath. The soul of man then, the human consciousness viewed in its highest manifestations, is condemned by cruel wrong to suffer under oppressors. Who are these oppressors? Shelley evidently means this, that the wise and good and lofty in human nature is perpetually in chains because tradition and custom and government, the instruments of those who are malicious because ignorant and powerful, are ever striving to repress higher development and destroy higher wisdom. This is for the present the law, as it has been the law in the past, that the evil hates the good and is physically the stronger. Here, then, we have the first half of the revolutionary doctrine. The world, as it is, is bad, and must be changed.

The higher consciousness of man is content to endure this wrong, because it knows the end must come. In the fierce anguish of new or cruel oppression, it may, indeed, vent itself in cursing, not wishing other evil to happen to those who are evil than the fact of their baseness, but condemning them in its wrath to that, and leaving off all effort to save them. In calmer moments, however, it sees how much to be pitied are those who are evil. It withdraws its curses; but it has no thought of yielding. One great comfort it finds continually in the companionship of nature. All things mourn the oppression of man, as they will join in his rejoicings when he is free. To the higher consciousness all nature has a voice, is in league with the loftiest aims. But the soul of man has yet other comforts. The strivings of great thinkers to pierce the mystery of things, the outpourings of generosity and love, of poetic fervor and devotion to liberty — all these things are continual prophecies of the coming emancipation. Thus, in courage, and hope, and defiance, the unconquerable spirit lives on, and awaits the day of freedom.

But now, what and whence the deliverance? Can the apostle of the Revolution show us the means and the result of revolution? Evil has sprung up, and now rules the world. How is that evil to be destroyed? Is it not, as much as good, a necessary part of the universe, fixed beyond our power? If not, what are the laws whereby we can remove it? Prometheus can not destroy the evil himself; he is chained. He knows not how long the oppressor's rule will last; he knows only that it must some day end. I have heard of few stranger conceptions than this, emanating, as it does, from a reformer's mind — than this, I say, of the chained Prometheus, the hope and embodiment of all that is good, the divine genius of reform, unable to see a moment in advance the coming of his deliverer, only assured that a deliverer must some day come, and meanwhile inactive, unable by any word or sign to hasten the accomplishment of the deliverance, a slave of fate, a child of accident.

And yet to me welcome is day and night;
Whether one breaks the hoar-frost of the morn,
Or starry, dim, and slow, the other climbs
The leaden colored east; for then they lead
The wingless, crawling Hours, one among whom —
As some dark priest hales the reluctant victim —
Shall drag thee, cruel king, to kiss the blood
From these pale feet, which then might trample thee,
If they disdained not such a prostrate slave.

What means this self-contradiction of the revolutionary spirit? Why is Prometheus, the representative of progress, a prey to accident, helpless? Is this merely the result of the fable, or the expression of Shelley's doctrine of life? Partly, of course, both; but mainly the result of the doctrine. Shelley need not have chosen Prometheus for his hero had he not wished it. He need not have bound himself with the chains of the old story had he not been willing. But, in fact, the world is to Shelley just this: a theatre of the sublimest accidents; a grand conflict of contrasts; a place where the triumph of good or of evil is a matter for joy or for lamentation, for enthusiasm or for horror, but never a definite end, to be reached or avoided by definite means. Shelley, the lyric poet, here appears in the strongest light. With the events and the experiences in the *Prometheus* we are held spellbound. Even their sequence, also, is sublime. But this sequence is as irrational, or super-rational, as it is sublime. Whether we hear about the dim and obscure Necessity, that some day the liberating hour should come, and the tyrant should fall, or whether we look merely at the grandeur of the event itself, the sudden outburst of the universe into a pæan of harmony and an ecstasy of sacred love — whatever we may do, we can but call the entire occurrence a mere happening, a wild chance. We rejoice that the chance has found such a

poet to sing it. But we doubt whether this means anything at all for our poor, real world of practical life. Do
reforms really come in this way? we say.

Angry we are at our own question immediately. Of
course, this is an ideal picture of things. Of course, the
poet leaves out of account the forces of reform, and
sings the glorious fact of reform itself. His picture is
true, as far as it goes. It pretends not to discourse of
causes and effects. And yet we must feel that this is not
enough to have said. There is a defect, not an artistic,
but an ethical one, in this poem. The doctrine is, despite all, only the orthodox revolutionary doctrine again,
the teaching that you need but strike off the chains and
the reform is accomplished; that you need but love fer-
vently enough, and hate is quelled; that, in a word, the
world is a game-table, whereon a good throw of the dice
must now forthwith be expected, because we have so
long made bad throws.

That this was Shelley's doctrine appears, I think, from
all his poetry, and from what we know of his life. His
faith in the good, and in the triumph of the good, was
sublime in its earnestness; but in its foundation it is
much the same as the gambler's faith in luck, or as the
ordinary stock optimism in which people always indulge
when they wish to be considered especially clear-sighted.
To say that in all things evil there is a soul of good; that
the purpose of evil is simply to adorn and embellish good
by contrast; that the deep desires of the human heart
are certain to be realized — all this is supposed to be a
sign of special profundity. Deeper, I think, would be
the insight that were willing to recognize the problems
of destiny as real, permanently real, and so forever insoluble problems; while itself only showed us what, in
this checkered life, the truly and eternally good is, and

bade us seek and increase that good as we are able. But all this shall be but an objection to Shelley's age, not to himself as the embodiment of it. To say that his optimism would have been shallow had it not been so deeply earnest, is to recognize the great truth about him, that he was undeveloped in his thought, but enviable in his ideas.

The revolutionary spirit as the gospel of the accidental was, I have said, especially fitted for Shelley's nature as a lyric poet. The effort he makes in Laon and Cythna (*The Revolt of Islam*) to set forth the doctrine of revolution at length and in order shows, I think, more than ever the truth of this observation. What a monstrous world of loveliness and horror, of glory and shame, is this into which the poet here introduces us. Yet just this is the conception of the world which he learned from his time, adding only the touch of his own genius. One sees in this poem especially one great defect of the doctrine in question. If the belief in sublime accidents leads us to hope that men will suddenly be reformed, and the world suddenly turned from darkness to light, the same belief, making certain as it does the possibility of terrible accidents, leaves only too much room to dread that the good will give place to evil, the world return to its former errors, and life once more be shadowed. If progress be mainly negative and cataclysmic, what horrible reverses will not humanity have to endure throughout all time; the higher the development, the more terrible the disaster.

It is strange to see how this doctrine, which one might suppose, after all, to be in Shelley the result of immaturity and of over-haste to teach his fellowmen, is in fact derived from his father after the spirit, in process of time his actual father-in-law, William Godwin, who had interpreted the doctrines of the Revolution to the young men of Britain in a book published first in 1793, and known as *Political Justice*. Godwin's first period of literary activity, the one from which of course Shelley learned most, is distinguished by a vast confidence in the power of liberty to cure all ills. Shelley drank in eagerly the spirit of the doctrines long after the author had come to see reason to modify the latter, and he was certainly not wanting in effort to put ideas into practice. His expedition to Ireland for the sake of aiding Catholic emancipation and arousing the people is well known, and has, within a few years past, been investigated at length by Rossetti and McCarthy. Very fascinating is the preserved correspondence with Godwin at this time. Godwin had never met Shelley, knew him only by letter, but was not a little disturbed at witnessing the zeal of his young follower. He feared all manner of consequences, and used every effort to dissuade Shelley from continuing his work as an agitator. But Godwin's efforts would have been to little purpose had not the poet come to feel that, after all, his vocation was not in Ireland. Yet only by degrees did Shelley abandon his projects of immediate social reform. Probably he never gave up the idea of being a great reformer some day; and if he had lived, doubtless in the days that followed his name would have been heard in fields other than what are commonly known as poetical. A passage with which the young enthusiast closes a certain *Declaration of Rights*, a brief printed broadside composed during his Irish expedition, will serve to show us how his doctrines sounded when they are expressed, not in poetry, but in prose:

Man! thou whose rights are here declared, be no longer forgetful of the loftiness of thy destination. Think of thy rights, of those possessions which will give thee virtue and wisdom, by which thou mayest arrive at happiness and freedom. They are declared to thee by one who knows thy dignity, for every hour does his heart swell with honorable pride in the contemplation of what thou mayest attain — by one who is not forgetful of thy degeneracy, for every moment brings home to him the bitter conviction of what thou art.

"Awake! arise! or be forever fallen."

Evidently Shelley just here feels as much a hero as if he were Satan himself on the burning marl. He always had a proper and praiseworthy admiration for Satan.

But enough of criticism of the revolutionary gospel as Shelley preached it. We see here the mistake into which our century has ever been apt to fall, a mistake which just now we seek to correct by studying natural science and history — those two great teachers of law and moderation and doubt. The mistake lies in recognizing from one side only that eternal activity which we noticed at the outset — the life-power whereby men make anew at each instant their works of good and evil; in recognizing, I say, this one side of the truth, while forgetting the other side, to wit: the fact of what I have named the perennial laziness of human nature, which prevents men from forming their ideas at any moment differently from the way in which they formed them the moment before, unless both new method and new impulses are present to their consciousness. The Revolution said: Men make their lives such as they are; therefore, if men but willed it, the world would be happy; therefore, grant freedom of action, and nature will do the rest. But the truth is that men do will and must will to be as wretched as they are unless both knowledge and stimulus unite to bring them to a better mind; and even then the change will be slow, weary, full of anguish. We can never be sure that the life of benevolence and of nobility in aim is possible for the mass of the race until we see the result accomplished; and even in that case we have no reason to suppose that evil would be forever prevented, or the goal of progress attained.

The Revolution was at first optimistic. Shelley, as representing it, is in purpose at least an optimist. But the fault of optimism is its blindness, and its *naïve* trust in the power of good intentions. In our time our duty is to correct this optimism by recognizing the ever-present fact of evil in the world. Not for a moment excusing evil nor yet daring to forget or overlook it, we must make up our minds to endless conflict while life lasts. We look forward to no haven of peace so long as we deal with life in its practical aspect. In contemplation, in knowledge, in worship, there is indeed peace; but these things belong not to active life, and to give ourselves up entirely to them is to be false to our duty to mankind. As men we must be in continual war. And even final victory for the right is never certain.

But if the Revolution was imperfect, its spirit was noble; and we who inherit its problems dare not neglect to reverence its ambitions, its faith, and its pure intentions.

I turn to those other forms of Shelley's poetry wherein we may see embodied the intellectual and emotional tendencies of the Revolution. We have been looking at imperfections, not because we desired to pick flaws in Shelley, but because to note these things is profitable. Whatever belongs to our poet's genius we find above criticism. Only as the embodiment of the ideas of his time, or as immature and not wholly master of his material, does he seem to us now and then imperfect. But when we come to consider him as the poetic voice of the emotions of the century, or as seer to whom higher truth is often manifest, here we find him not learning from the age. His genius has full play. The time impedes him less and less.

To catch a fleeting experience in its marvelous perfection of emotional coloring, to crystalize it and make it eternal, to leave it a jewel in the world's treasure house for all time, that it may flash back in multitudinous rays (how well worn the poor figure is!) the light of all future life that falls upon it — this is the great work of the lyric poet. This Shelley has done, living as he did in the midst of a time of revived emotional life, and has done with a magic power at which we can only mutely marvel. Think of the "Indian Serenade," or of the "Lament," which has been already cited, or of the songs in the *Prometheus*, or of Beatrice's song in the last act of the *Cenci:*

> False friend, wilt thou smile or weep
> When my life is laid asleep?
> Little cares for a smile or a tear
> The clay-cold corpse upon the bier.
> Farewell! Heigh-ho!
> What is this whispers low?
> There is a snake in thy smile, my dear,
> And bitter poison within thy tear.

> Sweet sleep! were death like to thee,
> Or if thou couldst mortal be,
> I would close these eyes of pain —
> When to wake? Never again.
> O, world! farewell!
> Listen to the passing bell!
> It says thou and I must part,
> With a light and a heavy heart.

Even the bitter and uncertain conflict to which the Revolution introduces us seems not too hard, if in its pauses we can hear at moments such strains of music as this, breathing as they do from and for hearts that, without all the bitter conflict, might be dead and joined to the things of earth alone.

But if already, as one who notes down experiences, Shelley is a marvel and a benefactor, as a seer of truth he has claims upon our regard even greater. The Revolution has meant for so many souls doubt, distress, hesitation in the choice of ideals, or even blank materialism of moral aims, that it is at once strange and refreshing to deal with a soul whose consciousness of the worth of ideal truth never falters, and that is withal so familiar a guest in the world of the ideals as to be quite unconscious that what itself tells us is at all extraordinary. Most mystics and idealists of any sort are a little proud of the fact, and like to recount to us with childish simplicity how they know secrets that they in no wise intend to reveal, how they deal with matters quite out of the common reach. Shelley has this in common with Swedenborg, that he is a very unmystical kind of mystic, and pretends to know a world of fact by no means so foreign in import to our own world. Shelley's mysticism is, however, unlike Swedenborg's, purely poetical, and hence perfectly safe, being judged altogether by the standards of emotional truth. He introduces us into the region of high contemplation, the region of all most secure from the disturbances of the world of practical life; and in this calm abode he entertains us with thought never dogmatic, infinitely plastic, and colored with all the many hues of his light-giving spirit. Here it is that Shelley appears at times as the man of a fervor rightly to be named religious. There is the same contempt of the finite, the same elevation above the world of sense, the same beatific vision, that marks the best moments of the saints of all ages. *Adonais* is the record of such experiences. The picture of that higher life which he for a moment attributes to the dead is not easily surpassable:

> Peace! peace! he is not dead, he doth not sleep —
> He hath awakened from the dream of life —
> 'Tis we who, lost in stormy visions, keep
> With phantoms an unprofitable strife.

But as a seer, Shelley above all distinguishes himself in the character of a philosopher of love. In this realm so remote, and to most poets so inaccessible, of genuine unsentimental comprehension of the great passion, Shelley has obtained for himself the highest rank. And this is a subject of some importance for our present business, because the poets of the Revolution period have all been very wayward in their treatment of the higher affections; and, in the doubt and obscurity of mind attendant upon the revolutionary spirit, have run from the extreme of sentimental ecstasy to the extreme of scepticism in regard to the worth, the truth, and the enduring character of love. Shelley, in the *Epipsychidion*, and in many single passages, has dealt with the subject in a spirit of the happiest faith. Love is with him real, and of profound importance; but half the ordinary sentiment about it means nothing to him at all. Hardly a more profitable study in higher criticism could be mentioned than one that compared in detail, as Shelley himself has compared in general, Dante's *Vita Nuova* with the *Epipsychidion;* the philosophic love of the age of romance, given up as it is to deep self-questionings, with the free, overflowing passion of this favored child of the age of Revolution, who had loved, as he said, an Antigone in some previous state of existence, and now could never rest in the precious toil of pursuing her shadow through all the world.

But, to sum up, we find in revolution the effort to accommodate the activity of thought and practical life to the ever new demands of emotion and experience. The Revolution of the past hundred years has expressed especially the need of the individual for fuller life, and for a better knowledge of his place in the universe. To use an expression from Novalis, many ways have the men of our day traveled; their end has been the same. To conquer the doubt of the time, and find themselves homes in the strange chaos of ideas with which the modern world seems filled, has been their common effort. Shelley, as a representative of the revolutionary spirit, has two chief things to teach us: that in the world of active life we are in no wise near to a solution of our problems. In the enthusiasm of the poet, which vented itself in dreams of an ideal society, dreams unlike the reality, and useless if they had been the reality, we see mirrored the incapacity of the modern spirit to lay the ghosts it has called up. Optimism is a resort as useless as it is unfounded. We are in the struggle of the Revolution still. We know not how it is to end. It would be no struggle if we did know. We know not that good must and will triumph. If we did know, why lay our vain hands on the ark and meddle with a predetermined fate? But, as such bold efforts as Shelley's teach us, we are unable to know. Progress is full of mishaps and accidents. Our duty is to watch and fight, ever on the lookout for foes, as a tiger in a jungle that the hunters are beating might wander, still brave and confident, but ever looking this way and that for the gleam of the bright spears. In active life the lesson Shelley teaches is, save for the example of his heroism, and devotion, and high purpose, mainly a negative one.

But as a child of the Revolution, Shelley gives example, too, of the intellectual and poetical results of the age of unrest; and here he is our guide altogether. As contemplation is ever better than action, as thought is higher than things, as ideals put to shame the efforts made to realize them, so does Shelley, in the world of ideas, stand far above the unrest of the age, a grand model. Send us, too, O Life, such power to endure and to see! If only at rare moments we are favored as he perpetually was, those moments will outweigh all the years of conflict, and uncertainty, and pain, and disappointment that lengthen out our lives, weary children as we are of an age filled with the woes of doubt and with toil in the dark.

THE NATURE OF VOLUNTARY
PROGRESS

[1880]

FOR the somewhat ambiguous word progress modern thought has tried to substitute the less inexact term evolution. By progress in a series of events or of conditions is commonly meant a tendency in this series toward some final state that seems to a spectator better than any other member of the series. Progress is growth that receives the moral or æsthetic approval of the observer in whose judgment it is progress. But by evolution is meant any growth according to law, whether pleasing to an observer or displeasing. Two persons who cannot agree as to whether in a given series of events there is progress, may be forced to agree as to whether in the same series there is or is not evolution. By optimist we mean very often one who believes that progress is universal and never ending. But a pessimist might believe in evolution. Just as elsewhere in science words implying a knowledge of objective sequences are substituted for words expressing subjective impressions produced by these sequences, so here in the science of society we find true advance made when the abstract term evolution is introduced.

Nevertheless, in the following essay I shall find it convenient to use the term progress rather than the term evolution. For changes in the condition of mankind may be regarded either as following fixed laws of sequence or as having some relation to the wishes of men themselves. Only when we regard these changes in the former way can we be said to study simply the laws of evolution. When we consider the same facts in the second way, when, in other words, we ask what men's own desires have been able to accomplish in the structure of society, then it seems best to say that we are studying the laws of progress. For changes that realize the purposes of the men concerned are called by themselves cases of progress; and so viewing all these changes in their relations to these purposes we may apply to them all the general term voluntary progress. Whether or not we who observe such changes approve of them, at all events the men who made them approve of them. Thus we are at once rising above our own subjective judgments, and yet not abstracting altogether from the subjective element in the structure and growth of society. By studying the nature of voluntary progress I mean, therefore, investigating the way in which human purposes and desires modify the institutions and growth of society, when they modify them at all.

All cases of voluntary progress are also cases of evolution. But in studying the laws of voluntary progress we must not expect to find them the same as the laws of purely physical evolution. If we find them different, that does not indicate that the truth of the laws of physical evolution, *i. e.*, of evolution unaffected by conscious human interference, is in any wise brought into question. Furthermore, in studying voluntary progress we need not consider even the degree of influence that men may possess to alter by conscious interference the phenomena of society; we need only investigate the quality of their influence, the tendency of their interference when it succeeds at all. Finally, not every change in society that results directly or indirectly from conscious effort concerns us in the following; but only those results need be studied that are examples of the success of deliberate and persistent efforts. Hasty undertakings, unwisely conceived and soon followed by repentance, are not cases of voluntary progress. Even those who undertook, and whose efforts were effective, do not approve of the result.

1. *The Subjective Prerequisites of Voluntary Progress.* — The study of the phenomena of voluntary progress may best be begun by considering what are the prerequisites in the consciousness of mankind which make voluntary progress possible. Evidently men cannot consciously influence the growth of society until they themselves have attained the power of criticizing present conditions, of reflecting on means of bringing about a change, and of understanding and conceiving in some general form their needs. Analysis of the present state, discovery of laws of change, the formation of ideals, these belong to all voluntary progress. Voluntary progress is therefore especially characteristic of civilization and grows more distinct as civilization advances. That he is progressive at all, and more especially that his progress is largely modified by his volition, seems to distinguish the civilized man more and more as he rises higher.

2. *Consciousness attendant upon Voluntary Progress.* — With these prerequisites in mind we notice two principal tendencies that appear in all voluntary progress under normal conditions. These tendencies are inseparable, though, as we shall see, where one of them is especially prominent the other is often kept in the background of consciousness.

The two tendencies referred to I shall call Conservatism and Optimism. The uncommon tendencies that under some circumstances directly oppose these are the Revolutionary Spirit and Pessimism. But, as will be shown, these tendencies have never long been without mixture of the tendencies that they oppose, and may be regarded as but modifications of the normal tendencies.

a. Conservatism. — By Conservatism I mean the tendency to change old conditions to meet new needs, in such a way as shall involve the least possible expenditure of energy. But this expression needs explanation. Conservatism is commonly supposed to be simply submission to an existent order of things. Is this true? Let us in answer consider the conditions under which either conservatism or its opposite is possible. Evidently neither of them can be spoken of unless the society of which we speak is one whose members have some conscious power to affect its constitution. There is neither conservatism nor liberalism in a flock of sheep. Old customs are indeed followed by new generations of sheep, but without consciousness, without power to resist or approve. There can only be conservatism when men could change their social condition, and know that they could. When they have the power to change in some definite way their social order, and refuse to do so, then for the first time they show the conservative spirit.

But this power to change an existing order of things, what does that imply? Evidently an understanding of the existing order of things, the power of thought already well developed. An institution or a tradition is not an objective thing of sense. All kinds of symbols, or of effects, or of outward expressions of the institutions may be seen with the eyes, but the institution or tradition itself must be conceived. Now, however, when the social forms are comprehended in this manner, what will it be to cling to them, to wish to retain them unchanged? Plainly, such clinging to the old forms can only mean a tendency to arrange new experiences in the old way, and to do new things after the old plan. Having seen how given social phenomena are instances or results of certain forms, the conservative wishes to find that all new social phenomena are also instances or results of the same social forms. His attitude then is one of desire to organize his new experiences without taking the mental trouble to construct or to accept new forms for the process of organizing. Conservatism is therefore an effort to save energy of thought. New conceptions, new plans of action, involve more effort than is involved in the subsumption of new facts under old conceptions, or in the undertaking of new work after old plans. Were it as easy to change the forms of our thought or the plans of our actions as it is to change the matter of our thought or the concrete things with which and for which we act, there would be no conservatism. The conservative, like every other human being, delights in variety of experiences, welcomes the new, and hopes for better things; it is only the forms of his thought and action which he does not desire to change.

But if this be the explanation of conservatism, where is there room left for radicalism? If it be true that to change old forms is in general harder than to alter the material that comes under these forms, and if the desire to do all things with the least expenditure of effort be an universal human desire, where then is there room for a tendency whose nature it is to seek change of form, and whose delight it is to expend energy without stint? The probable answer seems to be that a steadfast and permanent tendency to destroy forms because they are established does not exist. There is, I take it, no absolute radicalism in voluntary progress. Men never desire, except in the heat of passing anger, merely to alter institutions or traditions. The Extreme Left in its wildest schemes wishes in fact to adapt present institutions to new experiences. It is true that change of social forms is a common object of revolutionary effort. But the change is sought only because in view of new experiences and of new needs it is believed that retaining the old form would imply a greater waste of energy than finding a new one, because the old form does not at all suit, *i. e.*, explain or generalize the new facts. For total contradiction between form and matter, between general plan and individual need, between conception and single experience, would be the greatest expenditure of energy possible. A new form must be sought, and that in the very interest of conservatism. The very thing that the conservative desired, viz., to do new things with the least waste of effort, is now gained by modifying the old plan. "He is the best conservative who lops the mouldering branch away." This might be the expression of the most radical thought; yet it does not essentially differ from the expression of the most conservative thought. The question between the conservative and the radical is always a question of fact, not one of fundamental principles. Both must admit, if they but fairly examine their consciousness, that they desire new things of experience, that neither wishes mere monotony. Both must admit that they wish the new things to be dealt with after such a fashion as to economize effort in mastering and using them. Both must admit finally, if they reflect, that it is harder to find a new fashion of dealing with things, than to employ an old fashion for new purposes, always excepting the case wherein the old fashion is entirely inadequate for the new purpose. The difference is then merely about the concrete instance. In this case, will labor be saved by this change of tradition or of institution?

In brief, then, the radical is for the most part the conservative whose experiences will not fit into the forms to which he has previously learned to refer all his experiences. He will cease to be a radical and become once more openly conservative, as soon as his experiences harmonize with his rules and traditions sufficiently to make the effort of carrying out fixed plans under varying circumstances once more less than the effort of forming new plans.

Experience verifies this construction very clearly. That conservatism applies only to permanence of form will appear, if we remember that what the people concerned regard as forms may appear to others, to ourselves for example, as mere accidental circumstances. Conservatism clings to what it regards as a form, and has of course no gift of infallibility. To what is regarded as purely material the conservative tendency does not extend itself.

That, therefore, freedom of action within bounds is characteristic of all conservatism, whether extreme or otherwise, is plain enough on the slightest reflection. But that radicalism, unless we mean thereby the violence of transient passion, and no more, is even in its extremest forms in spirit conservative, and desires change not from love of change, but by reason of the stress of new experiences and problems, is not of itself so evident. But already we can mention one or two facts that most clearly indicate this result. For example, experience shows that very many revolutions claim to be returns to old and forgotten or neglected rules or traditions. Religious reforms, for example, commonly represent themselves as awakenings to a new sense of the truth and importance of old teachings. Christianity was at first explained as an effort to fulfill in spirit the law that had long been encumbered by a mass of later unauthoritative tradition. The Protestant reformers of modern times have generally undertaken to restore primitive Christianity. The Puritan revolution began with the program of rescuing the English Constitution from the abuses brought into its operation by the Stuart kings and their advisers. Every now and then some modern thinker calls attention to his doctrines, and gains support or ridicule for them, by representing them as having the authority of some ancient system; and thus Democritus and Plato, or Lucretius, or perhaps Spinoza, in strangely modernized shapes, are brought into play as ghosts on the stage of contemporary controversy. Where a revolutionary movement cannot point to an historical tradition as its authority, it loves to invent a mythical tradition. The fiction of the Social Contract gave support to the doctrines of the French Revolution. The authority of a great religious reformer like Buddha, is heightened by a mythical tale of his life in many preceding states of existence, so that an appearance of continuity may show the new religious revolution to be but a revival of old tendencies.

In all these cases, no doubt, the revolution cannot fully justify itself by its appeal to tradition. If the tradition is mythical, all outside the circle of the new faith will remain unconvinced by it. If the tradition is historical, the old rules and traditions will seldom if ever suffice to justify the new ideas. The Puritans had at last to break with the English Constitution and dethrone the king. The apostle Paul soon proved to the early church that its theory about restoring the old law was inadequate to its needs. Protestant reformers, when they undertake to restore primitive Christianity, soon show by their results that their real object is something different. Yet this inability of the reformer to identify his reform with any tradition does not show that he makes an effort to break away from tradition altogether. His inability proves only that there are new social needs to be met. His effort proves that in trying to meet these new needs, he has sought to do so with the least possible change of existing traditions. And see how this effort gives rationality and organization to the spirit of the reformers. The old way known to the fathers, and since forgotten, the purity of the ancient faith, the authority of the ancients, how such ideals, appealed to by vigorous and revolutionary reformers help to give unity to this new movement, which would otherwise sink into a mass of vague tendencies, purely negative. It is the conservative element in revolutions that saves them from utter confusion. And even if they found their conservatism on a myth, the myth gives them unity. Nothing can more plainly show the purely relative nature of radicalism than these attempts, unsuccessful as they prove, to reduce the tendency towards change of forms as much as possible, by making it appear as much as possible like a mere effort to restore. But enough of these examples. Our thesis is that conservatism and radicalism are examples of a single tendency of voluntary progress, the tendency, namely, to satisfy changing needs with the least .possible change of plan, to gain as much new experience as possible with the least alteration of the ways of gaining it. Yet thus far we exemplify rather than prove the doctrine.

b. Optimism. — The second tendency mentioned above as found everywhere in voluntary progress is the tendency that for want of a better name we may call optimism. Optimism I define as the belief that things are in some respect growing better, and that human effort can make them grow better. Evidently the belief that a certain measure of success is to attend human efforts is a necessary part of all deliberate interference on the part of individuals with the social order. Interference, selfish or otherwise, is prompted by the belief that it can accomplish some end. Nor can this belief ever be founded wholly upon experience. Be the changes attempted great or small, no one can ever tell whether or not coming events will prove the changes successful. Confidence in success is to a great extent a matter of temperament and earnestness. Wherever that temperament and that earnestness is present which is adequate for the purposes of those who are to bring about social changes, we shall find that confidence in the triumph of the right which is here called optimism.

No doubt the strict meaning of the word optimism would imply more than merely this. Optimism, as a theory of the universe, is the assertion that our world is throughout very good. This assertion has long been out of date. But there is the disposition to regard things as tending towards the good, which everywhere accompanies vigorous civilization. Mr. James Sully has proposed for this tendency the name meliorism, but as yet the term shows no signs of becoming popular. As for its nature, this tendency is evidently either an aid to conservatism or a compensation for the absence of conservatism. The civilized man, we have said, seeks to retain the forms of his activity unchanged, or to change with the least possible expenditure of energy when it becomes absolutely necessary to alter the forms. But when the expenditure of energy required by the circumstances is very great, then one must reconcile one's self to the required rebellion against conservatism by a corresponding increased confidence that one's great efforts are to meet with becoming reward. And so the confidence must be greater in proportion as the change that has to be brought about is of wider scope and profounder influence. Optimism is especially characteristic of great reformers, of men engaged in conflicts, of new civilizations. Every religious journal published by a small sect will furnish an example of the way in which a heresy is the more confident of success and of coming universal domination if its present members are very few. To be sure such optimism is not inconsistent with much that is called pessimism. Reformers spend much time in denouncing the world that they have come to save. Heretics generally regard the rest of mankind as outcasts, and declare the existent state of things very bad. But such a belief does not constitute true pessimism. If evils are merely accidental, and if the reformer knows the way by which to remove them, then there may be much cause for grief, but none for despair. All upholders of revolution are believers in the success of human effort, are therefore optimists. The more ignorant and misguided the revolution, the more does its optimism appear in glaring colors. For in such a revolution, since wisdom fails, the faith of the reformer alone remains to distinguish it. No modern institution is more purely optimistic than the Sand Lot.

Optimism, when not the expression of the undisturbed and self-satisfied conservative spirit, is thus seen to be the effort on the part of conservatism to be reconciled to those sacrifices which the conservative spirit must permit. As conservatism was found to be universal but in a very relative sense, so we find optimism a universal tendency of civilized men, only very much modified by experience and reflection. There are, in fact, four stages of optimism, four forms in which it appears, each one more modified than the previous, because more enlightened. The first stage is that of the purely individual childish optimism, which may be expressed in the formula: "I shall prosper." Such optimism, if shared by all the individuals of a community, will express itself in an unbounded confidence in the future success of all that the community undertakes. But the feeling will be personal, not patriotic, not a willingness to sacrifice, but a belief of each one that he is destined to be happy. Such is the optimism of a mining camp. That the fact of misfortune modifies such optimism, and makes it, as in the case of the ancient Hebrews, a belief that only a good man is happy, and successful in his undertakings, this makes the optimism none the less purely selfish, and necessarily unable to stand in the face of the experiences of more complex civilization. Men soon learn that individuals are not of necessity destined to be happy, and the feeling of higher civilization comes to be more and more what we may call patriotic optimism, a faith that individual efforts, if lost for the individual himself, are not lost for his community, that the combined effect of everybody's efforts is progress and general good. This second stage of optimism is what characterizes communities, and nations, and sects, and great organized movements of thought, while they are yet growing and active. Beyond this stage the common civilized consciousness never rises. Yet those few who take interest in humanity as a whole and to whom the chief end is the good of mankind may be optimists in a higher but more modified sense. Such optimists see that communities and sects, nations and even races may fail utterly, but they believe that in the long run mankind as a whole improves, and that efforts in the service of humanity need never be wholly lost. Whatever the evils of life now, life they believe tends towards the good. In all their labors they are hopeful. On each one of these three stages it will be seen that something is regarded as bad in life though hope is still entertained that this evil may be removed. The sanguine individual suffers particular evils, but hopes for good in the end. The sanguine patriot sees fortune desert him or his friends, but believes in the final triumph of the nation. The sanguine humanitarian trusts that somehow good will be the final goal of ill, yet has to admit that the ill is at present very great. A fourth stage is possible which is a more modified, I will not now say a higher, form of optimism. This fourth form of optimism sees so much evil in the world and so little chance of remedy in the regular course of things that we commonly call it pessimism. Yet this belief is not one of entire despair; there is still hope for human effort. Only the effort must evidently be of an entirely new and strange kind, the good attained one that ordinary men would call very scant reward. This form of modified optimism declares common human life, with all its ordinary aspirations and ends a failure, and sees no reason to expect that it will be better by and by. But from this point of view there is still a way of escape. A new life, one with altogether different aims is still possible, and in this ideal life there is good. Such is the doctrine of Buddha, of asceticism everywhere, of the author of the "Imitation of Christ," and in modern times of Schopenhauer, and even of the newer schools of English poetry, whose doctrine, to be sure, is not an ascetic one.

This last form of optimism has itself several varieties. It may amount to a belief that human life, though a failure in this world, will be a success in another. It may form for itself a picture of some entirely unique life on this earth, which would be perfectly good, though only saints can live it. Or it may conceive of certain states of consciousness, which though they cannot fill the whole of life may from time to time come into life so as to make the rest of it endurable. Contemplation, or poetic enjoyment, or some other form of impersonal pleasure, may be chosen as the ideal. A world in which such things are attainable is not wholly bad, and since we may hopefully strive to attain them, we are still even on this stage after all the disillusioning process, not without the earnestness that in the first place was the soul of optimism. Absolute pessimism does not appear to exist as a permanent state of consciousness in civilized men. For several poets and philosophers the claim has been made that they were absolute pessimists. Perhaps they may have been for a time, for the greater part of their lives even; but they were commonly hard workers and acute thinkers. Study and thought are activities requiring earnestness and enthusiasm, and therefore some form of hope. It seems best to say, then, that while the most skeptical form of optimism hopes for little of that which men commonly call good, it is not without belief that there is some good in life, though that good be very hard to attain. If selfish activities are given up as hopeless, then in labor for the good of others there is found a permanent and attainable end. Or if practical life is despaired of, refuge is taken in contemplation. Or if thought is painful, art for art's sake is the last resort of the cultivated mind. The active man is never entirely without hope.

To sum up our results thus far. Conservatism and optimism attend voluntary progress everywhere. But in form they are modified as experience advances or as circumstances become more complex. Conservatism sometimes disguises itself as the wildest radicalism, and optimism sometimes appears as the dreariest hatred of the world. But throughout the effort of human consciousness is to preserve intact, as far as possible, the unity and simplicity of the forms of its thought and action. When the form must be modified, let the modification be the least possible. If the change must be great, let the confidence that the good will triumph be as strong as possible. But if experience be so complex as not to be reducible to known forms at all, if our ideas are so disturbed that skepticism results, if our needs are so complex that unity of plan is impossible, and if in the great changes that must be made we can have little hope of success, then at least when all else fails we seek the same that we at first sought, unity and simplicity of ideas and ideals, by breaking altogether with the traditional vein of life and setting up for our goal something entirely beyond the range of ordinary human vision. In all these stages we have exemplified many forms of voluntary progress, but always one and the same nature.

3. *The Law of Voluntary Progress.* — If the foregoing analysis is correct we have already discovered something of the nature of voluntary progress. We shall be led to believe that voluntary progress is characterized by a tendency to preserve social forms intact, and so to make them apply to new material. We shall consider again, if we agree to the foregoing, that voluntary progress takes the direction of change with the least possible expenditure of energy, when change of social forms is required. And yet further, as a corollary to these principles we shall expect to find that the resultant of voluntary progress is a simplification of the social structure, a change in the direction of homogeneity rather than in the direction of heterogeneity. When in any series of social changes we find growth towards the heterogene-

ous and complicated, we shall be led to believe that deliberate volition is not responsible for the changes in so far forth as they were changes in the direction of increased complication. And thus the law of voluntary progress will appear as in one important respect directly opposed to the law of purely physical evolution, social or extra-social, as this law is usually formulated.

4. *The Types of Voluntary Progress.* — Voluntary progress as the deliberate modification of the forms of human activity to suit changing needs, will have as many different types as there are types of human activity. The voluntary activities in which men are concerned in society are the forms or types which specially interest us in this essay. We shall have to speak of individual activities, but we shall do so only in so far as is necessary to throw light on social activities. In classifying the types of human action, we shall have for the first, to leave out of account such activities as are mainly determined in their nature and growth by external causes, although they may be in themselves voluntary activities. If we turn to those types of human activity which are largely under men's control, not only as regards single acts, but as regards the forms used, our attention is attracted by four distinct types of action manifest on the slightest consideration: (1) thought activities; (2) industrial activities; (3) political activities; (4) and moral activities. In all of these a concert of individual actions produces a resultant greater than the numerical sum of the individual contributions, or else different in kind from this sum. Thus by discussion and by the aid of tradition, the united effort of men produces thoughts which no individual thinking, however acute and continued, could ever have evolved. The resultant of united political activity is again the state, an institution differ-

ent in kind from the contributions brought by any one
member of society, whose power is therefore not the
mere arithmetical sum of the powers of its subjects, but
an organic product of all of them. And so in the case of
the other types of activity mentioned, which are none of
them purely individual, and all of them voluntary, and
all of them determined to a considerable extent in their
forms by the will of those who engage in them. In the
growth of these activities we shall expect to find voluntary progress.

5. *Voluntary Progress in Thought.* — For this part of
our study a definition of thought is needed. Thought is
the process of consciously forming beliefs. A belief is a
mental assertion to the effect that the individual who
believes has had a certain experience, or will have a certain experience, or under certain conditions would have
a certain experience, or that other conscious beings have
had or will have, or under conditions might have a certain experience. These alternatives exhaust the possibilities of belief. To believe that anything is, or has
been, or will be, is to believe in a past or future or possible state of consciousness in some being. The limits of
conceivably possible experience are the limits of belief.

On their subjective side, *i. e.*, in their relations to the
believer himself, beliefs are always the satisfaction of
individual wants. No belief can be said to be forced upon
any one in any other sense than that it is accepted because it satisfies a conscious want. I say no belief; the
content of consciousness at any moment, whatever we
feel to be present in our minds here and now, that is
forced upon us. But beliefs relate to past, future, or
possible contents of consciousness. The past, the future,
the possible, are not immediately given facts. They are
only assumed facts, fundamental persuasions. As such

they express fundamental wants of consciousness. We feel the highest practical interest in holding fast our faith that there was a past and will be a future, and that our judgments as to the possible have validity. The present moment does not satisfy us. It is poor and empty. It gains meaning only when we view it as one of a series, or as one fact in a world of facts. Therefore, if we say we must believe in past and future, we do not in general intend to refer to the "must" that expresses the absolutely binding force of present momentary knowledge; but the "must" expresses a felt need.

The adjective "true" is applied to a belief by the one whose intellectual wants it satisfies, at the time when it satisfies them. The satisfaction of an intellectual want is attended with the expectation of permanent satisfaction to be gained from the same belief. To believe sincerely in anything and to believe that we always shall believe in it are one and the same thing. Therefore, by the term truth men express a general conception of permanent persuasion. He claims to know the truth about any thing, whose convictions about that thing never change. The one who possessed absolute truth would be the one whose convictions never could change about any thing.

These considerations on the nature of thought are necessary to the understanding of voluntary thought-progress. But if this be the nature of thought as the process of forming beliefs, then thought-progress is to be studied much as we study political progress. A system of beliefs is held, just as a system of government endures, so long as it seems to the men concerned advantageous to cling to it. Beliefs change, like institutions, when they no longer accomplish the end of their existence. And voluntary progress in thought will exemplify those general characteristics of voluntary progress which we have already pointed out. That is to say, voluntary thought-progress will be possible only when men have advanced far enough not merely to possess, but to analyze and reflect upon their beliefs. Voluntary thought-progress will be conditioned furthermore by a knowledge of the way in which new beliefs may be formulated and systematized. And a third prerequisite of voluntary thought-progress will be the ability to form an ideal of a perfect system of beliefs in those matters wherewith the thinker is immediately concerned.

Besides these conditions the same tendencies that appear in voluntary progress elsewhere may be supposed to exist in case of thought-progress. Normal and ordinary thought-progress, if our conclusions are right, will be characterized by conservatism and optimism. The optimism will show itself in a belief that truth in the direction of research is attainable. The conservatism will tend to preserve established forms of thought, established methods or persuasions, with as little modification as is possible. The four stages or kinds of optimism distinguished above may also be distinguished in voluntary thought-progress. There is the individual or personal optimism of school boys and enthusiasts generally, the optimism of the paradoxical thinker. There is the optimism of the disciple of some master, or of the specialist. Here the individual knows he is fallible, but trusts in the power of his church, or of his school, or of his science, to attain truth. This corresponds to the optimism of the patriot. Then there is the still more skeptical optimism of the man who thinks that, though error is vastly in excess of truth in this world, yet the truth is certain to win in the long run. The fourth stage is what many would call universal skepticism or thought-pessimism. Yet it is a familiar fact that absolute skepticism, the doubting that one doubts, is an impossible frame of mind. And in fact the despair that mankind will ever attain absolute truth is not at all incompatible with an earnest devotion to the interests of science and philosophy. The effort to formulate and systematize and simplify and generalize our thought, need not be given up or pursued with less earnestness when we have abandoned the hope of ever perfecting and so ending our knowledge.

If we undertake now to explain in a single formula the nature of voluntary thought-progress, we shall, I conceive, be led to the following: Voluntary progress in thought may consist (1) in the modification of old principles or beliefs or conceptions to meet the demands of new experience. And since these old beliefs or notions are the expression of certain human interests, if the interests remain the same, the beliefs or notions will be altered only so much as is necessary to keep them from manifest contradiction with the new experience; and the alterations will tend, if possible, to simplify, unify, and render homogeneous the old beliefs, so as to make them directer expressions of the old systems. (2) Voluntary thought-progress may be the formation of new beliefs or conceptions different from any before possessed, for the sake of meeting the demands of entirely novel experience. And here the interest of thought will be the formation of such beliefs or conceptions as will conduce to the understanding of all the new experiences with the least expenditure of thought-energy. The result will be an explanation of the new phenomena by analogy with previous phenomena, and the formation of simple and general conceptions; and will here be a tendency towards unity of conception. (3) Voluntary thought-progress may be occasioned by a change in the interests which men take in experience. And here the progress will consist in an effort to express most simply and with the least waste of energy the new interests in terms of new or of old experience. Each one of these forms of voluntary thought-progress demands a further study.

a. Progress as the Modification of Old Beliefs. — At the time when voluntary progress begins, that is, when men first begin to reflect on their thought and its work, they find beliefs already existing. We have not, therefore, to explain the origin of belief, but only to see how volition modifies it. All these primitive beliefs, I say, express human interests. How do they express them?

In general, a belief expresses a human interest by concerning itself with those experiences only that appeal to this interest, and by bringing these experiences into such an order as shall make them most simply and clearly conceived. In the search for truth, *i. e.*, for enduring belief, our consciousness is (1) selective: it pays attention to those facts only that affect some one of our interests. And (2) on the other hand, consciousness is not merely selective, but also a faculty of organization. And to organize experience is to treat the greatest possible number of data with the greatest uniformity of method, and to regard them as examples of the fewest possible distinct forms of reality. Every belief will be, therefore, the simplest possible adaptation of the facts of experience to our desires regarding experience; the easiest possible compromise between prejudice and reality.

But if the same interests continue of which any belief is the expression, then modification of the belief can result only from the appearance of new facts of experience. When the form is no longer adequate to the matter, the same interest which realized itself in the old form will seek a new one. The change from the old form to the new one will follow the law of least expense of energy, the general law of conservative progress. Instances of this process in matters of vague popular opinion could easily be found. More interesting, however, would be an example furnished by a great epoch in the progress of thought.

As it is true that no single scientific idea springs from nothing, so it is true that the whole body of modern scientific thought grew by slow degrees out of previous non-scientific tendencies that were for the most part theological. Let us see how this growth originated. Every one would call the origin of modern thought a case of voluntary progress. In it were expressed human interests. But what interests? The mere delight in novelty of conceptions? History shows the contrary. In its earliest forms modern thought appears indeed as the revolt against authority, as the desire to free one's self from Aristotle and from the Church. But what interest was expressed in this revolt? The same in fact that was expressed in the philosophical movements in the early Church, in the movements resulting in the formation of the orthodox dogmas. The effort was to reconcile the religious consciousness of mankind with experience and with the universal desire for simplicity of conception. The early Church had found itself in the possession of certain vague faiths. These had to be formulated, i. e., reduced to unity and simplicity. This work had been done by the Fathers and the Councils. Now, however, the Christian part of mankind was brought, by the crusades and by the other world-historic events of the time, again face to face with the fact of the diversity of religious beliefs, and, by the knowledge of antiquity, into the presence of many thought-tenden-

cies long since forgotten. Variety, contrast, and contradiction, in experience, faith, and dogma, were thus
brought into view. The variety must be reduced to
unity, the contrasts understood as different forms of one
reality, the contradictions got out of sight. The first
great effort to do this took form in the second period of
Scholasticism, which found in the conceptions of the
Aristotelian philosophy, as added to and corrected by the
dogmas of the Church, the unifying principle which was
to satisfy the needs of belief. Later, when yet further
experiences refused to be reconciled with the scholastic
conceptions, there sprang up the Renascence philosophy. But this philosophy, though apparently in spirit a
revolt against the theology of the Church, was unwilling
to desert the faith entirely. The tendency to reconcile
new needs with old forms is nowhere better realized
than in the doctrine of the so-called double truth. The
Renascence philosophers tried to persuade themselves
that there could be two kinds of verity, one theological
and one philosophical. The theological truth they pre-
ferred to regard as of the higher order. But in addition
to the data of faith there were to be received the data of
reason. The contradiction which seemed to exist was
not to be admitted. Now, to a superficial observer, this
doctrine of the double truth might indeed seem to be
growth in the direction of multiplicity and contrast of
ideas. But in fact the doctrine was an effort to make the
real multiplicity and contrast given in experience seem
less than it actually was. When we reflect that the
thinkers of the Renascence were for the most part sincere in their doctrine of the double truth, and that by
the doctrine philosophical truth was viewed as truth of
a secondary, lower order, and theological truth as the
one highest revelation of existence, we shall see that in

so far as in this case there was a growth towards complexity and contrast of ideas, the growth was involuntary, and that in so far as there was voluntary progress, this progress was in the direction of simplicity and harmony of conception. Throughout modern thought we should find upon search this same tendency to reduce new doctrines to old doctrines, and to conceal as much as possible the magnitude of a change when it must be made. It is as if the new hated its own existence, and would only be reconciled to its place in thought when it was able to name its own ancestors and to show itself forth as the heir of ancient virtues and rights. Thoughts are like men, and dislike to be regarded as creatures of yesterday.

In fine then, voluntary progress in thought follows the plan of modifying old conceptions to meet new experiences, when any such modification is possible. And the laws of this kind of voluntary progress are: first, the modification is always a minimum, resulting in the most favorable compromise possible for the old ideas in view of the new data; second, the modification is, so far as it is voluntary, a change in the direction of unity, simplicity, and homogeneity of thought, as opposed to the increase of complexity which naturally would take place.

b. Voluntary Progress as the Formation of New Beliefs. — In previous paragraphs we have been considering the process that may be called adaptation, *i. e.*, the subordination of new percepts to old concepts. But wide as is the use of adaptation it does not satisfy all the demands of experience. Old conceptions sometimes fail altogether to apply to new experiences. In such cases we have the formation of a distinct science or branch of science not naturally growing out of any previous science; or of a new belief that is not a modification of a previous belief. The work of voluntary progress in this case is mainly inventive. Fundamental conceptions must be formed, such as will reduce the new phenomena to order. What conceptions are chosen? The answer is, the simplest conceptions possible. Of two scientific hypotheses equally suggested and confirmed by experience, we invariably accept the simpler, in case the difference between the two is at all marked. Why do we do this? Who has revealed to us that of two methods of doing the same thing nature always takes the simpler? No one. The so-called axioms, that nature makes no leap, or that nature takes the shortest way to every goal, or that nature permits no waste, either mean nothing, or they are merely postulates of our subjective thought, determinations to see in the world simplicity and unity, because simplicity and unity of thought mean saving of labor for us.

The result of voluntary progress in this case is, therefore, briefly stated, transition from complexity, heterogeneity, and vagueness of conceptions, to simplicity, unity, i. e., homogeneity, and definiteness of conceptions. Here then voluntary progress appears again as a simplifying process. The law of physical evolution as stated by Spencer seems thus to differ from this law of voluntary progress, in that while in both cases we have growth from the indefinite to the definite, we find in physical evolution growth towards the complex, and in voluntary progress growth towards the simple. If nature loves many contrasting forms of life, thought in expressing any one of its interests loves even monotony of form in its ideas.

c. *Voluntary Progress with Change of Thought-Interests.* — Yet experience is not the only changing factor in the formation of belief. Change of form may be caused not only by the appearance of new facts but also by an alteration of human interests. In considering what bearing these alterations of tendency have upon our understanding of voluntary progress, it is necessary to remember that the change of interest is itself not voluntary. Progress, in so far as voluntary, follows certain fixed directions; lies, as it were, all in the same plane. The causes which change the plane of voluntary progress, the directions of its efficacy, cannot be understood without an appeal to the laws of involuntary change; and into the study of these we have not here to enter. But when the change of interest has once occurred the further process may be in the main voluntary progress.

I mention the class of cases thus defined chiefly to point out that certain tendencies in the growth of beliefs which seem to contradict the law before stated, the law of conservative progress towards unity and simplicity with the least expenditure of effort, are in reality not exceptions to the general rule. In so far as they are voluntary they result from a change of interest. No one makes or changes his own desires. The change of his interests is an involuntary process. Of the tendencies referred to as apparent exceptions to the rule two classes occur readily to our minds. There is first the general rule that systems of thought once formulated and widely accepted, in process of time tend to disintegrate by a kind of internal decay of the school that accepted them. The second class of cases is the one referred to in the rule that opinions develop in rhythms, that the growth of thought is in returning cycles. To explain both these classes of instances I should adopt the same general method. In both of them we have change of interest.

As for disintegration, the first of the classes of phenomena mentioned, it is commonly the work of a new
generation. Young men learn from their masters the
elaborate doctrines of some system. The doctrines like
spider webs cover everything valuable in the world of
thought. If they are accepted as infallible there is little
more room for individual efforts. But young men must
have reputations, and they can make them only by
working for them. Could they have made their reputations by building up the old system, nothing would
have pleased them better. But that cannot be done, because it has already been done by their fathers. No
reputation is to be gained by defending the established
faith, therefore these young men with one accord tear
it down or sweep it away, and then fall to fighting over
the ruins. This is what we call disintegration. It is a
voluntary progress to be sure, but its peculiar character
depends upon the change of interest involved. I see,
therefore, in these instances nothing contradictory to
the general principle of the conservatism of voluntary
progress as laid down at the outset of this discussion. In
so far as voluntary, the new growth is conservative.
Only so far as it is physically forced by the working of
extra-volitional psychological laws, is it essentially non-
conservative.

The second case, that of the rhythm of opinion, the
general theory of reactions, is more difficult. To state
briefly and without proof the way in which I should explain the phenomena in question: I should declare reactions in thought-history to be the results, first of
purely physical causes, either political or economical,
and secondly, of the fact that the fundamental interests
of human thought in the explanation of the world are
not one but various. Any one of these fundamental

interests may be obscured at any time by special causes, but will be certain to reassert itself again after a while. For example: there are two fundamental methods of explaining the facts of experience, either by noting their relations in so far as the things explained are co-existent, or by noting the laws of their sequence. That is, in science we study either the nature of phenomena or the history of phenomena; we analyze the elements whereof reality is composed, or we relate the way in which real things change and grow. The type of the one kind of study is pure mathematical science, which analyzes elements altogether. The type of the other kind of study is our modern theory of evolution, which confines itself mainly to the study of the history of things. Now the antithesis between the mathematical and the historical tendencies in thought runs through the whole history of belief. Commonly one method is for a while in favor and then the other appears prominently once more. The change of interest is plain.

5. *Voluntary Progress in Industrial, Political, and Moral Activities.* — I have discussed at considerable length voluntary progress in thought, because I regard it as a typical case. We must now define what is the nature of voluntary interference with growth in industrial development, politics, and morals, and we must see how the simple method of explanation previously suggested will apply to them all.

In each of the three types of activity mentioned, there are human interests concerned. Industrial activities are the expression of the interest in supplying the physical wants of individuals. They are the most direct expressions in society of the instinct of self-preservation. Political activities represent the same interest on a higher plane of intelligence, with more foresight and more un-

derstanding of the way in which self-preservation is to
be furthered by the use of force. Moral activities result
from an extended interest in conscious life as such, and
express a desire for the preservation and bettering of
living beings because they are living beings, and not
because they are important to one's self. Voluntary
progress in carrying on any one of these three kinds of
activity will be possible only under the conditions mentioned at the outset. Furthermore, voluntary progress
here will, according to our previous postulate, be attended by the tendencies already explained, Conservatism and Optimism. And as a consequence, voluntary
progress in the forms of trade, of manufacture, of government, of law, and of morals will tend, in so far forth
as it is voluntary, towards regularity, unity, homogeneity, simplicity, and of course, definiteness of form.
And as a further consequence, every change of form will
be a change forced upon man by external nature, or else
springing from an involuntary change in those interests
which are themselves the basis of all voluntary action.
When the change is forced upon men by external needs,
it will follow the law of least expenditure of energy. The
change will be the least that will satisfy the demands of
experience. When the change is the result of an alteration of interest, it will again be the least change possible
that will satisfy the desires.

These are the conclusions to which we should be led
according to our theory. Let us now see how they compare with the facts. The great fact which seems to contradict our theory is the one expressed in the law of
differentiation of social functions, or division of labor.
There seems to be here a tendency towards the manifold,
and this tendency seems to result from conscious human
interference. Yet in speaking of division of labor we

surely must not forget the principle according to which labor is divided. In differentiating social functions, surely we are not differentiating social aims; and voluntary progress seeks homogeneity of action viewed in relation to aim. Because our occupations are various, no one imagines that our fundamental objects are as various as our labors. There is not one virtue for the miller and another for the schoolmaster and another for the official. It was a cruder system of ethics, an imperfect understanding of the meaning of division of labor, that led Plato to distinguish the virtues of one class from those of another, or Aristotle to the doctrine that some men are born to be slaves and must of right remain so. Again before the differentiation of trades, every man would have his own way of satisfying each one of his needs, of hunting, or fishing, or making arms. Or if there were uniformity of method among different individuals, that would be only because voluntary progress had already been at work, simplifying methods. But when trades are differentiated, then all of a trade work alike. The manifold wants that previously existed and that are by nature and not by volition manifold, are satisfied as before, but by uniform and simple means. Civilization, indeed, increases vastly the number of wants, and so the number of trades. But this evolution of conscious needs is not itself voluntary. In fact, we may distinguish in this matter of the division of labor two tendencies at work, one voluntary, tending towards unity, one tending towards multiplicity, but involuntary. Voluntary is the division of labor in so far forth as it is an organizing of labor. Whoever brings into a state of society where labor was undivided and so indefinitely heterogeneous in character, because dependent for its form and time and success upon the caprice and ignorance of individuals, a plan for assigning to each individual his particular work, and for giving him reason to carry it on steadily and systematically, such a reformer does not make the structure of society more heterogeneous, but less so. The same work was previously done, but done badly. There was the same variety of tasks to be performed, only no one had united the efforts of men and so none of the tasks were completely accomplished. There was the heterogeneity of tasks, and there was the heterogeneity of individuals, who did not cooperate because they could not agree upon their ends, and there was the heterogeneity of occupations for each one. Organization of labor is the unifying of labor. On the other hand, the division of labor is an involuntary process in so far forth as it corresponds to a multiplication of needs, such as must take place in civilization. If new trades arise because men need new things, there is indeed growth towards variety, but the will of man is not responsible for the variety. Whoever is able to distinguish between tendencies or desires and deliberate efforts to satisfy desire, will be able to see that the multiplication of interests is not itself a voluntary process.

When we pass from general considerations to a more special study of these classes of voluntary progress, we find in case of each special exemplifications of the law. There is space only for a brief discussion of certain phenomena of voluntary progress in political institutions. Here, to be sure, the facts are very complicated, but the tendency towards unity seems to me plain. The greatest foe to voluntary progress everywhere, and especially in politics and morals, is the selfishness of individuals. The tendency of selfishness is towards diversity, but only because of the diversity of individuals. The most selfish will, in so far as it has definite interests, sets towards unity. A higher order of volition is that which, recognizing the waste of labor involved in conflict, seeks to save labor by harmony. Political progress consists in harmonizing and unifying the desires of men. I regard that view of human nature as very one-sided which holds the normal condition of mankind to be even now one of warfare. Conflict of interests is deliberately tolerated only so long as no way out of it is seen. The normal condition of men who seek progress at all may be considered as a condition of continual search for such aims as are broad enough and mighty enough to fill the whole of their lives. Show men one who is stronger than they, and they will follow and assist him, not because he has conquered them, but because they delight in strength. Now this willingness to join in whatever undertaking promises magnitude of result with unity of aim, shows itself in political growth wherever such growth is affected by conscious volition. The state depends not wholly upon physical force, but also upon the fact that its physical force takes certain definite and uniform traditional channels whenever exercised. The traditions of a constitution express the national aims as distinguished from the caprice of individual legislators or subjects. The state is sure of support so long as the constitution is adhered to and is not obsolete. Dread of the sovereign power is subordinate to the real gaurantee of national permanence, viz., desire for simple and uniform methods of carrying on the affairs of life.

If the state itself is the expression of the unifying tendency, political growth shows the same tendency. For it must be admitted that the normal development of any one government, when undisturbed by conflicting class interests, is toward centralization. But any one government in its normal development shows voluntary progress without change of the interests involved. And centralization means unity. Again the functions of government seem slowly but surely extending. Our own governments in this country are new, and their functions small. Hasty legislation, too, produces popular disappointment and reactions in favor of limiting even the few governmental powers already existent. In all nations ignorance of the means of organizing work under government direction limits the tendency, and makes socialistic ideals seem for the present idle if not wicked fancies. But slowly the unifying process goes on. Once every one was his own policeman. Later every one employed his own mail carrier. For a yet longer time every one was his own schoolmaster, or else found his teachers by supporting private enterprises. Now, police and mails and schools are largely in the hands of the government. England adds the telegraph service and the post office savings banks to the functions of government. Elsewhere railroads are under government control. Where will the process end? I see no limit but human ignorance and our present incapacity for organizing labor.

But, says someone, the ideal is after all progress towards human freedom. Human freedom is a personal affair. Man cannot be free; men must be. I reply that if individual freedom means limitless eccentricity, individuality without other aim than to be peculiar, then this tendency towards a savage diversity of wills and aims and thoughts is one that cannot be contemplated without horror. Individual freedom we indeed desire for all the world. But our desire means this, that, as we hold, in an ideal state every one would give himself up to whatever work were before him, every one would feel that the world's ends were his ends, and no human will would be coerced by another, because perfect submission would be the attitude of every one. That is, the desire for freedom as an universally desirable end, is nothing more than a desire for perfect harmony and absence of conflict. So long as there is conflict in the world, there never will be perfect freedom. In a conflict some one is always vanquished. The ideal of freedom is, therefore, just like the socialistic ideal when properly understood, the ideal of a state of things wherein men should be in harmony and wherein their ends should be one and their social forms so homogeneous as not to produce conflict. Both ideals are alike impracticable, and alike useful as ideals. There is, to be sure, no reason to suppose that men will not always actually be at variance, striving and miserable. That they will sometime be better off than they are now may be hoped; and when they are better off, there will be, no doubt, much more unity in government, language, and customs, much more centralization of the functions of government, much more organization of labor, much more interest on the part of every man in the welfare of the whole of conscious life, in fine much more of unity than there is now. For such is the nature of deliberate volition, this great agency of economy and unity. If that could work untrammeled the end would be certain. And on the other hand, there is no reason to suppose that men will ever be much happier than they are now, unless their deliberate volition interpose to make them so.

6. *Summary and Conclusion.* — That in voluntary progress there is a law of what we have called the Conservatism of Social Forms; that when forms are altered the alteration takes place with the least expenditure of energy; that voluntary progress adds to its conservatism some one of the forms of optimism; that voluntary prog-

ress is thus in every way characterized by a tendency
to simplify the structure of society; that evolution as
modified by the deliberate volition of men differs from
physical evolution in being everywhere a growth towards unity and homogeneity of actions considered in
reference to their ends; that finally growth in the direction of the complex is always involuntary growth, in so
far as it is growth in this direction: these are the principal results which this paper has tried to make probable
and to illustrate.

At the close of the whole investigation two reflections
arise. Is the universal goal of voluntary progress as we
have defined it one that is after all worth seeking? And
again, if worth seeking, is it ultimately attainable, or is
man condemned to an endless and hopeless warfare with
a nature that seeks limitless diversity of form, and that
delights in conflict, while he seeks unity of form, and
wishes harmony? As to the first question, it seems as if
the simplicity and unity which we all are seeking would,
if we attained it, appear to us a tedious and intolerable
monotony; that the goal of voluntary progress, if
reached, would be soon cast aside as worthless; and that
the change of interest of which we spoke above, would
eternally goad us onward in a never ending pursuit of
phantoms. I admit this contradiction, which I consider
inseparable from every theory of voluntary action. It is
the nature of the human will to be content with nothing
that it possesses, and to be always looking for something
new. A theory of ends and motives cannot be refuted by
saying that were the ends attained, new motives would
arise and new ends be sought. Pictures of enduring
happiness always fail. Happiness is best pictured as a
transient moment. Our theory suffers, in the contradiction pointed out, only what long since happened to

the old ideas of the state of the blessed in heaven, whereof Schopenhauer remarks that when every definite torment had been banished to hell, there was left nothing but the dreariest monotony for the picture of bliss. To say that no goal would satisfy us, is to say that unrest, dissatisfaction, is an eternal part of conscious life. Sometimes we are content to be forever active, and sometimes we rebel against the fact that we are finite, and say that conscious life is a failure. So long as we are at work we incline to the former opinion. Whichever one is the fairer, the problem involved is everlasting.

As to the second question, whether we can ever triumph over nature, and whether she will not always tear down whatever we build up, the only answer is, the *ignoramus et ignorabimus* with which a distinguished scientific investigator some years ago expressed his sense of the "limits of human knowledge." In so far as nature is responsible for the pain and evil that there is in life, I see no reason for being confident that good will ever triumph over evil in more than a very restricted sense. If at any moment there were triumph we could not be certain of its permanence. According to our present notion of the universe, we stand alone, a few specks of life in the darkness of infinite space, in the midst of nature forces whose resources we shall never more than very meagerly estimate, with an unknown future before us, in which what appalling accidents may happen, we can never even with faint show of accuracy foresee. But if the triumph of the good is uncertain, if voluntary progress is always a venturing into a mysterious future, there is no reason why we should on that account work less vigorously, or make our aims less lofty. It is a cowardly soul that needs the certainty of success before it will work. It is a craven who despairs and does nothing because what he can do may turn out a failure. Whatever future growth eliminates from human nature, it is to be hoped that one trace of the era of universal warfare will survive, namely, the courage that can face possible, even probable destruction, with the delight of a hero in resisting and planning and working so long as he can raise his arm.

THE PRACTICAL SIGNIFICANCE
OF PESSIMISM

[1879]

EXPERIENCE is too narrow to furnish us answers to all the great problems of life. We constantly take refuge, therefore, in theories, hypotheses, opinions, sentiments. I know of no thinker of any significance who is satisfied to state what he knows; every thinker, one might say every man of character, is driven, by the force of his own life as a thinker, to add to experience hypothesis, to fact opinion, to certainty conjecture.

And indeed no one who has reflected much on the phenomena of our consciousness will find in this tendency to anticipate or to complete experience a tendency in itself either exceptional or dangerous. All thinking in its very nature as mental activity, is necessarily a transcending of direct experience. We think of things and of laws, of causes and of effects, of obligations and of rights, of qualities good and evil, of matter and of mind, of time and of space, of the atom and of the universe; and yet these objects of thought are none of them objects of direct experience; they are one and all, as thought-objects, creations of the thought that thinks them. He who should desire to limit himself strictly to sense-experience in all his thought, would indeed have a very simple task; for he would then never think at all.

The tendency to transcend experience is, therefore, in itself not merely justifiable, but indispensable. We have only to look well to our footsteps that in leaving the path of experience we wander not into the wilderness of pure fancy. Experience without thought is, to use Kant's somewhat worn epithet, blind. But thought without a basis of experience is, as the same thinker had it, empty. To transcend experience you must first be in possession of experience.

I preface these remarks for the sake of indicating what I conceive to be the position of a certain doctrine or theory of life to which I propose to ask your attention. This doctrine transcends experience and is not ashamed to do so. One must judge it, if at all, as an hypothesis. One must see whether it has the proper basis in experience; and one must also see whether, in so far as it rises beyond the region of experience, it is a structure of true wisdom. One must treat with it upon its own ground, and expect from it only what it attempts to perform. I refer to the doctrine known as Pessimism. This, as a view of life in its entirety, is necessarily beyond the reach of immediate verification or refutation. Everyone must study the matter from his own point of view and must employ the power of his own insight. The best result he can hope to reach will be a probable result.

With this in mind then, we shall enter upon our task and consider as briefly as may be, four points: viz., First, What is the doctrine known as Pessimism? Secondly, Where and in what forms does it appear in human thought? Thirdly, What case, if any, can be made out in favor of a Pessimistic doctrine? Fourthly, What is the true value and significance of the doctrine regarded in its relations to human life? Upon the last point, I need not say, the most stress is to be laid; and all the other considerations but prepare the way for the one principal problem.

First then, what is Pessimism?

By Pessimism is meant nowadays a doctrine that sees in human life or in sentient life in general a preponderance of evil, that regards this evil as a necessary part of life, and that in consequence considers such life as there is as worse than no life at all. To be sure, this would not be Pessimism in the strictest etymological sense of the word. According to the etymology Pessimism would have to be the doctrine that regards the life that is as the worst possible or conceivable life; so that a worse state than the present could not be imagined. Yet this extreme view is seldom if ever held. It is enough that, in the usage of the day, Pessimism is the doctrine that looks upon the condition of sentient life as so full of evil, that a cessation of this life would be preferable to a continuance. On the one hand, then, Pessimism is a theory of life as we see it about us at present. This life is found by the pessimist to have in it an excess of evil over good. On the other hand, however, Pessimism is a doctrine of life considered in its nature, apart from any reference to time. The philosophic pessimist is he who finds an excess of evil over good, not merely in life as it is at present constituted, but in life as it must be at all times. Pessimism then declares that life, not your life nor mine, not this life nor that, not the life of the present, nor the life of the past, nor the life of the future, but life is in its essence and of necessity an evil, and were better brought to an end. Such is the doctrine as defined according to the recognized use of the term.

We note immediately one important mark that characterizes Pessimism as thus defined. Pessimism is, you will observe, in this narrower sense, not the expression of a mood, but of a doctrine. The philosophic pessimist, therefore, need not be of necessity any less fortunate or happy than the rest of his race. He founds his opinion upon observation or upon speculative doctrine. He intends this observation or doctrine to be perfectly impartial and all-embracing. He does not neglect the fact of happiness, but analyzes this like all other phenomena of feeling. He finds reason for holding that happiness is a transient and subordinate form of conscious life. Holding this view on general grounds he is not confirmed or refuted in it by his own personal experiences. If he is made happy by some event, that does not cause him to be the less a pessimist. He already knew that there is a thing called happiness, and that many share in its blessings. But he had studied this something called happiness, and had found it of less significance as an element of life than is its opposite, misery. His own passing mood is no refutation of his philosophic opinion. If you find him merry and self-satisfied you may not accuse him of inconsistency. His doctrine referred to the universe, not to himself. He may be an exceptionally favored being, knowing little of adversity. Only so much the more perhaps, has he had leisure to contemplate with calmness the nature of life, and to pass an unbiased judgment. I mention this here only that our minds may be quire clear as to the question at issue. I shall consider no mere frame of mind, no mere morbid outgrowth of individual misfortune, but a reasoned theory. One may no longer look upon Pessimism as a distemper to be treated pathologically when it is found in company with an unhappy career, or laughed at as an inconsistency if the pessimistic thinker himself has been a happy man. Pessimism in our day has risen from the heart to the head; and the problem is now an essential part of Moral Philosophy.

Historically considered, Pessimism is a very ancient tendency, but not a very ancient doctrine. Again and again, in literature of high antiquity, you meet with expressions that imply or that seem to imply, theories of life in the main pessimistic; yet a philosophic doctrine of

Pessimism is in Europe the product of the present century. The experience upon which Pessimism is more or less remotely based has long been noted and in part appreciated; yet a combination of circumstances has prevented any one from isolating, generalizing and formulating an abstract doctrine of Pessimism on the basis of these experiences. If one may be allowed to sum up in an abstract formula the numerous half-conscious pessimistic tendencies of literature, one may perhaps state the commonest prephilosophic form of our tendency thus: Evil predominates in life, because life is uncertain and brief. We constantly long for what is unattainable, simply because we desire to rise above the transient, yet are doomed to discover that everything is fleeting. However happy the hour may be, the morrow finds you mourning over its loss. However strong and promising the young plant, the decay of old age comes and checks all development. However desirable even the life of memory and restful contemplation, death robs one of this only remaining treasure. All flesh is as grass. Men are like the leaves of the forest.

In a hundred shapes you meet this same thought repeated in ancient literature. "Few and evil have the days of the years of my life been" — "The days of our years are three score and ten years; and if by reason of strength they be four score years yet is their strength labor and sorrow, for it is soon cut off and we fly away." These from the Hebrew writings that have so deeply affected the consciousness of the world in later times; and one need not stop to remind you of the comfortless gloom of the confessions of a worldling as they have been aptly called, preserved in the book of Ecclesiastes, or of the noble despondency of the book of Job. A like undercurrent of gloom was not unknown to Greek literature at an early period; and Greek philosophy, if it never formulated pessimism as modern philosophy has done, yet did very soon set about the study of the problems involved, and produced more than one doctrine that lacked but the universal insight of modern times to become Pessimism itself. Though to Buddhism belongs the melancholy glory of having made a doctrinal pessimism a fundamental religious dogma, yet we cannot take this development into consideration now, for to us Europeans Buddhism has been known only since the early part of the present century, and then but imperfectly.

The typical form of the pessimistic tendency as just described finds some variation in the mind of more than one of Shakespeare's characters; and we may take certain well-known expressions of theirs as representing yet another noteworthy phase of literary pessimism. Here we have no longer merely the fleeting character of human life, the inevitable decay, held up as the one source of evil; the negative criticism cuts deeper. It is not that life were better if there were more of it; but when Shakespeare, in the course of his all-embracing studies of human feeling, finds occasion to copy and to embody the pessimistic mood, he chooses often to express the pessimist's emotion in the form of an attack on every moment of life. There is, we read in some passages of Shakespeare, no significance in any part of life, much less in the whole. We are such stuff as dreams are made of. Life is but a tale told by an idiot, full of sound and fury yet signifying nothing. Or again, the whole consists in this, that from hour to hour we ripe and ripe, and then from hour to hour we rot and rot; wherein of course the one process is just as important and just as contemptible as the other. Here you have a new thought introduced. The worth of life is to be judged on the basis of an examination of the significance of the individual moments.

Modern literary pessimism just before Schopenhauer took still a different form, that of the so-called *Weltschmerz*, or pessimism of personal despair. This, the pessimism of Goethe's Werther, of Heine, of the Byronic period in England, is in no wise a philosophic view of the universe; but arises in and expresses simply the individual disgust with life. In the introduction to Alfred de Musset's Confessions of a Child of the Century, you have a picture briefly and feelingly drawn of this mood. *Weltschmerz* became then at this time a kind of epidemic, founded not in a sense of the universal in life, but rather in a common experience of the evils of protracted war, bad government, unsettled beliefs, artificial society, and the lack of objective stimulus. We must not confound this tendency with the one first represented by Arthur Schopenhauer, the founder and greatest expositor of a pessimistic philosophy in Europe. We therefore leave now the pessimism of the heart and come to that of the head.

Schopenhauer finds the essence of life to consist in the active or desiring principle of consciousness, called by him the Will. Life is made up, according to Schopenhauer, of a continual flight from one object of desire or interest to another. What we know serves as but the instrument of our will. Knowledge is always a subordinate phenomenon of mind. We are constantly in some degree in a state of longing. Without a consciousness of desire, of unrest greater or less, no life. Now pleasure is satisfied desire. Without a desire preceding, no satisfaction, and so no pleasure. Hence, pleasure is negative. The only positive element in consciousness is the longing.

Resist, overcome, deny or put to rest the longing, by
moral or physical means, and you have what is called
satisfaction or enjoyment. What we always enjoy is then
the momentary freedom we attain. When we feel pleasure it is that we have for the time one desire the less.
What then is the worth of life? The highest worth conceivable is precisely zero. The end of life, the desirable,
the highest pleasure would be attained were we free
from all desire. But to be free from all desire were to
cease to live. On the other hand, however, pain is the
consciousness of yet unsatisfied longing. Pain then is
necessarily united to all desire. Pain accompanies all
life. Pain greater or less is the birthright of every man.
Pain and strife each one inherits from his parents; these
are at once the marks and the punishment of the true
original sin, which is the desire for life. So long as one
lives he desires to live; for that is his nature, the blind
impulse he cannot control. But so long as he desires, he
suffers. The positive quality of life is its painfulness.
Happiness means at best more or less relief, more or less
rest from the inevitable toil. Happiness as a positive
possession there is none.

In the briefest statement, this is the basis of Schopenhauer's pessimism. You see that we have here a doctrine founded on an analysis of consciousness. With
the analysis you will doubtless disagree; but with the
general method of attacking the problem you must
needs be content. There is no other way of studying the
worth of life than by examining the very root and substance of conscious life.

Schopenhauer's theory of the negative nature of pleasure has been modified, elaborated, and strengthened
by a lengthy empirical examination of the facts of life in
the numerous writings of the still young but already

famous Edward von Hartmann of Berlin, whose *Philosophy of the Unconscious* has just entered on its second decade of life (first edition published in 1868), whose following is large and in a way influential, and whose doctrine is in many respects quite original. But I cannot go further with this historical account. You see at any rate that the pessimistic assault on the worth of life has taken two great forms, that of personal mood or impression, that of reasoned analysis of consciousness. The former led of necessity to the latter; and with the latter alone we shall now concern ourselves.

It simplifies the problem of the worth of life if we begin with the individual. Take any individual, as Caius. Consider him for a moment as the center of the world. See what would be meant by the worth of life for him. See in how far he may hope to obtain the goods of life in case he is favored by fortune. If it is impossible that in this simplest conceivable instance his life should be made worth living, then we may well despair of seeing the problem of life solved where the clashing of the interests of various individuals is introduced. If, however, the problem finds satisfactory solution here, we may with hope and reason search further.

You note that I do not suppose Caius alone in the world, but only, for the moment, of more importance than any one else. Let the relations of life be as complicated for him as you will; only let us make those relations subservient solely to his interests. Can Caius as monarch of all things attain to a truly satisfactory and worthy life?

First then, as monarch of all things, Caius can obtain for himself all sorts of sense-gratifications. We suppose his physical organism sound, his wit uncommonly great, his capacity for enjoyment as keen as possible in case

of a human being. His life is long. Death ends it to be
sure; but death comes to him easily, and Caius is above
slavish fears. He can live in ease and plenty if he so
wills; he can enjoy the help and society of his fellowmen
to his heart's content; for are they not his own? Now if
Caius chooses the life of sensuous gratification, and
gains his end, will his life viewed in itself be worth
living?

We answer no, not because the books for children say
no; but because we can see by examination that nothing
to be called worth can here be found. Our argument
shall take into account, of course, only this life and only
Caius; yet the worthlessness of sense-gratification can
easily be made evident. For each moment of enjoyment
unless remembered as enjoyment and counted as his
own enjoyment is worth nothing to Caius. Our sense-
enjoyment can be spoken of as valuable only when we
know afterwards that we personally have enjoyed.
Make me intoxicated or give me nitrous oxide so that
my memory is for the time destroyed, and then tell me
afterwards that I showed signs of feeling very pleasant
sensations while I was in this state; and this past enjoyment will be counted by me as of no worth. I did not
enjoy anything, I then say. Else would I remember.
There may have been transient sensations of pleasure.
They are now nothing to me. They are no more mine
than are the pleasures of Alexander the Great. For me
they are insignificant, since my memory does not preserve them. Nor would I choose them in future. Ob-
livion I might seek to avoid violent pain; but I never
would look either backwards or forwards with any interest to a feeling of pleasure that must vanish from
memory the very instant it had been felt. Self-consciousness then at least must be present, if I am to de-

clare a certain pleasure of sense at all a worthy event in life. I must remember and say, this I enjoyed; this was mine.

If sense-gratification is worth nothing without memory and self-consciousness to retain and to recognize it, what will the pleasures of Caius be worth to him in so far as he does retain and recognize them? Will they then be valuable objects of pursuit? Still the same answer. Even here a little analysis shows them of no value. For here Schopenhauer's argument recurs in a modified form. To know I had or shall have pleasure, is to compare my present with a past or future state. But when I remember gratifications past I am usually more or less in a quiescent state without great present pleasure. My memory is at the same time a recognition of the difference between the ideal and the real satisfaction, between the memory and the present. My memory of my own past pleasure is then of its nature a desire to repeat the experience. The like holds true of the expectation of future pleasure as our own. We recognize the expected pleasure as to be our own only by feeling a desire to reach it, an incompleteness in the present state. Or in Schopenhauer's form again, the pleasure appears as gratified desire, and the desire as a sense of pain or incompleteness in the present. Hence, if Caius does remember and recognize his past sense-gratifications as his own, he does so only by recognizing his present condition as imperfect, and his pleasures as possible means of completing his imperfection. His pleasure is turned to gall by the very mental process that makes it his own, for that very mental process implies that it is no longer his own.

Hence, then, the dilemma. If Caius lives the life of sense-gratification, he will either fly on from moment to moment, never reflecting, never pausing to attain a clear self-consciousness; and then his gratifications are as worthless as the unremembered pleasant sensations of a drunken man, and die as soon as they are born; or he will reflect and recognize his gratifications as his own, and then they will appear as past, as not now his, as no longer within his reach, or as future, as not yet attained, as objects of longing; and thus he recognizes the pleasure as his own only in so far forth as he feels the present lack of it, feels want or pain. Whichever horn of the dilemma Caius accepts, his life of sense-gratification turns out worthless.

This argument would apply equally well to all forms of individual enjoyment that Caius might choose to pursue, unless there be an exception in favor of the consciousness of fullness and breadth of self-development. This latter object of life we must yet consider. Perhaps Caius, giving up the search for enjoyment, proposes to seek for completeness depth and force of life, in a word, for a grander and higher self. We all have some notion of what such a search means. It is in part the search for what we call manifold experience, it is also what we understand under the search after the formation of a high character. It is the striving to be individually all that we possibly can.

If Caius then, instead of passing his life in the search for pleasure, determines to seek a perfected Self, and to make that his object, will he now be able as monarch of all resources to attain to a satisfactory and worthy life?

That the individual pleasures could never sum up into a worthy life we saw, because in order to give the individual pleasures worth at all, reflection was necessary. And reflection is of its nature opposed to enjoyment, and so recognizes pleasures as of worth only by opposing to them the empty and worthless present of the reflection itself. So that as much is lost in longing or lament as is gained in satisfaction. A like argument applies however to the worth of a successful struggle for self-development. To recognize our self-development as in itself a worthy object of striving, we must be able to do two things: First, to see some absolute worth in a given grade of self-attainment or self-perfection; Second, to compare our state at any one time with our previous state of development, or with a higher stage of development. These two things are necessary, I say, the first as a condition for our finding self-development a worthy end at all, the second as a means of measuring our progress in reaching the goal. At some stage of our evolution we must be able to say, "here I have attained an absolute good"; else wherein lies the worth of striving? But, at each previous stage we must be able to measure our progress and to say: "in that direction lies the goal; and I am so and so far from it." Now this second power of mind, the power of contrasting our actual attainment with something lower and with something higher, is necessary indeed to our progress, but it is of its nature opposed to our ever regarding any attained state as an absolute good. Reach a given state, and no matter what you thought of its worth before you attained it, you are no sooner there than you forthwith begin to compare it with other states. Higher it is indeed than previous states of attainment; but that furnishes no reason why you should regard it as of absolute worth. The same desire for the higher that has led you to it, drives you beyond it. You see how much lower it is than some state just beyond, and on you press once more. This ceaseless activity may be very praiseworthy from the point of view of the ethical teacher; but what is the significance of the matter, when viewed as a mere fact of nature, apart from its practical usefulness? The significance is that there can be no worthy end attained in this activity of self-development, because there is no end attained at all. Goals of endeavor here turn out to be illusions. They are goals so long as you have not reached them. Reach them and you find them no goals at all, but unsatisfying and imperfect conditions from which you flee in unappeased discontent. Nor let it be said, as so many have said, that the true worth in this case lies not in the states attained but in the struggle to attain them. What this can mean, I know not. It may be true enough that struggle is better than lethargy; but our present question is: What is either of them worth? Perfect rest after toil may be indeed worth less morally than the toil. But we wish to know now what the toil is worth. Toil, conflict, endeavor, these imply object, do they not? No one believes in toil and conflict that are known to be perfectly objectless. But now what is the object? The attainment of some higher state? Yes, we suppose some one to answer. Then the higher state gives worth to the struggle? Yes. The higher state is an absolute good then? Yes. Why then would it not be well to remain in this higher state when you have reached it, to enjoy the fruits of victory, to rest? Oh, that would be lethargy, indolence. To try to remain in the higher state without pressing on further would be to fall from that state, to cease to enjoy it. When we have attained the prize of this conflict we must forthwith begin a new conflict. We may not stop to enjoy the prize. So then, this conflict is all for the sake of a prize that you can never hope to enjoy. You seek constantly for a higher state in which you will never be able to rest peacefully.

You are warring for an illusion. You fight for a kingdom that exists but in your dreams.

But, one says, as Caius, in seeking this self-development gains some higher state, he is able to enjoy this state at the very time he is battling for a yet higher state. He need not rest in order to enjoy; he enjoys the attained, even while he is striving for the next higher. To this I can but answer that, if Caius is really in earnest I know not what such sham fights can mean. Caius has sought for the end A; his search has been earnest; he has attained it. Now we find him fighting for the higher end B. We question him: Caius, are you in earnest about the goal B, or is this only shamming, just to keep your fighting arm in trim for war? No, he says, I am in earnest. I want B most truly. Does not A satisfy you then, Caius? No, how should it? I possess A; and nobody can be satisfied with what he possesses. The satisfactory is always what a man has not. Do you then enjoy the end A at all? I do, in this sense at least, that I would not part with it. I should feel its loss sadly. But Caius, is this true enjoyment of A? Must not the sum of conscious life be either positive or negative? Can it be both at once? If the longing, the lack you now feel as to B, is as great as the longing and lack you once felt as to A before you sought for B, perhaps greater, how has your condition been bettered by gaining A? How can you be said to enjoy A, when the sum of your whole consciousness of satisfaction and longing is still negative, and at least as great a negative quantity as before? Our condition of weal or woe is measured not by what we have, but by what we want; just as the toil in mountain climbing for a given day is measured, not by our height above the sea level at the moment of starting, but by our depth below the point at which we aim. What would be my

gain if, in climbing the sides of an infinite mountain, I
left untold thousands of feet of elevation behind me, and
yet eternally seemed to see my desired goal just one
thousand feet above me? The one thousand feet lacking
would be worth more than all the thousands attained.
Thus, then, Caius, you are now wretched, having A.
Nor will you be less wretched, possessing B; for beyond
B there is a C, and beyond C a D; and the alphabet of
the infinite never reaches its Z. While you seek higher
individual attainment, you shall long and suffer, and
never attain.

Nor is this the only argument in the case. Our satisfaction in a lower condition is doubtless much greater
than our satisfaction in a higher condition when we attain that condition. For our satisfaction in our attainments is decreased with the increase of our insight.
When our attainments are so small that we ourselves
have not yet the power of self-measurement, our satisfaction with our condition may be considerable. But at
a certain point in our progress we attain the power to
estimate, quantitatively and qualitatively, the actual
amount of our possessions. With this power to estimate,
comes the consciousness that our powers are finite.
Before we estimated, our mental possession seemed indefinitely great. As soon as we estimate, we learn how
limited the whole treasure is. No development after this
can ever restore to the individual his former naïve confidence in his own immense worth. In other words, in
that Caius sets about the task of self-development, he
only passes further and further, at every step, from the
only stage in which he could fairly enjoy his self-development.

But finally, leaving out of account the impossibility
of any genuine satisfaction in the growth of Self, leaving

out of account both that an infinite series of goals will exist, and that self-criticism will on every higher stage destroy all the fruits gained by the striving upwards, omitting, I say, all reference to these things, there will yet remain another cause for dissatisfaction with the results of self-education. Other selves than Caius will exist; and be he master of these others or not, he will strive in vain to equal with his own growth the immense riches of life embodied in these hosts of humanity. Do what he will he shall forever feel that in life there is a vast ocean of knowledge and power, of which a single self can only dimly dream, can never fully conceive, and certainly never possess. And the consciousness of his own worthlessness in view of all this will go far to rob Caius of his hoped-for satisfaction in himself; even if nothing else opposes his desires. Contentment with self is only possible when one is unconscious of how much life there is outside him. Let him know of myriads of other selves, each desiring development like his own; each possessed of some experience that is not his; each the possessor of peculiar excellences; each the victor in its own great battles: I say, let one appreciate this, and a high opinion of his own insignificant fragment of the universe is impossible.

We have gone over somewhat hastily the field of the supposed individual goods. Our model Caius has been left to follow his own devices, has been observed and criticized. I have not pretended to say what Caius himself will hold of his life. Perhaps he will think it worth living. There is no telling the extent of a man's illusions. I have only argued from the point of view of an external observer that the life of Caius is not at all worth living. We who reflect and suppose ourselves in full possession of the facts, must decide, I claim, that all Caius' aims have failed, and that viewed with reference to himself only, it had been better for him had he not been born.

The argument about Caius, you see, is not an argument that he is wretched in the sense of knowing his wretchedness. I only claim that Caius, or any other man who lives for himself, could he but once be enlightened, could he but once view his life all through at a glance, could he but see the shadowy nature of all his pleasures and the illusiveness of all his goals, would be overcome with the conviction of the worthlessness of the whole business of living. He would then need no philosophic judge. He would declare himself wretched without further question.

But let us look at the consequences. Caius was the best conceivable case. He was the ideal man, living for himself. What is the real state of things among men? Are all such beings as Caius? Quite the contrary. A mob of individuals, hurled together as it were at random out of the infinite storehouse of the possible, every variety of disposition, every grade of weakness, of incapacity, of disease, of ignorance: such is Humanity. Every one, to speak in the rough, among the teeming mass of creatures comes into the world with a desperate desire to make it subservient to his ends. By hard treatment, by toil and bruises, and bloodshed and tears, he learns by and by that there are some things he cannot accomplish, some barriers he cannot break down, some enemies he cannot subdue, some aims that can never be realized. In his narrow circle he learns to live, if the task be not all too hard for him; and then discontented, groaning, hoping for better times, complaining of mythical lost happiness, cursing his lot and any of his fellows he may think more fortunate than himself, he wears the gloomy days away until the last sigh escapes him and men put him out of sight and forget him. An exaggerated picture you say; but remember that this is the actual prosaic, dead-level experience of untold millions. You need not go a mile from where we are now sitting to find in the streets scores of such individuals as I have described. This is the average lot of humanity. We who are better off are so because these are worse off. Their reluctant labor gives us leisure to be happier than they. And this swarm of living beings is not content with its present sum of misery. No, it must go on breeding at the wildest random, through every possible combination of the discordant dispositions found among its numbers, breeding offspring to increase and to perpetuate the sum of brute passion, of ignorance, of disease, of suffering. Here is the great rule. Exceptions are all the cases of prosperous people, of happy homes, of knowledge, of power, of contentment. And these exceptions, what are they but as the individual we have just been considering, as Caius. The best life, viewed with respect to the self that lives, is a failure, is worthless. What then is the worst life, or even, if you will, the average life?

Thus far I have laid no stress on pain; that great fact of life — Pain may not be eliminated as pleasure was by not reflecting upon it. Pleasure lulls reflection to sleep. Pain quickens it. Hard it is for the subject to say with full consciousness, now I am happy, now I enjoy. Happiness flies by unheeded, and time joyfully passed seems short.

But pain forces reflection. Easy it is to continue suffering and yet to reflect, to be impelled to reflect, I it is who suffer, I am the one in agony. Now pain is a fact of the widest importance. Everywhere you find it. Yet beyond a certain point pain is a foe to all that makes life worth living. Moral endeavor of the highest sort will fall powerless before it when it is long continued and distracting. Leaving all else out of account this one great fact of suffering would be enough to make us doubt the worth of life. Contemplate a battle field the first night after the struggle, contemplate here a vast company the equal of the population of a great town, writhing in agony, their groans sounding at a great distance like the roar of the ocean, their pain uneased for many hours, even death, so lavish of his favors all day, now refusing to comfort; contemplate this and then remember that as this pain to the agony of the world, so is an electric spark drawn from the back of a kitten to the devastating lightning of many great storms; and now estimate if you can the worth of all but a few exceptional human lives, such as that of Caius.

Briefly and imperfectly I state the case for pessimism, not even touching the economical and social argument, drawn from a more special consideration of the conditions of human life. Such then, is our individual human life. What shall we call it and whereunto shall it be likened? A vapor vanishing in the sun? No, that is not insignificant enough. A wave, broken on the beach? No, that is not unhappy enough. A soap bubble bursting into thin air? No, even that has rainbow hues. What then? Nothing but itself. Call it human life. You could not find a comparison more thoroughly condemning it.

But the practical significance? This I can briefly state. The practical significance is not that men should go and hang themselves. Just the opposite. He is a poor judge of the merits of the case who counsels this. The indictment has been, mark me well, against human life regarded as individual life. This is evil. But you note that I have had nothing to say about other facts of life;

about the worth of love, of sacrifice, of the worship of the beautiful, of the purely intellectual delights, of the devotion to ideal ends. These things I have not touched upon. And why? These things belong not to individual life. Sum them all up, in their practical aspect in one term, Holy Living. And then of this I shall say that Holy Living is living not for Self, but for the quelling, the putting down of Self, and for the building up of peaceful, harmonious, but entirely unselfish life. The object of such a life is found in its own perfection. The pessimistic argument does not touch it, because such a life is not one of restless striving or of fleeting desires, but of calm, of resignation, of broad earnestness. It is affirmed then that in so far as one lives in unselfish love of others, in sacrifice for the sake of the higher prosperity of the world, in sacrifice if you will for the sake of true sacrifice, in contemplation, in the delights of thought for thoughts sake, in a word, in the Ideal, that in so far as one thus lives, he lives not as an individual, but as a mere representative of the higher life. Such a higher life is beyond the pessimist's criticism. Such a life we should seek.

Thus then, the moral of Pessimism can be easily stated: First, Pessimism leads us to the settled conviction that all life for Self is worthless. The development of Self is opposed by every obstacle. The best possible result would be simply zero. Expect then, nothing from Self or for Self. Labor to cast self aside, and to live in the universal life, having only this one object, that the best and highest should be attained, no matter who attains it.

Secondly, Pessimism is opposed to all half-way schemes for reforming the world. Do not make men unhappy by telling them that were they a little more wealthy or politically a little freer, they would be happy. Tell them that they can find happiness only when they cease to seek it for themselves. Talk no more of golden ages. Talk of golden deeds.

If this be best told men through a particular creed, let it be so told. But let not the creed talk of future happiness for individuals in another world. This is but to substitute a ghost for a shadow. Let the creed be hard and bitter. The individual soul will resist it, but once conquered, will be the better for it. To know how poor are our own lives, is to know how lovely is the Higher and Holier Life beyond Self.

PESSIMISM AND MODERN THOUGHT
[1881]

THE problem of the worth of life is often regarded among men of the world as one that the healthy have no wish to discuss, and the unhealthy no right to decide. But surely reflective beings must sooner or later be led to consider the worth of conscious life; for self-criticism is an essential part of all mental growth, and cannot rest until it has taken into consideration the whole, as well as the parts, of our activity. But as every new step in critical thought is made by means of a negative criticism of old positions, the question of the worth of life must distinctly appear for the first time in the form of what is inexactly called pessimistic doubt about human life. The doctrine popularly named pessimism, the doctrine that evil is on the whole triumphant, is consequently the immediate subject of the following discussion, whose ultimate aim is the suggestion of some thoughts on the method of estimating the worth of human life. Our plan will be to give, first, a study of certain modern views that bear on our problem; secondly, a critical examination of the bases of these views. We shall preface a very brief account of what is meant by a worth-estimate of human life.

No one familiar with the spirit and objects of modern discussion will find it improper that we should confine ourselves throughout to the study of human life as we know it in this world. Our life this side death is, at all events, the one subject of present moral interest. We are accustomed to bound our desires, even when they extend beyond the limits of our own lives, by the limits of the probable future life of our race. The future means,

to the modern man, future generations. Our position is
that of Faust, and from that position alone can we
clearly reason and definitely hope:

> Aus dieser Erde quillen meine Freuden
> Und diese Sonne scheinet meinen Leiden.
> Kann ich mich erst von ihnen scheiden
> Dann mag was will und kann, geschehn.

I. WORTH-ESTIMATES IN GENERAL

Pleasure and pain being familiar facts of consciousness, there arises a frequent desire quantitatively to
compare different pleasures and pains. Whether this
color is as pleasing as that one, this Christmas as merry
as the last one, this novel as delightful as another,
whether seasickness is more disagreeable than a toothache of equal persistence, whether a broken arm is a
greater pain than a wounded conscience, such questions
as these are often discussed among men. The only
means of deciding them directly is by an appeal to inner
personal experience. Discussion, by arousing sympathy,
jealousy, or obstinacy, or by appealing to the desire for
the approval of others, often alters the natural judgment in such matters. But natural or artificial, the
ultimate judgment is based on inner experience. The
difficulty, however, in imparting and understanding
these elementary worth-judgments lies in the fact that
the objects compared are not always clearly defined. It
may be regarded as axiomatic that the result of a direct
comparison of two present facts of experience is decisive
of their relative value as pleasures or pains. If, at the
same time, two colors are before me, or if, in immediate
succession, I hear two different sounds, or smell two different flowers, my decision as to which is just now the
better of the two compared experiences, is a decision

beyond appeal. But most of our worth-judgments are not founded on direct comparison of facts of present experience. Two Christmases are separated by at least one year. Toothache and seasickness need not unite at the same time for the torture of the man that compares them. And so through a long list of cases. A worth-judgment is thus often founded on the comparison of a present with a remembered experience, or of two or more remembered experiences with one another. Here the direct judgment is as such indeed above appeal. If the experience A appears to me in memory as superior to B, then so it appears. But one may still doubt whether A if present would seem preferable to a present experience of B. The actually made judgment does not and cannot decide upon this latter point. Of the relative worth as pleasures or pains of A and B in themselves we cannot judge, since A and B are experiences (*e. g.*, Christmases, toothaches, sea voyages, novels) separated by a considerable interval of time. Our judgment of their relative worth concerns them merely as they appear in memory.

We have some means of determining the nature of the illusions to which memory is subject,[1] but these means are insufficient for the purpose of eliminating the disturbing element introduced into our worth-judgments by the lapse of time. Our best effort in this direction is usually made when we have asked ourselves to decide quite deliberately what we should probably do in the way of choice, were the experiences in question now to present themselves for our decision. We substitute deliberate weighing of the remembered for living choice of the present experiences, and our decision is in the

[1] See Mr. James Sully's late book, *Illusions: A Psychological Study;* in particular ch. x, on "Illusions of Memory."

end a choice between two conceived actions, *i. e.*, a volition.

Completely hopeless is any attainment of direct judgment when we have to consider the total worth of a long series of experiences, such as are contained in a year or in an epoch of our lives. The sum of any number of successive impressions of pleasure and pain is never given in consciousness. Experience knows of no true summation of experiences. The sum of a series of enjoyments, or of sufferings, is a purely ideal thing, invented by subsequent reflection. You can sum up two heaps of bullets by putting them together and counting them. Facts of consciousness are not bullets to be kept, heaped up and counted. They die as soon as they are born. You might as well seek to sum up the successive tongues of flame in your fireplace as to find the sum of the ever-moving, upspringing, and dying contents of restless human conscious life. What we mean by the sum of a series of pleasurable and painful experiences is commonly simply the total impression of them that remains in memory when we overlook the past. When one says that it was "worth while" to take a certain journey, to read a particular dull book, to learn a certain foreign language; when one poet says that it is better to have loved and lost than never to have loved at all, or when another poet tells each of us to count over the joys of his life, and then to "know, whatever thou hast been, 'tis something better not to be"; in all such cases we have to do with no real summation, but with an estimate based on the qualitative difference between the present total impressions of two represented sets of experiences. Not even such a rough summation is there here as is made in case of a hasty estimate of the size or weight of a present material mass. For the parts of the material mass coexist, and the total impression is made without any considerable lapse of time during the survey of the parts. But the worth-estimate is concerned with non-coexistent objects, separated by large periods of time. The one estimate is capable of verification; the other is beyond verification. The estimate of the actual size of a material object is the goal of inquiry. The most careful estimate of the mathematical sum of a long series of pleasures and pains would really be of no importance whatever if it chanced to disagree with a worth-estimate based upon a mere feeling or total impression of the acceptability or non-acceptability of the series of impressions as a whole. Prove to me that during a certain mountain walk I had in sum more pain than pleasure, and you will not prove to me that my walk was a failure. I may still have the total impression of the acceptability of the whole experience, an impression resulting from the fact that I have nearly forgotten the vexations of the walk, and have retained a vivid memory of the views and of the mountain air. This total impression you shall in vain seek to overcome with your estimate. I should not care for your sum if you were to make it with the exactitude of a recording angel. My mere feeling of the worth of mountain-climbing decides the whole matter.

Thus, then, our estimate of the worth of any large fragment of human life is founded, not so much on an estimate of the mathematical sum of its separate experiences, as on a total impression of the worth or significance of the entire series, when viewed from some other moment of time. The knowledge that this total impression is the basis of all judgment of life, is at the bottom of the *hæc olim meminisse juvabit* of the man in present misfortune. Hope says that even if our unhappy experiences exceed in number and intensity our

happy experiences, still the future will arbitrarily turn
the scale by regarding the whole series of experiences as
essentially good. And so no man, unprejudiced by a system, tries to apply a strictly utilitarian test to the judgment of the worth of his own experience. The utilitarian
test would require a strict summation and balancing of
pleasures and pains. Such summation is in fact never
possible. If it were possible, the balance sheet of joy
and misery would be for most men of no use whatever.[1]

Worth-judgments concerning human life, as a whole,
are, therefore, not reducible to assertions about the
mathematical sum of pleasures and pains. What, then,
determines these judgments? Our historical study is intended to answer in part this very question. So much is,
however, clear: that a worth-judgment about human life
is the result of an act of mind, somewhat resembling an

[1] This problem of the "Hedonistic calculus," is discussed by
Mr. Sidgwick, Methods of Ethics, 1st ed., bk. II, ch. iii, sec. 2,
p. 120, sqq. The fundamental importance of the whole question seems to be hardly appreciated by most utilitarians. To
tell us to seek for the "greatest possible sum of happiness,"
when the balance of pleasures and pains can neither be made,
nor, if made, accepted by most unprejudiced men, as expressing their sense of the worth of their own experience: this
is simply to tell us to behead the Cheshire cat that has no body.
The connection of the subject with the present question appears very well in v. Hartmann's essay, "Ist der Pessimismus
wissenschaftlich zu begründen?" (Philosoph. Monatsh., bd. XV,
hft. X, p. 589, sqq.), where the author coolly assumes (p. 591),
"that objection to this Hedonistic estimate of the worth of
life . . . does not affect the truth of pessimism, which has for
the first to do only with the proof of the fact that the balance
of pleasure in the world gives a negative result." In other
words, "Off with the cat's head," whether or not it has any
body.

ordinary practical volition. *This life is good, this life is evil*, these opposing judgments are two opposing attitudes of will. The ultimate decision in the matter is not to result from a mathematical estimate, but from moral insight. The nature of this insight does not yet appear. But we must be clear as to what we are seeking, viz., not a balance sheet of evil and good, but a watch word to determine our principles of action; an everlasting yea or nay, that shall relate to the whole of life.

II. Pessimism and Modern Poetry

Ethical "criticism of life," to borrow Mr. Matthew Arnold's phrase, takes in this century many forms. Chief among them are poetry and speculative philosophy. The poetry of the nineteenth century has been largely the result of the movement in mental life for which is chiefly responsible the revolution, political and social, at the close of the eighteenth century. The revolution meant for the poets the suggestion of a splendid or terrible future for the human race, and the present realization of a fullness of emotional life unknown to the earlier decades of the century. Here was material enough for magnificent dreams and for stirring life-pictures. The schools of poetry that expressed the spirit of the age were, however, weighted with something that proved fatal to very many promising talents; and this something was the tendency to reflection. To have an emotion is one thing, to sing it a very different thing; but to sing it even while you are speculating about its philosophic significance is the saddest of all the tasks imposed by the envious gods. Yet such is the task to which are condemned more than half of our best modern poets. They can not have the pure emotion; or, if they can have it, they can not sing it purely and simply. The demon of reflection is continually whispering in the singer's ear: What is all this good for? Whence comes it? What has it to do with the inmost nature of things? What bearing has it on the conduct of life? The singer, unless he is a chosen one of all, stammers and blunders; or, recovering himself, takes refuge in grand metrical digressions of a semi-metaphysical nature. In fact, because the revolution itself expressed tendencies largely speculative, and because thought-problems were never before so widely known or discussed as they are in this century, the poet in mirroring his own age is forced to seek such union of thought with emotion as was never before demanded of the verse maker.

Emotion tinged with speculative reflection results in the writing of what is called romantic poetry. High or low, grand or inane, nearly all sincere modern poetic effort is in this sense romantic. A sort of secondary, artificial freedom from reflection we find in a few classic modern poems; a few natural songs from time to time spring up unaffected by the reflective spirit. But on the whole, for good or for evil, romanticism is triumphant: for good, when the thought and the emotion unite to form a perfect whole, a colored but still unblurred crystal, a *Prometheus Unbound* or a first part of *Faust;* for evil, whenever the thought mars the purity of the feeling, the feeling the definiteness of the thought.[1]

Of all the subjects of reflection in the romantic poetry, none is more familiar than the question of the meaning and worth of human life as a whole. The first and natural answer of the modern poet to this question is well known. Human life means for him the emotional side of life. The highest good, when found, must be an emo-

[1] The rest of Sec. II was incorporated in ch. v of *The Religious Aspect of Philosophy.* — Ed.

tional good. The romantic poet, criticizing life, must aim to make clear what kind of emotional condition is the most satisfactory one. Notice that in this view we have no mere truism. Many forms of Hedonism would oppose the doctrine that in the intenser emotions can be found the ideal states of consciousness. The common sense of men of the world sees in the more moderate pleasures of polite leisure, in the attainment of practical knowledge, in a successful professional or business career, the sources of permanent satisfaction. Several schools of ancient philosophy regarded tranquillity as constituting the essence of a blessed life. But to all this the spirit of modern poetry was from the outset violently opposed. Tranquillity, once exchanged for storm and stress, is not again regarded as the goal. Active emotion, intense in quality, unlimited in quantity, is what the poets of the revolution desire. One need only mention *Werther*, *The Robbers*, *The Revolt of Islam*, *Manfred*, *Faust*, to suggest what is meant by this spirit of the revolutionary poetry.

Life, then, can be of worth only in so far as it is full of the desirable forms of poetic emotion. But is such fullness of life possible? Is the view that makes it the ideal a tenable view? Must not the consistent following of this view lead ultimately to pessimism? The answer to this problem is the history of the whole romantic movement. Here must suffice a sketch of some of the principal results of the movement.

The stir of modern life, then, has awakened sensibility, quickened desire, aroused the passion for freedom, disturbed old traditions. Above all, the theological ideals of life have been for the romantic poet disturbed, perhaps shattered. His highest good must be sought in his own soul. What is the consequence? First, of course, a sense of splendid independence, a lofty spiritual pride. The joy of freed emotion is equaled by few delights on earth. The self-worship of poetic genius is surpassed by few forms of conceit. Shelley, rejoicing in his strength, writing *The Necessity of Atheism*, and defending, in all innocence of evil, adultery and incest, is a good example of the expression of this spirit. Lavatar's account of the nature of genius is another instance: "As the apparitions of angels do not come but are present, do not go away but are gone, as they strike the innermost marrow, influence by their immortality the immortal in men, vanish and yet still influence, leave behind them sweet shuddering and tears of terror, and on the countenance pale joy, so the operation of genius. Describe genius as you will — name it fruitfulness of soul, faith, hope, love — the unlearned, the unlearnable — the inimitable, the divine — that is genius. 'Tis inspiration, revelation, that may be felt, but not willed or desired; 'tis art above art, its way is the way of the lightning." [1] I cannot quote a tenth part of this rhapsody, wherein the self-admiration and the mutual admiration of the young men about Goethe, in the years just before and after 1780, receive a characteristic expression.

This pride leads directly to the effort to build up a wholly new set of ideals. The patience of the statesman, of the student of science, of the business man, is unknown to these forceful young men. They must make a world of their own, and in a day, too. At the same time they are without any definite faith. In fact, definite faith would endanger for them the freshness of their emotions. They fear any creed but one self-made. And they can more easily tear down than build up. One of

[1] See the passage at much greater length in Koberstein's *Gesch. d. deutch. Nationalität*, bd. IV, p. 26 of the 5th ed.

the most interesting of the young geniuses of that age [1]
is the early lost Novalis (Friedrich v. Hardenberg), a
representative, like Shelley after him, of the emotional
or romantic poetry in its pristine innocence. A truly
noble soul, joined to a weak body, oppressed by many
troubles, unable to grow to full manly spiritual stature,
he shows us the beauty and imperfection of the emotional movement in close union. He writes pages of
vague philosophy, which afterwards impressed the
young Carlyle as an expression of a sense of the deep
mystery of life. You find delight in wandering through
the flowery labyrinths of such speculation; but you
come nowhere. Only this is clear: the young poet persists that the world must in some way conform to the
emotional needs of man. And he persists, too, that a
harmonious scheme of life can be formed on a purely
romantic plan, and only on such a plan. He actually explains no reality and completes no scheme of life. He
hints, at length, that the Catholic church is the best
expression of the needs of man. With this unsatisfactory suggestion, the little career of wandering ends in
death. But in what could it have ended, had life continued?

Perhaps in what was called by the close friend of
Novalis, Friedrich Schlegel, the romantic irony. This is
the next stage in the growth, or, if you like, in the decay
of the romantic spirit. Emotion is our guide and our
goal. But what is emotion? Something changeable and
by nature inconsistent. Each emotion sets up a claim to
fill the whole of life. For each new one, the earnest
poetic soul feels willing to die. Yet each is driven away

[1] The age in question extends from 1770 to 1830. No special effort is here made to follow chronological order. Our purpose is to cite illustrations, not to give a history.

by its follower. The feet of them that shall bear it out are before the door even while the triumphant emotion is reigning over the heart within. Fullness of such life means fickleness. Novalis, upon the death of his betrothed, made a sort of divinity of the departed, and dated a new era from the day of her death. His Diary was for a while full of spiritual exercises, suggested by his affliction. He resolved to follow her to the grave in one year. Within this year he was betrothed anew. If such is Novalis, what will be a lesser spirit? Conscious of this inevitable decay of each emotion, Friedrich Schlegel suggests that one should make a virtue of necessity and declare that the higher life consists in a sort of enthusiastic fickleness. The genius must wander like a humming bird in the garden of divine emotions. And he must be conscious and proud of his wanderings. Activity, or rather agility, is his highest perfection. The more numerous his emotions, the nobler the man. The fickler the man, the more numerous his emotions. This conscious union of nobility and fickleness is the romantic irony, which consists in receiving each new enthusiasm with a merry pride. 'Twas not the first, and will not be the last. We see through it, even while we submit to it. We are more than it, and will survive it. Long live King Experience, who showers upon us new feelings!

So much for an ingenious and thoroughly detestable view of life, in which there is for an earnest man no rest. This irony, what is it but the laughter of demons over the miserable weakness of human character? The emotion was to be our god. It turns out to be a wretched fetich, and we know it as such. 'Twas mine, 'tis his, and has been slave to thousands. It is gone, though we trusted in it. It was our stay, and it has flowed away ike water. This is not fullness, but hollowness, of life.

And how shall the romantic irony supply the vacancy? This irony is but the word of Mephistopheles about the ruin of Gretchen: *Sie ist die erste nicht.* Not the first change of emotion is this present one; not the first breaking up of the fountains of the great deep within us; but what misery in that thought! Then there is nothing sure, nothing significant. In our own hearts were we to find life, and there is no true life there; only masks with nothing beneath them; only endless and meaningless change.

The consciousness of this result is the next step in the self-criticism of the romantic spirit. The consequence is what Hegel in the *Phänomenologie des Geistes*, described under the name of *Das Unglückliche Bewusstsein,* and what is more familiarly known to us as the Byronic frame of mind. The very strength of the previous emotion renders this consciousness of the hollowness of emotion the more insupportable:

> When the lamp is broken
> The light in the dust lies dead.

The brighter the lamp, the deeper the darkness that follows its breaking.

The romantic despair thus described took many forms in the poetry of the early part of the century. To describe them all were to go far beyond our limits. A few forms suggest themselves. If we are condemned to fleeting emotions, we are still not deprived of the hope that some day we may by chance find an abiding emotion. Thus, then, we find many poets living in a wholly problematic state of mind, expecting the *god stronger than they who, coming, shall rule over them.* Such a man is the dramatist and writer of tales, Heinrich von Kleist. "It can be," writes this poet to a friend, December,

1806,[1] "it can be no evil spirit that rules the world, only a spirit not understood." In such a tone of restless search for the ideal of action, Kleist remains throughout his life. No poet of the romantic school had a keener love of life problems purely as problems. Each of his works is the statement of a question. Kleist answered his own questions at last by suicide. Others have other ways of fleeing misery. Ludwig Tieck, after running through the whole round of romantic questions, rids himself of his demons by turning his attention to other literary work, and lets most of the old romantic ideals alone. Friedrich Schlegel finally escapes from himself by means of scholarly toil and Catholic faith. Hölderlin takes refuge in a mad-house. Shelley manages to endure, while he lives, by dint of childlike submissiveness to his emotions, joined with earnest hope for yet better things. Schiller joins with Goethe in a search for perfection in the ancient Greek world. There are many fashions of quieting the restlessness that belonged to the time, yet what one of them really answers the problems of the romantic spirit? There is still the great question: How may mankind live the harmonious emotional life, when men are driven for their ideals back upon themselves, when traditional faith is removed, when the age is full of wretchedness and of blind striving, when the very strength of poetic emotion implies that it is transient and changeable? The conscious failure to answer this question is more or less decided pessimism.

Could modern poetry free itself from that reflective tendency in which we have found its most prominent characteristic, the pessimism could disappear with the criticism of life. But this is impossible. Omit part of

[1] I quote from J. Schmidt, *Gesch. d. deutchen Literatur*, bd. II, p. 472.

our lyric poetry, some of our comedy and of our satire, and the rest of our best nineteenth-century poetic work is a more or less conscious struggle with pessimism. The grounds and the nature of this struggle have been set forth in the foregoing. The poet once for all accepts the emotional criterion of the worth of life. Determining to see in the harmonious emotional life the best life, feeling as the most certain of principles that "there is a lower and a higher," the poet seeks to picture the perfect existence thus defined. Failure means for him pessimism; not v. Hartmann's really quite harmless "*eudämono-logischer Pessimismus,*" but the true pessimism of the broken will, that has tried all and failed. The life that ought to be, cannot be; the life that is, is hollow and futile; such will be the result of disappointed idealism. In our time, the idealistic poets that are not pessimists have all, nevertheless, fought more or less consciously the same battle with pessimism. Think only of the *Excursion,* or of the *In Memoriam,* or again of *Faust,* that epitome of the thought of our century.

But before we allow ourselves a word on the relation of *Faust* to our problem, let us look a little closer at Byron. *Faust* is the crown of modern poetic effort. If that fails as a solution, all in this field has thus far been lost. But in Byron there is a confessed, one might even say a professed, moral imperfection, whose nature throws light, not so much on the solution of the problem of pessimism, as on the problem itself.

The development of Bryon's poetry has two very marked periods, the sentimental and the critical. The sentimental Byron of the years before 1816 is not of very great historical interest. The Byron of *Manfred, Cain,* and *Don Juan,* represents an independent phase of the romantic movement, whose faults are as instructive as its beauties. This period of Byron's poetry is of course but very roughly described by the word critical, yet that word is at any rate suggestive. A sensitive man, and yet heroic, strong in spirit, but without fixed ideals of life, a rebel by nature who yet finds no greater soul to lead him, no faithful band to follow him in any definite effort for mankind, Byron is a modern likeness of him that in the legend afterwards became St. Christopher. Only Byron seeks the strongest without finding him, learns to despise the devil, and never meets the devil's master. Worn out with the search, the poet flings himself down in the woods of doubt and dreams *Don Juan*. We look in vain for the right adjective with which to qualify this poem: it is so full of strength, so lavish of splendid resources, and yet in sum so disappointing. It has no true ending, and never could have had one. It is a mountain stream, plunging down dreadful chasms, singing through grand forests, and losing itself in a lifeless gray alkali desert. Here is romantic self-criticism pushed to its farthest consequences. Here is the self-confession of an heroic soul that has made too high demands on life, and that has found in its own experience and in the world nothing worthy of true heroism. We feel the magnitude of the blunder, we despise (with the author, as must be noticed, not in opposition to him) the miserable petty round of detestable experiences — intrigues, amours, dinners — in brief, the vulgarity to which human life is reduced; but the tragedy is everywhere to be read between the lines, not in what is said. The romantic spirit has sought in vain for the satisfactory emotional state, and for the worthy deed to perform, and now rests, scornful and yet terrified, in dizzy contemplation of the confused and meaningless maze of sensations into which the world has resolved itself. "There is nothing there to fear or hope," this spirit seems to say.

> "When Bishop Berkeley said there was no matter,
> And proved it, 'twas no matter what he said."

Or again:

> "To be or not to be?" Ere I decide
> I should be glad to know that which is being;
> 'Tis true we speculate both far and wide,
> And deem, because we *see*, we are *all-seeing*.
> For my part, I'll enlist on neither side,
> Until I see both sides for once agreeing.
> For me, I sometimes think that life is death,
> Rather than life a mere affair of breath.

In *Manfred* the same spirit seeks another, and not quite so successful a form of expression. The only peace that can come to this world-weary spirit, Manfred expresses at the sight of a quiet sunset. The only freedom from eternal self-examination is found in an occasional glance at peaceful nature.

> It will not last,
> But it is well to have known it though but once;
> It hath enlarged my thoughts with a new sense,
> And I within my tablets would note down
> That there is such a feeling.

The famous last words of Manfred,

> Old man, 'tis not so difficult to die.

coming as they do after all Manfred's vacillation upon just this point, indicate the final resolution of despair to brave all possible wretchedness from without for the sake of feeling within, in all its strength, though but for a moment, the fierce defiance of the rebellious Titan. Hungry for deeds, finding nothing to do, fearing the possible future life, and hating the present, the hero at last resorts to an untrue but stirring assertion of absolute personal independence of all the hateful universe here and hereafter:

> Thou didst not tempt me, and thou couldst not tempt me.
> I have not been thy dupe, nor am thy prey —
> But was my own destroyer, and will be
> My own hereafter.

This is pessimism that overleaps itself and falls on the other. The outcome of self-analyzing romanticism is the determination to build afresh a world that shall be nobler than this poor world of decaying passive emotions. Feeling will not do. Manfred attains something by action, even though he first acts in the moment of death. Doing work of some kind is, then, that to which we are necessarily driven. But if the action of defiance can make death tolerable, why might not some kind of activity make life tolerable? Is not the worthy life then to be found, not in emotion, but in work? Is not the ideal state the ideal activity, not the ideal feeling? This suggestion is at the foundation of the prototype of Manfred, the Faust of Goethe.

Praise of the first part of Goethe's *Faust* is nowadays superfluous. Doubtless the work is a torso,[1] but so is the life of man. Extravagant encomium of *Faust*, such as that wherewith Hermann Grimm has marred, as with a showman's harangue, the conclusion of his otherwise most instructive *Lectures on Goethe*, seems as out of place as applause in a cathedral. The poem is grand and profound, because the life problems it so truthfully portrays are grand and profound; in form, if you except digressions, it is sublimely simple and unassuming. Its

[1] Cf. the opinion of M. Edm. Scherer as quoted in Mr. Matthew Arnold's essay, "A French Critic on Goethe," in the *Mixed Essays*, p. 291.

imperfections are as open to view as is its grandeur. The doctrine of the poem may be thus briefly suggested. Here is a world wherein nature, the expression of divine intelligence, is perfect, wherein man, by the same divine wisdom, is left in darkness and confusion. The angels, who simply contemplate nature's perfection, are the "true sons of God." But they do nothing. They only see and think. Man is to act. By his action he is freely to create such perfection as already passively exists in nature. That is, his life is to become an harmonious whole. The postulate of the Lord is that this is possible. Mephistopheles holds the opposite opinion. The question is to be solved by the case of Faust.

Faust is a man in whom are combined all the strength and weakness of the romantic spirit. No excellence he deems of worth so long as any excellence is beyond his grasp. Therefore his despair at the sight of the great world of life. So small a part of it is his. He knows that he can never grow great enough to grasp the whole, or any finite part of the whole. Yet there remains the hopeless desire for this wholeness. Nothing but the infinite can be satisfying. Hence the despair of the early scenes of the first part. Like Byron's Manfred, Faust seeks death; but Faust is kept from it by no fear of worse things beyond, only by an accidental reawakening of old childish emotions. He feels that he has no business with life, and is wholly a creature of accident. He is clearly conscious only of a longing for a full experience. But this experience he conceives as mainly a passive one. He does not wish as yet to do anything, only to get everything.[1] But at the same time with this desire for a

[1] Cf. the lengthy discussion of this point in Friedrich Vischer, *Goethe's Faust, Neue Beiträge zur Kritik des Gedichts*, especially p. 291, and p. 304. "*Er* (Faust) *weiss also für jetzt nur von der Lust.*"

tempest of new feelings, Faust has the consciousness that there never can be a satisfactory feeling. Mephistopheles, stating the case of the contented man of the world, assures him that the time will come for enjoying good things in peace. Faust indignantly replies that pleasure can never deceive him, the tolerable moment never come. In making this very assertion, however, and in concluding his pact with Mephistopheles upon the basis of this assertion, Faust rises above his first position, and assumes a new one. The satisfactory pleasure can never be given to him, and why? Because he will always remain active. Satisfaction would mean repose, repose would mean death. Life is activity. The meaning of the pact is of course that, for good or for evil, all the existence of a man is work, and that no one is ever wholly lost so long as the power of accomplishment remains his. But if work is the essence of life, then satisfaction must be found not in feelings but in deeds. The world is good if we can make it so, not otherwise. The problem of Faust is, therefore, the discovery of the perfect kind of activity.

With this insight the romantic spirit has risen beyond itself. The essence of romanticism is the desire for fullness of personal experience. The essence of this new spirit is the eagerness to accomplish something. The difference is vast. Faust, following this new tendency, might be led to an obscure toiling life of endless self-sacrifice. His pessimism (for in the early scenes he is a pessimist) might give way before unquestioning heroic devotion to some great end. Does this take place? We know too well the answer. The whole poem is indeed a conflict between the two tendencies of Faust, but the first, the desire for manifold passive experiences, is until the last scenes of the second part predominant. Faust is active, but his activity is mainly a continual pursuit of new experiences. Even at the end he is not active as other men are active; his work is done by magic; and the accomplishment for whose sake he is at last willing to say, *This is the highest moment*, is an anticipation, not a reality. In the real world the satisfactory work is never found. And thus the solution of the problem is not fully given, though the poet, while suggesting it, has done more than any other modern poet. The revolution had furnished as life-ideals grand emotion and heroic action. The two cannot wholly be harmonized. The highest forms of activity imply self-sacrifice, drudgery, routine, cool-headed calculation, realism. The highest forms of emotion, pursued by themselves, intoxicate and ener-vate. It is the purpose of Goethe to lead his hero through the various stages of emotional life for the sake of mak-ing him prefer in the end a mode of action to all forms of simple emotion. The result is to be a man above the deadness of ordinary work-a-day realism, yet as devoted to toil as the stupidest realist. There is to be a free sur-render of a full self to the service of some high end. Nothing is lacking to the conquest over pessimism, ex-cept the clear statement of that for which the converted Faust is to work. The goal of activity once found, the problem will be solved, and the devil's wager lost. But the dim allegorical suggestions of the second part will not suffice to give us the account of what is wanted. Faust is to work for human progress, and progress means the existence of a whole nation of hard-laboring, fearless men who fight forever for their freedom. To have been the father of such a people is the highest blessedness. Good, indeed, we say; but to have wrought by the devil's aid, through magic and oppression, is this the highest? Is this the type of the best activity? And is the great problem after all really solved? For what is the ultimate good of the eternal warfare with nature in which mankind are thus left? Faust leaves behind him a nation of toilers, whose business it will be to build dikes to keep the sea out. A worthy end of romantic hopes, truly! That Goethe himself is not wholly content therewith, is proven by the epilogue in heaven, which means, if it means anything, that the highest end of human activity is something very fine, but altogether inexpressible, invisible, inconceivable, indefinite, a thing of ether and fog. One longs in this last scene for the presence of Mephistopheles, who surely has as much right there as in the prologue, and who would be sure to say, in his terse and sinewy fashion, just the right and the last word about the whole business.

The incompleteness of *Faust* is the incompleteness of modern thought. The poet is silent about the final problem, because modern thought is still toiling away on the definition of the highest human activity. And so we naturally turn from our hasty survey of the poetic movement of the revolutionary period to a sketch of certain forms of speculative thought regarding this problem of pessimism.

III. PESSIMISM AND SPECULATION

At the outset of our discussion, we rejected the view that estimates the value of life as an accountant estimates a man's assets, viz., by summation and balancing. The only useful speculations on the worth of life are those that regard life with reference to some accepted goal; itself a state of consciousness in some animate being. Given the goal, we can compare therewith the work actually done in human life, and see how nearly the desired state has been approached. The desired state may imply a series of experiences, in which, upon summation, there is found to be an excess of pain over pleasure. Yet this state may be demanded as the highest state, and the implied series of experiences may be accepted as a means thereto, without any question on the part of the acceptor as to the balance of pleasure and pain. The worth of life is judged solely with reference to the goal.

What determines the choice of our goal need not here be considered at length. It is enough to note the following principles: 1. If we choose any end as the end to be sought, our work towards that end is accompanied by an unrest, *i. e.*, by a constant disposition to alter the content of our consciousness, so long as we are at work. The attainment of the goal means the cessation of the unrest. To seek the goal and to seek to quiet the unrest are, therefore, one and the same thing. 2. Unrest has no absolute worth. For otherwise, unrest itself would be our goal. But unrest is not the goal; it is the consciousness that we are seeking our goal. The goal has worth in itself; but the unrest has worth only as bringing us near the goal. 3. If we have fixed upon any goal, so that we judge life as good in so far as it approaches, bad in so far as it does not approach, the goal, then our estimate of the worth of life is by implication fixed, and can be altered only by an alteration of the goal. But the choice of the goal is an act of volition. We cannot prove to another person that so and so is the goal. We can tell him what our goal is, and can hope that we shall find or awaken in him a sympathy with our enthusiasm. The choice of an object in life defies logical demonstration. Men catch from other men moral ideals, or now and again originate new ones for themselves. Never do they receive their moral principles as they do their mathematics, by rigid demonstration. The ultimate axioms of conduct are practical volitions; while the ultimate axioms of science, if volitional in nature, are yet volitions of another order. 4. But, in accepting several goals at once, or in altering a previously accepted goal, we are, to a certain extent, influenced by a logical consideration, viz., consistency. If two accepted goals of action are found to conflict, we seek to harmonize them by compromise, or by the elimination of one of them. If one goal is found, upon analysis, to imply a self-contradiction, we alter it. If, upon better understanding of what an accepted goal implies, we alter our position towards it, our reflection has influenced our volition. Thus, there arises a sort of moral dialectic, and the independence of our will, in accepting a particular object as the goal of our striving, is limited by the reaction of our thought upon each new ideal that we set up.

These principles being admitted, the discussion of the worth of life reduces to the following questions: 1. Are the goals of ordinary human action such as can be clearly defined at all? 2. If defined, will they be found to be consistent, or inconsistent and mutually destructive? 3. If this is the case, can any process of dialectic purification reduce them to unity, and set up a consistent and universal ideal of life? 4. If this last ideal is found, is it to be regarded as attainable?

The first question is generally answered with a qualified, sometimes with an unqualified, affirmative. That at least some of the popular objects of human life are definable, is implied in nearly every discussion of the subject, whatever the result of such discussion. In so far as such goals of action are not definable, the life that seeks them has, from our point of view, no definable worth.

Given an affirmative answer to the first question, the second presents itself in two forms. It may relate to the objects of the life of some one individual, as given to and for him. Or it may relate to the various ideals of various people, considered in their social relations. In both its forms we must answer the question in the same way. The various ordinarily accepted aims of human life, both in individuals for themselves and in society at large, do conflict. Vacillation, inner struggles of all kinds, show us how disunited are our own individual ideals of life; aggression and cruelty, even discussion, even the forms of compact and alliance, show how great the conflict, or the danger of conflict, between various human aims. But if life as a whole is to have worth, these conflicts, it would seem, must, on the whole, be brought to an end. For they mean hindrance and extra unrest even to the victors; total failure, endless unrest, to the vanquished.

The third and fourth questions are the places of the greatest controversy. If one may be permitted to affirm anything about people's answers to questions that they themselves did not in so many words formulate, one may with fair certainty say that on his negative answer to our third question depends, in part, Schopenhauer's peculiar form of pessimism, while on the affirmative answer thereto depends the optimism of the most of the Hegelian school, as well as the optimism of the evolution philosophers. For the Hegelian, all conflicting human ends finally, through a dialectic process, harmonize in one highest end, the self-consciousness of the Absolute Spirit. For the believer in physical evolution, all human ends will at length harmonize in the one end of giving self, through the perfect satisfaction of our fellows, the greatest satisfaction possible. Such at least is the sense of a late formula propounded by a thoroughly competent authority. But for Schopenhauer such harmony is impossible. The greater our knowledge, the better shall we see, according to Schopenhauer, that warfare is of the essence of the will, and that the various objects of the will, not only are incompatible, but must forever remain irreconcilable.

But if the third question were answered in the affirmative, if the one goal were fixed upon, the fourth question would remain. This fourth question, viewed apart from the third, is answered negatively by Schopenhauer, affirmatively by the evolution philosophers, presumably with a *weder noch* by most of the Hegelians. Let us look for a moment at the matter. Given any goal, then life is of worth in so far as it approaches that goal. Endless unrest would be failure. But now, says Schopenhauer, life is will, and will is unrest. Given any goal as the highest, then attainment would mean absolute rest. Absolute rest would mean cessation of will, and so death. But if attainment of the absolute end means death, then in life the end cannot be attained. Life can, therefore, never have absolute worth. Whatever is a goal with nothing beyond cannot be life, but must be death. Whatever life has no final goal within its reach, must be an eternal failure. On such a basis is Schopenhauer's pessimism built up.

Let us consider the subject in another way, making ourselves more independent of Schopenhauer's metaphysic, and taking a course that leads to a direct attack upon that stronghold of modern optimism, viz., upon the ethical significance of the doctrine of progress. Some people at one time liked the phrase "perfectibility of man," instead of the more modern phrase "evolution of humanity." But when men looked to history for proof of this "perfectibility," one trouble in their way was the sad fact that the perfectible creature has never yet been perfected. If not quite "*so wunderlich als wie am ersten Tag*," he is still not a little defective; in fact, mostly a blunderer, and often a knave. "The progress of man" seems, then, a more satisfactory term wherewith to sum up the facts of history. But too many optimistic congratulations must not yet be exchanged over this fact of progress. It is a fact; progress is for the better, and worship of savage innocence was a mere sentimental whim of the strait-laced eighteenth century. But what follows thence about the nature of life? Alas! too little. This worship of progress is only another bit of sentiment, useful in its place, but of not very tough moral fiber. Stouthearted men in this great, dark universe, must be ready to take their own view of the worth of life, quite apart from their knowledge of a link or two of the myriad-coiled chain of the world history. For reflect: this bit of life that we here know, is but a fragment (a cross-section as it were, with a little piece added lengthwise) out of an eternity of events. Here is an endless sequence of causes and effects. Now, on any hypothesis as to the powers that direct the universe, so much is certain. After an infinity of time (of progress or of retrogression, or of endless circular motion? Who shall say?), the world spirit or the world force has brought forth this present world of human life, with all its vast imperfections. The world plan or no-plan (we need not here discuss which) involves as a possible result, after the lapse of infinite ages of change, all the failure and worthlessness and blind struggling that is here about us in these oppressed millions of wasted lives, in these thieves and cut-throats, in these filthy, in these halt and blind, in these stupid wretches that make up the lower classes of society, in these heart-sick, lonesome wanderers that seek the out-

skirts of civilization, in all these fellow-beings to whom
our hearts go out in pity even while we despise their
weakness. This is one result of the infinite ages. Take
the worst wretch ever heard of — a Guiteau or a Judas.
It took just an eternity to produce him. Now, this being
so, it is enough. What the world plan is we need not
judge. What it may imply, we by this example see. It
may imply always just, as it now realizes, the existence
of what we in this discussion are regarding as evil,
namely, hopeless striving ending in failure, fierce conflict ending in mutual destruction of the fighters. Here
helps no progress. This world may get better for a while;
what are a few million years in an eternity? But there is
no evidence to show that progress is eternal and regular.
If progress had gone on from eternity, where would be
room for imperfection now? Much as many efforts in
theodicy become inconsistent with orthodox theology in
that they necessarily imply that the evil of this world,
being an essential of finite and rational existence, must
continue into the next world and enter heaven itself,
even so this optimism of progress proves too much. If
evil is possible and actual after infinite ages of progress,
then a further infinity of progress might never remove
the evil. And why, then, is progress a very cheering
fact? But if the infinite past has not been all progress,
then what hope for the future? The most probable
view of the universe as a whole would seem then to be
the view, according to which growth and decay go on
forever in cyclic rhythm. At any time in the past or
future we should expect to find much such a universe of
striving and imperfection as we now find, the forms infinitely various, the significance wearily the same.

So much for the skeptical consideration of our fourth
question. To return now for a few final words about our

third question. In the present writer's mind there is no doubt that the third question can be answered affirmatively; that there is an ultimate goal, to which, by simple self-knowledge, by immanent criticism of human desire, all the various and conflicting goals of action can be reduced. Whether all men will ever come to recognize this one goal, whether by any process of dialectic purification the many will for all men be stripped of their deceits and seen in their reality as but one, we do not know. That makes little difference for the purposes of our third question. Nor can we go far now into the defense of this as our goal. We must content ourselves with a mere statement. The one goal is the rendering as full and as definite as possible all the conscious life that at any moment comes within the circle of our influence. Devotion, then, to universal conscious life, is the goal of conscious life itself; or the goal is the self-reference or self-surrender of each conscious moment to the great whole of life, in so far as that whole is within reach. Separation from other conscious life means failure. Conscious union with other conscious life means for every conscious being success in proportion to the fullness, clearness, and definiteness of that union. This union is the highest goal, not for itself logically demonstrable as such, but deducible from the other actual goals of mankind when they are analyzed in their true meaning.

This being the goal of action, the fourth question recurs. Is the goal attainable? The trust in progress is, as we just saw, no secure support. Progress seems to be a fact of very limited scope, magnified rather unduly in our eyes by a certain praiseworthy enthusiasm of contemporary thought. No hope then there. Critical thinkers can not be permanently caught with such chaff. Optimists or pessimists we must be here and now, in and for this present earthly life in this nineteenth century. Everybody then must finally settle the question with his own soul. Discussions like the present but try to state the problem, that each may have its terms before him. And what is the problem as our discussion has defined it? Here is our final statement:

If the goal is conscious union of every conscious being with the great whole of conscious life, and if rest is impossible until that end is attained, and possible if that is attained, can we hope under human conditions to attain this goal? The answer is: in perfect union and harmony with the whole of conscious life we can at moments feel ourselves. Self-sacrifice chief of all, and in the next rank hard work for any impersonal end, or the mere contemplation of active life, the union with others for the doing of work that involves no warring with an opposite party, even warfare when carried on for the good of the whole of conscious life; whatever, in a word, impresses on each his own insignificance and still more the grandeur of the great ocean of conscious activity below, about, and above him: all such deeds and experiences serve to accomplish what is meant by union of each being with the whole of life. Yet such union is perfected only in moments. For the rest of the time selfishness, self-conceit, struggle with hated equals, in a word, unrest, are predominant. And of mankind as a whole, this is even more true than of those individual men who have a fancy for ethics. We must look forward then for ourselves to a life-long—for the universe to a seemingly eternal — process of unrest, broken by transient moments of union with the whole of conscious life, by moments, that is, of devotion, of cheerful absorption in noble work, of strength in the admiration of other strength; by moments of sympathy and of self-sacrifice. Whether in sum there shall be more pains than pleasures in this series of conscious states, who knows? And who need care? Are we registering machines or men? We are viewing life solely with reference to the highest goal. What matters the rest of it?

This being our result, is it optimistic or pessimistic? Surely not what most people mean by the former. A life of endless battle, with temporary triumphs here and there, is no complete triumph. But is it complete failure? The goal never is finally attained, but is repeatedly attained, though but temporarily. The result is not the despair of disappointed romanticism, for we passed beyond that when we found that without activity no real triumph is possible. Nor is it that confused representation of an indefinite something with which the epilogue in heaven in *Faust* torments us. This sense of oneness with universal consciousness is a very simple experience: you can know it easily if you will but do a sacrificing act with purely unselfish motives, or if you will but give yourself up to the enthusiasm of a great popular cause, or if you will sit down and comfort a fellow-being in distress. Much nonsense can be talked about the matter; but, after all, the soul of true living is such experience. *This life is my life:* it is a rich moment when we say that of some other being, and were it but of a chirping, nest-brooding bird in the woods at twilight. Nor is our result a mere acceptance of activity as in itself enough. No, the activity is unrest; but through the unrest comes occasional rest. As for Schopenhauer's objection that the unrest predominates, we admit the fact. Schopenhauer's inference is that the will to live ought to be quenched. We reply that this is a matter not thus to be decided. As we first chose our goal by independent volition, so now we may choose how much hindrance of our endless efforts to reach the goal will be regarded as compensated by our occasional successes. Not the comparison of the two sums is desired, but the verdict of volition upon the worth of two sets of experiences. Which will you choose? That last question is simply unanswerable, except by a direct act of will. Here are the facts: A goal, viz., self-forgetfulness in the contemplation and creation of the fullest and clearest universal conscious life; a struggle to reach this goal, a struggle with blind nature, with selfishness within, with hatred without; this struggle alternating with periods of triumph; the process of alternating struggle and occasional triumph an endless process. How like you this life? It is the best that you are apt to find. Do you accept it? Every man has to deal with these queries quite by himself, even as with his own eyes he must see colors. It is our province merely to suggest the ultimate questions.

It has been the aim of the foregoing essay to present the question of pessimism in various historical lights, and to suggest a method of dealing with the problems involved. That these problems are deeply rooted in human nature seems plain. Unfortunate is the public apathy and light-headedness which declines to consider serious moral questions until accident forces them upon our notice. Pessimism is often regarded with horror; yet an earnest pessimist would be better than a sluggard of any creed.

TESTS OF RIGHT AND WRONG

[1880]

ETHICAL phenomena, like all other phenomena wherewith human thought deals, may be studied in either one of two ways, viz., by an historical examination of their genesis, or by an analysis of their structure as they now exist. Either way of studying phenomena is made easier by the practice and insight gained through pursuing the other, yet the ways are essentially distinct. To know the origin of things is not the same as to know their nature. In this paper I shall first undertake to compare in general the results gained by the two methods as applied to testing the distinction between right and wrong, and shall then discuss this distinction as it is seen from the point of view of the analytical method.

The historical method of philosophizing, understood in the most general sense, is the method especially pursued by those who support the doctrine of evolution. The analytic method is the one that was long in favor in philosophy, though nowadays it is often unfairly neglected. By the historical method of philosophy, to be sure, I do not mean to include all the ways of working of those writers whose study is history. Many historians are above all devoted to the analysis of social structures, and take interest in questions of genesis only in so far as these throw light on the constitution of things. But on the whole writers on social science make most prominent one or other of two postulates. The postulate of the historical school is: The forms of things are determined by the growth of things. The postulate of the analytical school is: The history of the world is nothing but the series of various possible groupings of the permanent elements of the world. It is plain upon reflection that neither of the two schools can ever conquer the other. There is no direct conflict. Both ways of thinking are necessary and well founded. The historical method bases itself, like the science of experimental physics, on the general confidence in the uniformity of nature. The analytical method, with its postulate, has the same ultimate foundation as the science of mathematics. The one method says, certain laws of change are fixed. The other method says, certain elementary statical relations endure forever. Both must be admitted, as far as they go, to be possible ways of unifying human experience. Both lead to such truth as mortals can reach, viz., to clearness, to simplicity, to harmony, to unity, in our conceptions. But the two methods show us the universe in different lights. The historical or Herakleitean method studies things as in flow, the analytic or Eleatic method studies the same things as at rest. And any effort on the part of one method to exclude or refute the legitimate proceedings of the other must lead to onesidedness and mistakes.

But to speak now especially of ethics. The historical method if carried to its farthest extent and if successful, would give us a complete account of how the moral ideas of men grew up. Taking as known the condition of a mind actuated by simple and unmoral motives, such as the desire to avoid an immediate pain and to gain immediate pleasure, the historian would show us how, as the conditions of the environment grew more complex, the consciousness of men must grow more complex also, and how somewhere in the growth there must appear those sentiments which we call moral. That these sentiments are qualitatively different from those out of which they grew, would interest the historian but little. That they grew out of the assumed previous state would be his thesis; and he would show that they must grow out of this previous state, by finding the uniform laws according to which they actually have grown. For the historical philosopher, "must follow" means "does follow in all cases where given conditions are present." Whether analysis would show the subsequent state to have been contained in the previous state as an element or part of it, or whether the resultant is of an entirely new kind, wholly unlike the antecedent, is for the historical philosopher a very subordinate question. Uniformity in sequence does not mean that a thing follows from something that was like it, but that a given simple sequence of two things, like or unlike, will take place whenever certain conditions are present.

The analytical moralist, on the other hand, is especially interested in the moral consciousness as it is. The facts of history mean for him not evidences of genesis, but experiments whose use is to show the component parts of the moral consciousness by bringing moral agents into very various relative situations. The study of ethics is for him the distinction, description and criticism of the different ethical tendencies in human character, as they exist in themselves and in combination. Therefore, how the moral consciousness grew is for him a problem not of the highest importance.

We cannot say that the one of these methods which is followed by an ethical philosopher determines his conclusions as to the true test of right and wrong. Utilitarians for example have sometimes been analytic students of Ethics, as Bentham was, or again, have often been students of the genesis of moral ideas. In like manner those whose ethical doctrine is founded on the notion of a divine origin of right and wrong are no less students of genesis, than is Mr. Spencer himself in his *Data of Ethics*. But if the method does not determine one's view of the moral principle, it certainly modifies greatly one's treatment of particular moral doctrines. One-sided pursuit of either method blinds us to the facts on which the other is based. Moreover, if the analytic student forgets that analysis is only a part of the truth, he is apt, through neglecting to study the evolution of moral ideas, to fail in his analysis itself. And, on the other hand, if analysis is neglected for the sake of studying the evolution of morality, one is led to superficial generalizations, and in the presence of many important problems is left helpless.

To exemplify first the fault of the one-sided use of the analytic method: it is plain that if one determines to base his system of ethics solely on an analysis of his own moral consciousness as it now is, he will probably fail for lack of a sufficient variety of illustration. His analysis will be unsystematic, crude, not clearly intelligible to other people. His code will be provincial in the narrowest sense. Or if liberal, his liberalism will not be based on an intelligent appreciation of the diversity of human life, but on pure accident. Another man whose system was formed in like fashion will fail to find ground for agreement with the first. Their mutual intolerance will be a mutual refutation. Their best remedy will be an appeal to history to come to the aid of analysis. Let them view the history of humanity as the expression in time of the various possible forms of human character, as furnishing therefore a sort of self-dissection of the world spirit. Let their ethical doctrine be based on the results of this natural analysis of conscious life. Thus may the essential and the accidental in morality be separated from each other, and the analysis be given an enduring character. To be sure, each man's self-analysis must be the foundation of all his philosophy. Nothing can be more certain than what we really observe in ourselves. But for suggestions as to what we should seek in ourselves, this process of historical analysis is invaluable.

On the other hand, look at the problems introduced and left unsolved by the one-sided following of the historical method. Suppose that we trace one's acknowledgment of duties towards one's fellowmen to the growth of the social impulse. We may succeed in giving a very good psychological account of the genesis of moral ideas. But one great purpose of ethical discussion will be left unaccomplished. No sufficient test will be furnished for distinguishing right from wrong in many cases of conflict between duty and selfishness, or between one and another duty. Not merely in its practical or hortatory aspect, but in its theoretical investigations ethical science will thus be incomplete. Take a particular instance. By the historical method of ethics, stealing is shown to be a vice, by pointing out that civilized society could not exist if men had to distrust one another's honesty altogether or in great measure. It can be shown that through the experience of the consequences of theft, there has gradually grown up the instinct to disapprove of theft and to avoid committing it. As a rule, the truly civilized man does not steal. So much history can show us. All this makes honesty appear as an end of society, a demand on the part of what the late Professor Clifford called the "Tribal Self." Yet this study of evolution does not get rid of the fact that what makes the call of morality as morality binding on each one of us, is his own inclination to be moral. Take

away my sense of morality and my wish to do right, and
you may frighten me into legality, but you will not
make me virtuous. Now suppose for a time that I especially desire to steal. · Suppose moreover, that I see
clearly that civilized society could not exist if men had
to distrust one another's honesty. Suppose, however,
that I am just now quite indifferent to that fact. My
theft will not be discovered, I shall not be punished; and
my act, though belonging to a class of acts which if
numerous enough would ruin society, will in point of
fact leave society where it was before. Now my knowledge of evolution has taught me the true end and use of
morality, namely, the existence and good of society. It
has not taught me that this social end must always and
everywhere be my only end. On the contrary, it leads
me to believe that the social end tends to be realized
notwithstanding all resistance. At all events, though I
hope society will grow better, in fact, I feel that my one
undiscovered insignificant wrongdoing will not injure
society at all, but only the one person from whom I steal.
He will get no redress, and may never even know what
hurt him. Society will not be attacked at all. As for the
evil that bad example does to society, there is no bad example in this case, because by hypothesis nobody knows
of the act. If everybody did such acts, there would, indeed, be no society; but everybody does not do such
secret acts, and there is no danger that many will ever
be done. Why must I refrain from an act simply because its universal performance would endanger society?
If everybody chopped wood or played with sand continually, there would be no society either. People actually do chop wood when the action is profitable, and
play with sand when they have nothing else to do. Even
so, if people only stole when they could do so absolutely

without suspicion and at a time when their neighbors were generally honest, stealing would endanger society as little as other rather uncommon acts such as chopping wood and playing with sand. Historically then, there is no moral fact discoverable that makes my theft bad for me unless I just now happen to regard it as bad. My end is just now not the universal social end, it is a selfish end. Enlightened selfishness leads me indeed to see in society something of the highest importance for me. Enlightened selfishness does not lead me to refrain from harming my neighbor in a case where revenge or counter injury is impossible, and where my act cannot be interpreted as a direct attack on society, nor as an example to others. In brief, the result of the historical account of morality is such that from it alone I can draw no reason for condemning any wrong act that is done in secret, that is beyond discovery, that is uncommon, and that is therefore directed against the individual and not against society. If my analysis of my own purposes does not show me the right, the history of social purposes will not in this case help me at all.

The difficulty which all of us feel in accepting this argument as valid arises simply from the fact that none of us are content with a purely historical account of the moral consciousness, but that we appeal to analysis of the moral consciousness as it is whenever a case of doubt arises. Plainly stated, however, the fact is, that the now favorite historical account of morality does exhibit the moral consciousness as, according to its origin, merely enlightened and exalted selfishness. Now this history of the evolution of morality is no doubt, correct as history. But as a fact the moral consciousness now existing turns out, upon analysis, to be something qualitatively different from enlightened selfishness. Enlightened selfish-

ness leads me to serve society because society is valuable
to me, or even to work for posterity if I take pleasure in
thinking of posterity. But enlightened selfishness cannot teach me to do or to avoid any act that does not
affect society as a whole, and that does not bring me
reward or save me punishment, unless the doing or
omission of this act suits my inclination. My moral
consciousness does demand that I should do right and
eschew wrong, even though I am not inclined to do so,
and even though directly or indirectly the most enlightened selfishness cannot teach me that the least advantage will come to me from a particular right act, nor
the least harm result to me from a particular wrong act.
How and with what reason and consistency conscience
makes such great demands upon us, only analysis can
show us. History is powerless before the fact that whatever the moral consciousness of men has sprung from it
is more than enlightened selfishness. Analysis must
come to our aid, and show us what then this "more"
really is. Historically I judge of acts as more or less
"evolved."   An act on a lower stage of evolution is
attended with less knowledge of consequences, with less
thought of tendencies. On a higher stage a man looks
further into the future and regards the indirect as well as
the direct results of his acts. That is all. If an act of
cruelty or of injustice is contemplated and desired, I
cannot see that the man who refrains from the desired
act because it seems wrong to him, can be proved by the
historical method to be any better than the man who
with like impulse, regarding the act and all its consequences, and finding that in the particular case the act
because of its secrecy will never hurt society at large,
and seeing, too, no chance that he will suffer himself because of it, resolves to do it. Both men had the evil

desire alike. In one it was checked by a vague feeling. In the other it was deliberately carried out after consideration of all the consequences. If we are to take the civilized moral consciousness as it is and analyze it, perhaps we shall find out why one man does what is called right, and the other what is called wrong. If we merely question the doctrine of evolution, it can at best tell us that in some future time such acts will cease with the evil desires. Meanwhile, the problem remains so long as the desires do.

The difficulty in question becomes a very practical one if we remember that many harsh words are spoken, many unjust criticisms passed, much back-biting and coldness and sneering permitted in this world, just because enlightened selfishness can show no harm to the evil doer or to the structure of society resulting from such acts. Not often is stealing made attractive by the rare circumstance that we have a good chance and run no risk; but we often speak ill of a man or laugh at him in case we know he cannot harm us in return. For that circumstance often occurs. Society is not revolutionized by our deeds, nor perhaps, would it be bettered if we refrained from them. Only the poor fellow we maltreat is the worse for it, and we personally with our delight in our own powers of speech are greatly amused and even benefited. Perhaps a future society will eliminate all this; but meanwhile it is a question whether in our present state evil tongues are not useful to keep every man at his post, and whether our own sneers and harsh words are not a valuable practice for the battle of life. What baseness is thus cloaked and justified!

In fine, then, the historical doctrine of morality is of very great value as history, but it leaves certain important problems unsolved. It assumes what the history of evolution can never prove, that acts should be avoided in case their consequences would be bad were such acts universally done. This postulate of the Kantian Ethics could never have been discovered by the theory of evolution. An observer from another planet, himself without conscience, but endowed with all insight, would surely condemn no act or desire of mine unless he saw its consequences to be ultimately bad for me. An act that tended in the long run to injure self he would call foolish. If I wished to hurt my fellows, and if no harm came to me from cautiously gratifying my wish in certain ways, he would praise me as a skillful and clever being, a fine product of evolution, even as I now praise for her skill and do not condemn for her cruelty a cat that lies in wait for little birds. Even as a social being I would seem to him praiseworthy if I could use social forms to injure other people without harming myself and without in any way weakening the stability of these forms. He would see indeed that such acts to be successful must be either insignificant or rare. So much the more would he praise me for knowing and respecting the boundary that I cannot pass without defeating myself. Such an observer from another planet is the historian of the moral evolution of humanity, in case he refuses to study the inner meaning of actions, and to analyze the consciousness of man in its own present structure. The worth of general morality he can prove. The binding force of all individual obligations he cannot demonstrate. The rules of the social philosopher admit of important exceptions. The moral law knows indeed doubtful, but never truly exceptional cases.

We now turn to the analysis of the moral consciousness, an analysis not carried on in an intolerant or exclusive spirit, but as an aid and complement to the theory of the evolution of morality. Let us state its problem, and do what we can towards indicating the way in which it may be solved.

THE PROBLEM OF ETHICAL ANALYSIS

Problem. Given a world of moral agents, required to define most generally their mutual relations as moral agents, and the kind of work morally devolving upon each. By moral agent I mean a being not hindered by external interference, acting solely according to the laws of his own nature, and possessed of the sense that distinguishes between right and wrong. This sense is well known. What the term denotes is perfectly clear. If any one·pretends to doubt let us show him plain instances of the distinction between right and wrong. If he is a moral agent at all, he will exercise his moral sense in apprehending the instances. It is right to do a man a kindness where you expect no return. It is wrong to roast a man alive on a gridiron. It is right, if you own a ship and are free to use it, to send it out to rescue a shipwrecked crew from a desert island. It is wrong to explode dynamite under the dwelling of a peaceable citizen merely to show him how much you dislike him. It is right, if you are entirely master of your time and fortune and life, to go into a pestilence stricken city to nurse the sick. It is wrong to put obstructions on a track to wreck a railway train. It is right to speak kindly to a crying child that you meet in the street. It is wrong to beat a dog for the sake of hearing him howl. These are simple instances of moral distinctions. Everybody competent to speak upon moral questions will make them. Clifford in his two remarkable ethical tractates (published in the posthumous "Lectures and Essays") was surely right in assuming such distinctions as the starting point of ethics, and in regarding them as matters of simple consciousness for all moral agents, like colors and tastes for all beings with normal eyes and tongues. The denotation, I repeat, of the words "moral sense," "moral consciousness," "moral distinctions," etc., is perfectly plain. It is their connotation that is in question, and this we must determine by analysis. Clifford's ethical essays seem to me disappointing in that after their luminous beginning they go on to a one-sided use of the historical method. The acceptance of the distinctions as data seems to me to imply the need of analyzing them as they are in consciousness. If we would be thorough-going in our analysis of the moral consciousness, we must undertake a brief analysis of consciousness in general. The distinction between right and wrong must be based, nearly or remotely, on the ultimate facts of mental life. Yet our analysis of consciousness need not pretend to be exhaustive. We can limit it in one direction forthwith. To distinguish right from wrong is to perform an act of knowledge, to make a conscious judgment. Therefore, in analyzing mental life we may for the present purpose, restrict our attention to those phenomena of consciousness which are grouped under the general name knowledge. That right and wrong differ is something known. How do we know anything whatever? How does knowledge come to us and appear in our minds? Let us attempt a brief answer. If it carries us away from ethical inquiry for a moment, we shall return the better qualified to understand the tests of right and wrong. For the nature of knowledge in general determines the particular nature of ethical knowledge.

The Nature of Knowledge in General

To know clearly is to judge the agreement or the disagreement of two or more things, the qualities or the existence of something, or the relations in coexistence or in succession of different things. Clear knowledge appears as judgment with subject and predicate conceived but not necessarily expressed. The clearer the knowledge, the more plainly the act of apprehension takes the form of a judgment. But in the act of judging about things, three elements or constituents of knowledge are involved. At least one of these is present in all knowledge, and the others may be present. Let us look at these constituents more closely.

1. Whenever we know, our act of knowledge is possible only in so far as something is given to us as a fact of momentary experience. This *fact* or *datum* suggests the judgment and gives the material for it. When I judge "This paper is white," "This book is mine," "Washington was the father of his country," "A triangle is a plane figure having three sides"; in every such case there is, when I judge, something given in my consciousness, something that I passively receive, and cannot at the time alter. The perception that I call by the name "paper" or "book," may be an illusory perception. Yet at the moment it is given, and I cannot resist the force that puts it into my consciousness. Perhaps Washington never existed, and history is a myth; but quite certainly my present idea of Washington and his character is a datum, which I accept as a simple fact, whether there is a corresponding reality or not. It required once no little mental activity for me to understand what was meant by the word triangle. Now my ideas of triangle and three-sidedness seem perfectly familiar, and

whether they be good or bad are given as they are at the moment of my judgment about them. In short, the content of feeling or perception or idea in the present moment is absolutely forced upon me. No scepticism can make me doubt it, and no resistance make it seem for the moment other than a fact. Without data no knowledge. Whenever there is knowledge there are simple data of consciousness.

2. But now when I judge: "Washington was the father of his country"; "tobacco is a narcotic"; "space has three dimensions," and the like, I do more than accept a given datum of consciousness. I assert that this datum stands for more than itself, that not only it is, but also something else not now given is represented by it. This persuasion is the persuasion that a present judgment has some sort of "objective validity." Now reflection will show that the datum itself as datum cannot carry with it a certificate of objective validity. Not only may such judgments as those cited sometimes prove to be illusory, but it is sure that all of them go beyond their data. A fact of consciousness is given, a color, a pain, an idea of Washington, a concept of space. Nothing but a pure fact of consciousness. Whatever validity is ascribed to a judgment beyond the sphere of the moment in which it is made is not certified by the data of consciousness themselves as data, but is a product of some mental activity, working on the data, and evolving from them what is not in them. Every judgment of objective validity is ampliative, *i. e.*, it predicates more than the data alone can justify. Thus I have an idea of Washington. This is a datum. By my own activity I project this idea, as it were, into a past time, and ascribe to it validity for that time. I say, "this idea of Washington stands for a past fact in the experience of

the race. Washington really existed." Without the projecting activity of mind, without the disposition to see in data more than they contain in themselves as data, reason, belief, what men call truth, and action, principle, effort, virtue, in a word, spiritual life, would be impossible. The data by themselves signify nothing at all. All real significance is given them by the activity which postulates that they stand for a reality not contained in themselves.

But this ampliative activity involved in all serious judgments upon data takes two principal forms. It takes first of all not the form of a wish or desire that something may turn out to be so and so, but appears as a simple acknowledgment that something is so and so. The simplest case of active judgments is perhaps to be seen in judgments of memory. Though in any present moment only the content of this moment can be actually given, yet we commonly suppose or assume that part of this content, the faint part called a representation, stands for a past that was given as actually as the present is now given. To declare that there has been a past time at all, is to attribute to some element of the present a reality that does not belong to it as present. It would be easy to show that a great part of the judgments about an objectively real world depend upon the recognition of the past as having once been actually present. Therefore, memory is a part and basis of all important beliefs about the real world, and we may say that there is in most knowledge as a second element, in addition to what is given, an acknowledgment of something that is not given, but that is said to be remembered or believed as a part of past experience. In knowledge, then, not only is something given, but very commonly, too, something is acknowledged or accepted as real or valid over and above what is directly given. And the whole past is a characteristic subject of this simple acknowledgment. Whatever is acknowledged we regard as absolute and unchangeable. The past does not alter. The most transient experience is eternal in so far forth as it is eternally true that this experience actually was when it was. Two elements of knowledge have thus been distinguished, viz., (1) That which is Given, the Datum, (2) That which is acknowledged or admitted as real, the *Positum*. There remains in many cases of judgment a third element corresponding to the second kind of ampliative activity in judgment.

3. When I judge: "The sun will be totally eclipsed at some calculable date:" "The tides will continue to fall and rise at certain intervals"; "Two and two will always make four"; in all such cases I do more than acknowledge that present data stand for truth not given as a part of them. I actively expect future experience. It is plain that without expectation of a future, my acknowledgment of the reality of past time would have little worth. Unless I acknowledge something more than is datum of a present moment, there is no real world at all for me to work in. Unless I do more than acknowledge my *posita*, there is no work to be done in the real world when I have it. Expectancy is the third element of knowledge, and for action the most immediately important element. You cannot rigidly prove the validity of any expectation, because you cannot reduce what is expected to a mere datum. There is no chance of demonstrating that any present moment is not the end of all time. For the future is not a datum. If it were, it would be no future. Nor is the future simply acknowledged as real. It is expected. That the expectation is attended with the utmost confidence I admit.

But the confidence simply expresses the vigor of the mental act whereby we postulate at any moment that there will be a future. There may be some kinds of judgment without active expectation, but these are not the practically important judgments. Judgments about the possible are generally, I apprehend, syntheses of what is acknowledged with what is expected. Science and philosophy, popular every day beliefs, and all, even the most exalted faith are thus built up out of judgments about data, judgments about that which is acknowledged as real, about that which is expected, about that which is conceived as possible. Judgments of possibility play a great part in all thought, and especially in all abstract thought, but do not as I conceive, form a class by themselves. Thus, then, the special province of judgments about data is the present. Past experience is the particular field of judgments about what is simply acknowledged or posited as real or valid. To future experience refer the judgments of expectation. Both the judgments of acknowledgment and those of expectation contribute to our ideas of possible experience. And all conceivable truth is contained within the limits of the past, future, and possible experience of conscious beings.

THE NATURE OF CONDUCT

Having thus considered how knowledge takes place in our conscious life, we have to speak next of the relation conduct bears to knowledge. Knowing is, we have seen, itself activity. Even judgments that are confined to the data are the results of an activity of comparison and distinction. Judgments of acknowledgment and expectation are by so much the more cases of activity, for in them something is postulated beyond and above the data. But if knowledge is activity, nobody would call simple knowledge a species of conduct. Conduct is activity directed towards an end. To form the idea of an end, a somewhat complex synthesis is necessary. In a present moment of experience there must be at least one desire, *i. e.*, a certain sort of feeling, itself apprehended as a datum. There must be also a simple judgment of expectation. For when we act we expect future experience of some sort, and wish to affect that experience. There must be also a judgment of possibility, *i. e.*, an acknowledgment of some fixed objective relation of which we propose to avail ourselves, coupled with an expectation of some particular case under that relation which may occur if our act is properly directed. Out of all this complex state of consciousness we form by synthesis the idea of acting for an end. To act for a purpose is to seek satisfaction for a momentary desire, by making real one of several possible experiences. When we determine to act for an end we conceive of the possible experiences, we expect that at least one of them will become real; and we determine to make one of the number real, expecting that it will satisfy our desire. If more than one desire is present at the moment of action one only conquers or is chosen, and so the act satisfies that one. Conduct or action for an end is then, made possible, (1) through desires, (2) through judgments of expectation, (3) through judgments of possibility, (4) through the entirely unique moment of choice or conquest of one desire over opposing ones, that moment, which we cannot further describe, and which we call by the name of Will. It matters not now whether we conceive this Will as free or not.

Now conduct is of the simplest form when at the moment of choice one desire only is in consciousness, when there is but one possible way of fulfilling it, and when the expected experience fills a single instant just in the future. If I lift my arm for the sake of showing that I can do so, or put a piece of candy in my mouth for the sake of its flavor, my conduct is of the simplest form. Suppose, however, that instead of conforming my action to an expected future of one instant only, my conscious expectation at the moment of acting covers a good deal of future time. Thus, when I am about to put candy into my mouth, suppose that I expect not only the coming moment, but think of the next few hours. My conduct may be modified. For every definite expectation of future experience is accompanied with a definite acknowledgment or memory of past experience, and the future expected is always more or less like the past remembered. My memory in this case may be of past indigestion resulting from eating candy. My thought may be thereupon one of possible future indigestion. A new desire may contend with my desire to eat candy. My conduct whether in eating or in refraining will be of a more complex character. There will be more elements in it. The same thing is true no matter what the particular object of conduct is. The general principle follows: That conduct is as a rule more and more complex according as the future experience that is expected at the moment of acting is more and more extended. For expectation of an extended future experience is commonly attended with an acknowledgment of a past experience proportionately extended, and acknowledgment of past experience includes the consciousness of pleasures and pains included in this past experience, and so is attended with a consciousness of desires manifold and various in proportion as the conceived past is more and more extended. To expect a single sweet taste I need but to remember one or two moments in the past.

To expect definitely a term's work, I need to remember a term's work. To expect definitely a sea voyage, I need to remember a sea voyage. To expect definitely the content of a future century of the world's history, implies an activity based upon whatever definite conception and acknowledgment we have of a past century. And so in general our idea of the future whose coming we expect is proportionate in extent and definiteness to our memory or our conception of the past whose validity we acknowledge. And thus the complexity of our conduct is determined by the extent of time we take into account. The present moment is given. To act with reference to it alone, is not conduct at all. Conduct is first found when in the present we act with reference to at least one future moment, forming our expectation of what this moment may be through an act of acknowledgment of what some past moment was. And conduct increases in complexity and definiteness according as we act with reference to a more extended time, posit a greater past time as real, expect a greater future time as yet to come.

Observe that in all this we are not speaking of the evolution of conduct from the simple to the complex, but are only defining conduct according to its different grades. We are greatly aided, however, in this analytic work by the lucid discussions of Mr. Spencer's *Data of Ethics*. The use of all this long way of argument will I hope soon appear.

Conduct Approved or Disapproved

Conduct is attended with knowledge. Knowledge is directly of the present, and only by acknowledgment or by expectation is there a knowledge of past and future. Conduct is more complex according as the present moment is conceived as standing in relation to a more extended past and future time. By means, therefore, of the process whereby thought always transcends the data of thought and postulates or constructs what is not perceived, does conduct become first possible at all, and then, with knowledge, more complex.

But now, how do we judge conduct as good or bad? First, in so far as it accomplishes its ends. Secondly, in so far as the past and future acknowledged and expected in the moment of conduct are more extended and are more definitely taken into account. If desiring to taste candy I throw it into the sea my conduct is absurd. I should have put it into my mouth. My conduct is not such as to produce the desired effect. If wishing solely to avoid indigestion, I knowingly eat unwholesome things, my conduct is absurd. I should have eaten wholesome things. But not alone for its failure to adapt itself to ends is conduct judged. Far more important in an ethical point of view is the approval or disapproval of conduct because of the nature of the ends themselves. Conduct may be not only absurd, but low, contemptible, detestable, wicked, according as its ends are more or less plainly evil. And how may the ends of conduct themselves be evil? In reply let us see how they may be graded in value at all.

An act is complex according to the extent of time that was taken into account in performing it. It is good or evil in a similar ratio, according to the extent of conscious experience that it is designed to affect, and according to the way in which it is designed to affect that experience. At the moment of deliberately doing anything I conceive of its future consequence. Suppose the act is pulling the trigger of a gun. Suppose I conceive of the amusement that may be expected from pulling the trigger, and of the hurtful consequences that may follow from a careless discharge of the gun. Each of these conceptions is an expectation of future experience. Now suppose that, after all, the expectation of momentary pleasure overbalances for me the fear of future hurt from the discharge, and I pull the trigger. The result, perhaps is serious injury. My act is to be disapproved of. Why? Not because in it deeds were wrongly adjusted to ends. On the contrary, my end was the amusement of pulling the trigger, and I attained my end when I pulled it. Because, then, the chosen end was not the right one. Why not right? Had I known nothing at all of the danger, never before having seen a gun, had I felt the same desire for amusement and performed the same act, no one would blame me, though one might deplore my ignorance. My act was wrong because, conceiving as I did of two possible experiences, one of slight pleasure, the other of great pain, I chose to make both real, because the little pleasure seemed worth more to me than the great pain could overbalance. My stupidity was inexcusable. I conceived of both consequences. I knew the dangers and yet I chose them. How was it possible for me to do so? Plainly, because the danger, though conceived and expected, seemed less real to me than the pleasure. Here was my fault. Ignorance would have screened me from blame. Awkwardness in adjusting my acts to my ends would have brought me pity or ridicule. Deliberate neglect of one of two expected experiences brings condemnation upon me. Knowledge gave me certain expectations. Desire colored them falsely. Knowing what I did I yet chose the worse for the better experience, disregarding the expectation of evil consequences, and viewing it as less real than the expectation of good consequences, I chose against light. My end was ill. My act is to be condemned. Condemned, be it noted apart from its actual consequences. If a lucky accident were to keep the gun from going off or injury from resulting, although I ought to have expected both, my act is just as bad, for its intent was the choice of great danger and small amusement, instead of safety and a trifling sacrifice. Acts are approved or disapproved according to the expectation with which they are performed, not according to results.

I have taken a simple instance of disapproval to illustrate how conduct is judged with reference to its ends. To summarize: Conduct is approved when it is such as is performed with full and equal attention to all the future experiences conceived at the time of performance, as possible results of the act in question. And to pay full and equal attention to all possible results signifies choosing the act so that all its conceived future consequences, near or remote, shall form the most desirable aggregate. Or again, conceive all the expected consequences of an act, near and remote, as now and here present and given. Choose the act so that these consequences should form the most satisfactory present experience that is possible. This is the first rule of conduct, simply stated: In thy acts treat all the future as if it were present. Let not a consequence believed by thee to be probable, escape thy notice because it is so remote. Suppose that thou hadst to suffer all the consequences at once and at this very instant. What act wouldst thou then think most desirable? Consider and choose that. On such a basis as this are acts judged with reference to their ends.

Moral Approval of Conduct

But thus far I seem to have been speaking only of maxims of prudence. Conduct would be approved on grounds of worldly wisdom if all expected consequences were treated with equal regard to their intrinsic desirableness. What we may call the illusion of perspective in time would be avoided. However remote the consequences, prudence demands that if known they shall be estimated with equal scrutiny. Now how may this maxim be transformed from one of selfish expediency into a maxim of moral conduct? We may now reap the fruit of our previous analysis of consciousness in general. One of the most serious problems in all ethical discussion may perhaps, thus be solved.

When I estimate the consequences of my acts, for whom are these consequences? Do I mean the consequences for me, or for my fellows, or for all of us? Am I to measure the personal consequences for myself first and then for my neighbor? Let us reflect. Here is the conflict of egoism and altruism, left unsettled in our preliminary study, now facing us again. Can we bring it to a close? I answer, we have the means for a theoretical solution of the puzzle. The practical solution belongs, perhaps, to far-off centuries.

What do I mean by myself, and the consequences for myself? What by my neighbor, and the consequences for him? Let us not fear such questions. They need careful attention, but they are forced upon us, are not to be avoided. What do I mean by myself? Do I mean a being, existent above and through all the changes of consciousness, identical, the subject of all my thoughts and experiences? Perhaps that is what I mean, but one thing is plain, such a permanent, identical being is never

given to me at all in experience. For let us return to our
first analysis. Given is the content of one present moment, no past, no future. The past may be acknowledged as having been, the future, may be expected as
yet to come. The present only is datum. Therefore, no
identical absolutely existent being can be directly given
in my experience. Given may be a feeling of personality,
a peculiar interest in a particular kind of conceived past
and future experience and an emotion of sefishness or of
self-respect. But my existence as a permanent real entity is no more and no less given in consciousness than is
the existence of my neighbor. I acknowledge certain
past experiences, and with some of these I group a certain feeling of interest, and find the conceptions of them
very vivid; and these conceived experiences I call mine
and the acknowledgment of them as real I call memory.
So quite vividly and with a peculiar interest I expect
certain future experiences to be real, and these I call my
future, and the expectation of them I call personal hopes
and fears. But my conception of a real past and a real
future does not stop here. I also conceive and acknowledge as real many past experiences that are not mine,
and expect the reality of many future experiences equally
different from those that seem so vivid as being future
deeds or states called "mine." The lack of the feeling of
self-interest in conceiving them does not make these conceived experiences less acknowledged and expected real-
ities. The difference is an emotional one, not one of
thought. I know my neighbor to be as real as my self.
His experiences are no more given to me than my own
past and future experiences are now given. Yet none the
less I posit their reality. How and why I do so does not
matter. I know not how and why I should postulate my
own past and future as real, when they are not given.

The fact is I do so postulate them. And the fact is that I do conceive of my neighbor, with all his past and future as real like myself.

By myself I mean then, a certain aggregate of comparatively vivid (*i. e.*, acknowledged and expected) experiences, with whose present conception there is joined a certain peculiar feeling of interest, commonly called the selfish interest. By my neighbor I mean an aggregate of conceived (*i. e.*, acknowledged and expected) present, past, and future experiences, with whose present conception, itself comparatively faint, I do not join the selfish interest. So too, the whole world of conscious life I conceive as also at some time real, as past and future, as in some way like this present conscious moment, as variously grouped, as filled with different conflicting selfish desires; and I conceive all this though nothing of the entire conscious world, myself included, is given me but this one insignificant present moment. So wonderful is the work of conscious activity.

This much for our definitions. Now for their application. The essence of approved conduct, as we saw, is the treating in a present given moment of the conceived possible contents of future consciousness as if they were even now data, and the determination of actions according to the result of such treatment. In determining my actions by the conceived future results, what results am I to consider? Those to myself? But these results are not conceived as in themselves more real than those to my neighbor. The difference is that the results to myself are conceived with a certain peculiar feeling of interest which makes them seem more real and which is not a part of the conception of the results to other conscious beings. Ought this feeling of self-interest to affect my action?

Think of the parallel case of prudent conduct. At some moment I am more interested in eating candy than in avoiding indigestion. Yet the conceived evil of indigestion is known to be greater than the conceived good of a sweet taste. Or I am more interested in pulling a trigger than in avoiding the risk of injury. Yet the conceived injury is a greater evil than would be the loss of the pleasure. Now my conduct in these cases is approved if I treat all the consequences as if they were present, disregarding the prejudice created by my momentary interest, and then choose such consequences as are in this view intrinsically most desirable. My conduct is not approved, if I give myself over to the illusion of time-perspective, or choose a conceived consequence, not for its intrinsic desirableness, but because I am the slave of my momentary interest. Approved action consists in weighing all future consequences according to their conceived value, not according to the value that my passion gives them.

Now it would only be carrying this principle out to its full extent if I treat in like fashion the conceived future experiences of my neighbor. In these I have not the same selfish interest, but I do postulate them as equally real and unreal with my own conceived future. My existence as an enduring entity is not more immediately given than is the existence of my neighbor as an enduring entity. The same activity that postulates by expectation my future, postulates his future as well. The consequences of my act for me, are not more real than they are for him. If then, I am to order my conduct according to all future experience regarded as equally an object of striving, I must include my neighbor's future with my own, and order my conduct accordingly. If the injury produced by carelessly discharging a gun is not an injury in my future, but in the future of another conscious being, none the less is it expected as a real injury. And if all conceived future states are to be taken into equal account in my conduct, then all my fellow-beings are equally objects of my care with myself. My interest in them is not so strong, but real future experience for them and for me is equally real, *i. e.*, is equally expected though not given. Selfish feeling makes a difference. Insight views all as equally real. Thus mere consistency brings me to the following considerations: Whatever experience is to come, will come. All conscious moments of painful and pleasurable experience are equally real when they do come. No conscious moment is a datum for any previous moment, but can only be expected in that moment. All future consciousness then, as equally to be expected, as equally real when it comes, as equally unreal till it comes, is equally an object of present striving. Every present act should, therefore, be ordered for the welfare of all future conscious life, in case it should be ordered for the welfare of any future conscious life at all. That any moment or series of moments of future consciousness is at present more interesting than another is of no consequence. The essence of conduct is the putting of insight before desire, when naturally desire is before insight. And the insight into the identical nature of all past and future life as conscious life is the result of our analysis of the nature of consciousness. This analysis does not give as a result Me, an absolute entity, distinct from all the World in which I work, but the World of conscious life postulated as all equally real or to be realized, as all equally an object of striving, as in every one of its countless moments of pleasure and pain equally worthy of regard. The inevitable result of this insight is the postulate that conduct can be approved only when its end is the good of the whole world of future experience as this world is conceived at the moment of action. The universal end of conduct is the only end free from illusion. Every other end implies the conception of experiences as certainly future and yet the contradictory conception, the product of a desire, that some of these expected experiences have more reality than others. This is the illusion of selfishness. The Ego, however, is not more a datum than is the Alter. My future is as much a mere expectation as is your future at this moment. The reality of the one is the reality of the other. Work for one must become work for both, or else be indefensible.

Now to be sure this insight and its consequences cannot be rigidly proven. They can only be shown. My claim is that here is expressed the essence of that moral sense with which we began our analysis. Condemnation of cruel and commendation of kind acts, is like the condemnation of imprudent acts and the praise of self-control, in so far as in all cases the act of one moment is condemned when it disregards the claims of expected moments, and praised when it views all expected moments as if they were real and present. All the cases of moral approval or disapproval of acts are cases of approval of the insight to which all conceived conscious life is as one, and of disapproval of the contradictory state of mind for which a conceived future is yet treated by desire as if it were not conceived at all.

The moral sense then is based on this maxim: All future consciousness is to be equally regarded in our conduct, because all is alike not given but only expected, and all is alike real when it comes. Therefore the rule of conduct is: Act as thou wouldst wish to have acted were all the consequences of thy act for all the world of being here and now given as a fact of thine own present consciousness. Or again: Choose thy deeds so that their outcome shall seem the best possible outcome when all the results are viewed at once as a whole in their intrinsic good or evil. Thus conduct is made absolutely consistent.

Notice now these things about our result. Acts are judged according to their purpose, not according to their actual outcome. Only the future of which I conceive can affect my conduct. Whatever really comes of my deed, the deed is right if by intention, at the moment of action, I took into account all the expected future consequences to myself and to all other beings, and treated these conceived results as if they were alike present and given at the moment of action. The results that I did not conceive of I could not take into account. Notice again that all conflict of egoism and altruism is set aside, by making all approved conduct equally altruistic. Every moment of right conduct acts for other moments as if they were present. And this process is carried on without limit. Notice further that work for others is shown to be but the consistent expression of the same tendency that is expressed in prudent work for self. The disregard of all interests but those in the intrinsic value of the expected experience is the essence of prudence. The same impartiality carried out in full is absolute altruism. Notice in fine, that this result follows from our analysis, and could never be obtained from the history of the physical evolution of morality. For the history of evolution, the individuals are absolutely separate beings, each moved by selfish desires. From these selfish desires moral acts could be deduced only by exhibiting the acts as enlightened selfishness. The incompleteness of this view we saw before. But for the analytic view no such restriction appears. We examine consciousness as it is, not as it grew; and we find in it no absolute ego given, no organized self, who must be served above all. We find instead a present moment, acknowledging past moments and expecting future moments all different from itself and excluded by itself. Conduct is work at one of these moments for other conceived coming moments. Consistent conduct is work at any one moment for all conceived future moments. Absolutely consistent conduct is the only conduct that meets perfect moral approval. No matter how great the conflicting interest, be it passion or laziness or general selfishness, right conduct is that only which, disregarding the conflicting present interest itself, looks to the intrinsic worth of the expected consequences. And so for this higher insight each moment of every life is judged in the presence of the whole of consciousness conceived as one being, or better, as one moment of being. Every moment-atom of this infinite life is approved if, knowing the other atoms, it recognized their claims in its action. For each deed of good done at any moment for another moment, the moral sense has the approving word that comes as it were from the very throne of the one infinite consciousness: Inasmuch as ye have done it unto the least of these, ye have done it unto me. This sense of the absolute worth of all experience, this insight into the unity of life, has been the continual theme of moral teaching and preaching, of all true religion, since there were minds to think. One has no new doctrine to teach about it. One can but restate and try to justify by analysis the old one. And I confess that for this purpose I know of no possible way other than that taken. If we give up this doctrine, I see nothing but moral scepticism before us, with the claims of self and of others left unsettled, with the illusion of selfishness perpetually tormenting us, with a sophistical torturing of history to make it prove what it cannot prove, that boundless self-sacrifice is a good, in brief, with all the half-heartedness of uncritical ethics. Let us throw these incomplete theories aside, or use them when we can as stones to build up a better building. Practically we shall remain what we were before. In everyday life the illusion of selfishness will lead us captive as much as ever. But in theory, perchance, upon the basis here proposed, we may raise a structure in honor of the true and eternal object of life, which is the good of the great conscious soul whose atoms of experience are the moments of our individual lives. For this One Absolute Being all our right work is wrought.

Such is the basis of the solution that I would propose for the ethical problem as above stated. That the solution is not fully given I need not formally admit, since the fact is plain. The relations of moral agents could not be fully treated until I had gone further into the question of the principles of choice among conceived consequences of action. But the general method of making choice is clear, and that alone formed the subject of my present study, which has been confined to the problem of egoism and altruism.

ON PURPOSE IN THOUGHT

[1880]

THE discussion of the fundamental problems of human thought can be carried on in any one of three distinct fashions. First, thought may be viewed as a fact of mental life, to be studied, like all other mental facts, according to the methods of psychology. The psychological mode of treatment tries to find out how human thought grew up, how it is related to the environment, and how in actual use it is combined with other mental phenomena. In the second place, however, human thought may be studied by means of logical analysis, with a view to discovering wherein consists the connection among the successive acts of a train of thought, what are the fundamental axioms of all thought, and what is the final result of all efforts to separate the formal and universal from the material and accidental elements of knowledge. A third method of studying thought-processes has often occurred to me as proper and fruitful, a method which I long considered quite the same as the method of logical analysis, but which I am now led to regard as in some important respects distinct therefrom. I mean the mode of examination which, for the sake of technical exactitude of terms I shall name the teleological analysis of thought. After we have studied in the fashion common in our day the history of thinking processes as they grow up in the individual or in the race, after we have gone yet deeper and studied the truly philosophical problems concerning the principles of knowledge, as modern logic brings them before us, we shall yet have open to our approach and still unconquered the problems as to the fundamental purposes of all thought, and as to the way in which these fundamental purposes are realized in the thought-structures that we have been examining. I do not claim to have mastered either the psychological or the logical problems of the theory of thinking. Yet after having noted as I studied these somewhat familiar but still stubborn questions the lack of appreciation which seems to exist in view of the importance of the third class of questions, I may not be wrong if I try to lay stress in this paper on the problem that I may thus briefly state: What is the final end of purely theoretic thought, and in what relation to the fundamental axioms or principles of human reasoning does this final end stand?

To study the purposes of human thought is impossible unless we know something of the structure of thought. My effort at teleological analysis depends, therefore, in some wise upon both the previously mentioned kinds of thought-analysis. Yet psychology and logic furnish rather statements of the problem than solutions thereof. Though nothing can be more fundamental in its sphere than the exhaustive logical analysis of the principles, assumptions, methods, and great results of thought, yet it is possible to go further than this analysis by viewing the whole material in a new light, and by asking new questions about it. Though, on the other hand, no mental fact lies outside of the province of psychology, yet psychology seeks mainly to give a history of the evolution of mental processes, not an analysis of their significance in view of any end. And furthermore, as psychology is in the widest sense of the term a physical science, that is, a science of explanation of effects by causes and of facts by laws, psychology is itself logically dependent upon the results of the philosophical analysis of knowledge, and, therefore, cannot supersede either the analysis of thought-principles or the study of thought-purposes. Our relation to the other modes of studying thought is, therefore, this: We treat the problems of the logical thought-analysis, but we treat them in a different way, asking ourselves not primarily, what are the forms and assumptions of thought, but what end has thought in making these assumptions? As for psychology, we regard it in this essay not as a logical basis, but a storehouse of suggestions. That it is worth while thus to distinguish the teleological analysis of thought from the psychological analysis and from the logical analysis, only the result of our efforts can make clear to us. I shall waste no time in an elaborate justification at this point.

I

The Purpose of Thought as the Attainment of Truth

What, then, is the end of human thought? Or has thought any one final purpose? An answer immediately suggests itself. Theoretical human thought, says this answer, has but one ultimate purpose, to wit, the attainment of truth. All thinking is to lead to knowledge, *i. e.*, to objective certainty. And knowledge or objective certainty means the possession of truth. Every other aim is subordinate.

This answer is plausible and sufficiently vague to be a good text for a popular philosophy. Let us try to make the notion more exact.

What is here meant by the possession of truth? Or, more simply, if thought had attained the goal here placed before it, in what state would it be? How does the imperfect state of mind that precedes the attain-

ment of the truth differ from the perfect state of mind
when the truth has been reached? Wherein lies the contrast between seeking and finding? In answer let us remember that by truth is commonly meant either the
agreement of a belief with some external reality, or else
this external reality itself. "Ye shall know the truth,"
means apparently the same as, "Ye shall know what
really is." But, "This belief is nothing more or less than
the truth" seems to mean "This belief agrees with what
really is." In either sense, the attainment of truth implies essentially the same thing; viz., an agreement between thought and external reality. This meaning is the
one I choose to give to the expression: "Thought has for
its end the attainment of truth." While I have no doubt
that some meaning could be given to the word truth
which should make this account of the purposes of
thought perfectly satisfactory, and while I am not disposed to hint that the purpose of theoretic thought can
ever be the attainment of untruth, yet I am forced to
see that if truth is taken in either one of the meanings
that I have mentioned, and if by "attainment of truth"
is meant the bringing of thought into correspondence
with a reality external to thought, then the statement
that the ultimate end of thought is the attainment of
truth cannot be regarded as at all satisfactory. My reason for rejecting so plausible and simple a statement of
the end of thought is one familiar to all students of
philosophy, and in no wise original with me. Yet for
the sake of clearness I must not pass it over too lightly,
but must state it as if Protagoras and Berkeley had
never existed.

If thought reached its supposed goal, and was in
agreement with external reality, would it be aware of
this agreement, or would it be ignorant thereof? If the

latter, if thought on reaching the truth did not know that it had reached the truth, then surely the end would not be attained. It is the nature of purpose that your actual success in carrying out your own purpose will be known to you. Otherwise you, who were alone concerned in carrying out your purpose, are never satisfied. And satisfaction and the attainment of a desired end, the fulfillment of a purpose, are the same thing. To say that one has accomplished his purpose and does not know the fact, can only have a sense if we mean that he has objectively done or accomplished something which, were he cognizant thereof, would in his mind produce the subjective state known as satisfaction with an achieved result. But this satisfaction was what the man must really have purposed, not the objective result without the satisfaction. Really to reach an end and to know that one has reached it, these express the same fact.

If the attainment of truth is the end of thought, thought must be able, in case it can reach the end, to know of its success. Imagine then, that a thought corresponds with an external reality. How can this correspondence be known? By comparison of the thought with the external reality? But the reality, being external, is not in thought at all. Nothing but the thought itself is known directly. How can we compare the thought with the thing outside of it to see if they agree, when one of the terms only is given, and when the act of comparison would imply that both the terms should be given. That I can compare two thoughts is plain enough. That I can see to it that these are thoughts about the same subject matter, is, if not so plain, at least conceivable. But that I should be able to know by immediate comparison the correspondence of two facts whereof one is known to me by and in the other, that I should be sure of the validity of my thought about external things when only this thought is given to me as a subject for judgment, and when the external things could only be objects of immediate knowledge by ceasing to be external, all this is entirely mysterious. If agreement between thought and outer reality be all that is meant by truth, and if by outer reality be meant anything whatever that is not and cannot be wholly in thought and of thought, an idea among ideas, then to say that the attainment of truth is the goal of thought is to say that thought seeks an end that could never conceivably be attained, an end of which no clear notion can be formed. And what is this but declaring that thought has no end at all, is entirely purposeless.

To be sure, nothing is as yet said about the existence of an external reality. Whether there be real things apart from thoughts is a matter that does not now concern my argument. I ask only, how is the mentioned purpose of thought to be formulated? And my answer is, the mentioned purpose of thought cannot be formulated, is no definite purpose at all. Never can one definitely figure or think out a condition of thought in which a correspondence between a present notion and an external thing not a content of thought could be known through actual comparison. At any moment only a content of thought could be known. Of an external thing only so much could be known, that it was no thought at all. Whether and how it might be in agreement with the thought, only an infinite mind conceived as identical both with the external thing itself and with the finite being's thought about the thing, could be supposed capable of knowing or even of clearly conceiving.

If actual and conscious agreement with external reality is not the end of thought, I am still quite prepared to admit that in the theory I am examining there is a considerable element of valuable suggestion. Knowledge of agreement with external reality may not be an intelligible end of thought-activity; but there may be some meaning in the expression that the end of thought is the attainment of confidence in the agreement of the thought with external reality. Confidence is a purely subjective affection. I may not clearly conceive what I mean by agreement between thought and things; yet I may be very confident that I can reach or have reached some ill-defined sort of agreement of my beliefs with a reality beyond consciousness. It is at any rate quite intelligible to say that all thinking aims at that kind of subjective persuasion which we commonly find among men. But this statement needs analysis. If certainty in the sense of conviction and confidence that we are in agreement with an external world, is the end of our thinking, let us see how we can intelligibly define the nature of this conviction towards which we strive.

I ask again: If the goal as thus anew defined is attained, if in our thinking we have passed beyond a state of uncertainty and suspense to a state of surety that our thought is valid and that it has some kind of correspondence with external reality, what is the nature of our conviction?

First, just as before, so here we shall not be able to say in what consists the agreement between our thought and the reality which is independent of it. We shall according to the present hypothesis, believe that there is some kind of agreement between the thought and the things. But how the thought can correspond with something of which we only know that it is not thought, this we shall never clearly grasp so long as we are finite beings at all. The confidence that is here said to be the goal of our thinking will be merely a persuasion that some conception which we have and which we do know, corresponds in an entirely unknown way with a reality of which directly we know simply nothing. Such a persuasion could surely give no other warrant for its validity than its own subjective evidence. If we call a statement of such an absolute ungrounded self-contained conviction an axiom, then we may say that in this modified form of definition the end of thought is declared to be the attainment of axiomatic certainty. The nature of the correspondence of which we are so certain will remain perfectly mysterious. Secondly, however, in attaining what is now said to be the goal of thought, we shall reach not merely this perfect and mysterious confidence that our thought in some of its forms agrees with an unknown reality, but we shall gain the power to compare other beliefs that in themselves seem not so certain with these absolutely unprovable and certain beliefs, and so shall come to possess not merely axioms, but systems of derived truths. The whole purpose of thought would then be thus described: Thought aims at finding and stating axioms, and at bringing all our beliefs into harmony and connection with the axioms. The end of thinking would be attained (*a*) if we could enumerate all possible axioms and could have a perfect certainty of their agreement with external reality, and (*b*) if we could show as to all not-axiomatic beliefs that they are in agreement with the axioms, and follow from the axioms.

We seem driven to modify in this way our opinion about the end of thought as being the attainment of truth. The real end of thought must be the attainment of some state of consciousness. In thinking we must be striving to reach some thought that is satisfactory. Therefore the real conscious purpose of thought must be something within the sphere of thought. Not objective correspondence with reality as such, but at most, subjective confidence in the correspondence of thought with reality can be consciously sought or conceivably attained with an actual consciousness of attainment. And thus the simplest statement of the goal of thought seems to be that thought seeks to change uncertainty into confidence, and beliefs that appear as though they might not be in harmony with reality into beliefs of which we are mysteriously but perfectly convinced that they are in harmony with reality.

Yet is this account final? Evidently thought tries to bring beliefs that are not axiomatic into agreement with and dependence upon beliefs that are axiomatic. But is it true that axioms express an unbounded and unfounded confidence in the agreement of our thought with unknowable "things in themselves" outside of thought? Is the conviction which our thought aims to reach a conviction that our known conceptions resemble in unknowable fashion unknowable noumena? This is surely, when stated, a very singular goal for human thought. Is it the actual goal?

Let us take an example. There is a well-known axiom of number which may be stated thus: "Results of counting are independent of the order in which the individual things are counted." Whether I begin with my thumb and count towards the little finger, or take the reverse order, I shall always find just five fingers on my hand. One order in counting is no better than another, unless we want to avoid danger of omissions or of repetitions. This is an evident truth, accepted with perfect confidence. Does it express any confidence as to an agreement between a thought and an unknowable external reality? My impression is that this axiom states merely an uniformity of experience. Given a set of objects in experience sufficiently permanent to be counted, then the law holds good that whatever the things counted, be they colors or sounds or ideas of colors or sound or men or imaginary beings or footsteps or odors, I can count them in whatever order is convenient, and yet be sure that my result is entirely independent of the order of counting. I have here to make no assertion, however vague, about things in themselves. I deal only with an assumption made with perfect confidence, about my experience, actual and possible, and about what must hold true of this experience. (Cf. Clifford, *"Lectures and Essays,"* Vol. i, pp. 326 sqq.)

Here is a case where perfect confidence is attained, which seems nevertheless to be not at all a confidence in an agreement of thought with reality beyond thought, but solely a confidence in the permanence of a certain relation or set of relations among facts of experience. Here, then, the goal of thought would seem to be the attainment of beliefs that express with full conviction certain enduring laws of human experience. The previous statements must be once more modified. Shall we say that thought has two distinct ends, first the attainment of confidence that it is in correspondence with an unknowable reality, and second the attainment of confidence that some universal and necessary relation among the facts of experience has become known? Surely no student of Kant will be averse to admitting, at least provisionally, that the second of these ends is the genuine and important end of the great mass of our thought, whose object is the determination of possible experience.

And it will be worth while for the present to omit all reference to the external and unknowable reality, whose agreement with thought may be in a vague but passionate way believed in, although what the agreement may be and mean is simply inconceivable. The more important end of thought, if not the one highest end, is therefore the attainment of certainty as to the nature and laws of experience. To the end as thus defined we now pass.

II

THE PURPOSE OF THOUGHT AS THE ANTICIPATION OF EXPERIENCE

Let us glance back at our previous results. We set out to discover if possible the goal of human thought. The first suggestion that met us was that theoretic thought always seeks truth or correspondence with external reality. The objection was that we may know well what is the meaning of correspondence between one thought and another, but cannot well make out what may be the meaning of a correspondence between a thought and something that is not a thought but absolutely external thereto. Since the correspondence could never be known and tested within the sphere of our thought itself, and since it seems absurd to suppose that the goal of thought is one that even if attained in some mysterious way could still never be known as attained, we were led to modify our first statement. It seems plausible that, as is quite generally the case with deliberate human activ-ity, thought has for its ultimate purpose the attainment of some state of consciousness. The highest good for thought would then doubtless be the reaching of confidence in itself, confidence absolutely fixed and perfect.

And, therefore, we were led to state the end of thought thus: "Thought seeks confidence that it is in agreement with objective reality." Yet we were constrained to admit that by this altered statement, by this substitution of perfect confidence in its own validity instead of the absolute validity itself as the actual goal of thinking, we had nevertheless been unable to escape the mystery involved in the assumption that thought agrees with what is not thought. And so our statement demands yet further study. At this point we were led to note that after all we are often content in our actual thinking with having attained beliefs, not as to the nature of the things in themselves, but as to the laws of human experience. The goal of thought turns out to be, in fact, much less the gaining of confidence that we are masters of the hidden secrets of being, than the gaining of confidence that we can anticipate experience, and that we have power to know the laws of phenomena. Leaving altogether our first form of statement we have, therefore, begun with a new definition of the goal of thought. "Thought, we now say, has for its main object the attainment of mastery over our experience, so that we may predict the same, and know the ways in which its data are necessarily connected."

The analysis of this statement comes next in order. What would be a knowledge of some permanent and necessary law of all experience? And how should we be able to gain such a knowledge? Or, to put our questions in the old way again; if the goal of thought in this direction is attained, what will be the resulting state of thought, and how will the perfect state of possession of assurance differ from the imperfect condition preceding?

To illustrate the whole problem let us take one important case, the so-called Axiom of Uniformity. In adhering to this axiom will any final purpose of theoretic thought be attained, and if so, how?

The axiom of uniformity states that of necessity there will be in our experience some kind of regularity and fixity of succession, and in fact such regularity that, under like conditions, like results will always follow given agencies. What is the theoretic use of this axiom? What is the justification of making any use of it at all?

Evidently the hardest part of the problem is to state the axiom of uniformity intelligibly, and in its simplest form, freed from all encumbrance. Once stated, if it be an axiom it will commend itself at once to our approval. And accepting it, we shall probably find out without difficulty its relation to the purpose of thought. The preliminary statement just given is, however, not simple and not convincing. What is the meaning of "like conditions?" Why is it certain that like results must follow from them? What is regularity of sequence in experience? In answer let us study in succession certain of the views as to the axiom of uniformity.

First, some one may assert that the axiom of uniformity means that if in experience we have noted often a sequence of the phenomenon *b* upon the phenomenon *a*, then we have a right to expect that *b* will again follow when *a* again appears in experience. This is the crudest form of the axiom of uniformity, the form corresponding to an *inductio per enumerationem simplicem*, and, therefore, merely useful as a basis for more elaborate forms.

Secondly, the claim may be made, that when an inductive sifting of experience has taught us that in many cases under observation *a* proves itself the indispensable antecedent of *b*, and *b* a constant sequent upon *a*, the effect of other conditions having been eliminated or allowed for, then the connection noted between *a* and *b* may be assumed to be causal and permanent, so that the appearance of a will entail the appearance of b, unless sufficient hindrance to the effectiveness of a arises from some other source c. With some such statement as this the analysis of the processes of induction might be content to begin its study.

Here is made a fundamental assumption that there will be found to be some kind of enduring union among phenomena, so that every experience shall point to some other experience as necessarily connected with it. What is the ground and the use of this assumption? Note, before going on to the answer, that the assumption as stated speaks only of regularity of succession in phenomena. Nothing is said of permanently existent things, but only of recurring sequences in experience. Now what purely theoretic purpose can be subserved by supposing that every fact of experience is joined in necessary ties with some other fact of actual or possible experience? Why not view the facts as facts, each by itself? Why not regard them as independent, and as capable of recurring in any order, however different from the observed order?

A natural answer would be that habit, association of ideas, has impelled us to expect that the future will resemble the past, the unobserved the observed. But this would not be a fair answer to our question. We ask not, how came we by our belief in the uniformity of experience? but what purpose does this belief serve now that we have it, are conscious of it and can criticize it? Hume's account of our belief in uniformity was a suggestive speculation in psychology. It did not answer the logical problem: "what is the authority of the belief?" nor does it satisfy us who now ask, what is the good of this belief?

A better answer is the one stated in his rather odd fashion by Professor Schuppe in his "*Erkenntnisstheoretische Logik*" (Bonn, 1878), in the chapter on "Notwendigkeit u. Möglichkeit" (Kap. x, pp. 195 sqq.; especially p. 198). Adapting his results to our present form of putting the question, I understand him to mean about as follows. The fundamental necessity of all thought is this, "dass wir weder von der Existenz der Welt noch von unserer eigenen Existenz zu abstrahiren vermögen." We can neither think ourselves away without thinking the world away, nor can we think of ourselves as other than beings in a world of conscious experience. But if this is the case, if we can imagine any succession of facts only under the condition of thinking ourselves as spectators thereof, it follows that absolute irregularity in the succession of facts is impossible. "Denn eben dies gehört zur Existenz eines Bewusstseins, dass sein Inhalt solch feste Ordnung hat." In other words, if we try to think away all regularity of sequence from the world, we shall be trying to think ourselves away; and it is useless to undertake this feat. The attempt to conceive of the irregular experience is made by our author in this wise: "Dann hört doch selbstverständlich jeder allgemeine Satz auf, jede auch die schlichteste u. einfachste Erfahrung, u. somit wurde ein solcher Mensch nicht dazu kommen seine Arme und Beine — gebrauchen zu lernen — Und dabei denke man noche an ein bewusstes Ich! Was für Denken wäre wohl möglich, welche Gedanken könnten entstehen, wenn wir auch wirklich eine Spur dumpfen Bewusstseins in solchem absolut regellosen Wechsel von Zuständen uns dächten. Die 'feste Ordnung' — gehört also unzweifelhaft zu den Grundbedingungen des bewussten Ich u. ihre Aufhebung hebt dieses u. somit die Welt auf." The surety of the principle of uniformity consists therefore, in the fact that without some uniformity experience would be impossible. The purpose of holding the axiom, therefore (to come to our own special question) is the desire of thought to employ itself upon the future as a subject matter, and the impossibility of conceiving a future at all without conceiving it as made up of uniform sequences.

This attempt is one in nature with the numerous efforts to see in the unity of self-consciousness the type and ground of the unity we postulate in the world. We will not quarrel with these efforts as a class. We remark as to this effort only that it does not express the whole, or as it seems to me the most important part of the actual purpose of thought in its assumption of the principle of uniformity. Thought seeks not mere general and indefinite regularity of experience, but absolute uniformity of perfectly definite laws. Self-consciousness would surely not be made impossible, hardly even affected, by a moderate irregularity such as would imply no fixed connection of any one cause with any one effect. Memory and historical account of facts whose connection and definite uniformity of sequence is not at all perceived, is surely possible. What would be added to the completeness of self-consciousness by an operation wherein for the mere history was substituted the scientific explanation of the facts? The advance would be great viewed from the side of the thinker. But the facts of experience and one's knowledge that they are facts would not be altered or even improved. I fail to find, therefore, in Professor Schuppe's account of the matter a sufficient basis for the use that he himself and human thought in general make of the axiom of uniformity.

If this effort to explain the aim of our thought in conceiving experience as uniform fails, another speedily suggests itself. If the former effort could not tell us why future experience must definitely resemble past experience in so far as concerns the sequence of events, may we not hope for better results if we regard the principle itself as demanding only an hypothetical uniformity of sequences, at once exact and formal, the uniformity of the sequence of fixed results upon the placing of certain given things in certain determinate conditions? Confining ourselves then still wholly to experience, may we not state the axiom of uniformity thus: "Like things under like circumstances behave in like fashions?" Here we mean by thing not a "thing-in-itself" beyond consciousness, but a certain determinate complex of experiences. The permanence of any law will then mean, not the permanence of any one kind of experience, but the permanence of relations among experiences. The previous account seemed to see in the axiom the assertion that there are limits to the variety of our experience. Then our author tried to prove that there are actually such limits to variety. The proof was successful, but the limits were too broad for any purpose of thought. Now we state in a purely hypothetical way that if at any time the same thing is found in our experience twice in the same circumstances we shall expect to notice the same behavior, and we shall expect with the utmost confidence. We ask again, what can be the purpose of thought in making this assumption?

"The same purpose," answers in substance Mr. Shadworth Hodgson, in his *Philosophy of Reflection* (Vol. ii, ch. ix, "On the Postulates and the Axioms of Uniformity") "the same purpose that we have in assuming the identity of everything with itself, to wit the purpose expressed in every act of attention, the purpose of noting what everything that passes through consciousness is. The axiom of uniformity is the postulate of identity applied to experience." I thus paraphrase Mr. Hodgson's discussion. To use now his own words (p. 103, ch. VIII): "If there were no uniformity in nature, there could be no postulates of logic; if that uniformity were not universal and without exception, the postulates could not be universally and necessarily true. For while we asserted A — it would or at any rate might be changing into not A — and the postulate" (*i. e.* of the identity of A with itself) "would be falsified." Again (p. 108) in stating the axiom of the "uniformity of the course of nature," Mr. Hodgson distinguishes this from the former axiom of uniformity, by saying that the axiom of simple uniformity "envisages single percepts" while the axiom of the uniformity of the course of nature "envisages sequences of percepts." Yet the two differ not at all in nature and basis. "That wherever A is found, it will be followed or accompanied by the same thing B, as it was the first time — this also depends on the postulate of identity. For if A were followed by B yesterday, and by not-B today, there would have been some relation in which A stands now, which it did not stand in before; that is, A would not have been strictly the *same A* in the two cases. We should find that some *respect* had been omitted, in which what we now call A was different from what we then called A. But if no such difference exists, and yet the postulate is true, then A must be followed by B, both yesterday, and today, and whenever it occurs."

Thus, then, according to Mr. Hodgson, the axiom of uniformity, whether the uniformity means logical identity of everything with itself, or regularity of sequence of consequent upon condition, always expresses the application of the logical postulates to the facts of experience. To think of the world as made up of things, is to think these things as united in fixed relations. To know the purpose of thought in thinking the axiom of uniformity is apparently the same as to know the whole purpose of thinking. For the axiom of uniformity rests upon and expresses the postulate of the identity of every thing with itself.

This opinion of Mr. Hodgson's is one that in various forms finds support in contemporary thought. In the current number of *Mind* I notice in Mr. Leslie Stephen's review of Mr. Balfour's *Defence of Philosophic Doubt*, an expression of opinion concerning the nature of the axiom of uniformity which seems very nearly identical with the view just set forth.

Whether omitted or not, this theory as to the nature of the principle of uniformity is certainly ingenious. Let us study it. The axiom in question is here supposed, we have said, to apply to things, and to experience considered as a succession of things presented in various relations, and under various conditions. The principle says that if the event A under certain conditions was followed by B, then under the same conditions A, if it recurred, would be again followed by B. A means an event identified as presenting a certain set of things, m^1, m^2, m^3 — in certain definite relations at some one moment. B means a consequent event, similarly identified. The complex m^1, m^2, m^3 — under the set of conditions c^1, c^2, c^3 — is seen to be followed by the resultant complex denoted by B. The assertion is made, according to the principle of uniformity, that every recurrence of precisely the same complex of m^1, m^2, m^3 — under the same set of conditions c^1, c^2, c^3 — will of necessity be

followed by the complex B. The question arises, how
can this assertion be made sure? The answer of Mr.
Hodgson and of those who agree with him seems to be,
when you separate it from all the technical expressions
of any system, essentially as follows. B having once
followed must always follow A. For suppose that instead of the complex B there followed in a new case a
different complex B^1. Then, since in our first experience
we meant by m^1, m^2, m^3 — and by the set of conditions
c^1, c^2, c^3 — (all of which made up A) precisely that set
of things and conditions that was followed by B, and
since, in brief, our definition of A was that it was the
complex upon which B followed, and since in this supposed case B^1 and not B follows, therefore not A but
something else, say the complex A^1, must have preceded.
Therefore, since A is A and not A^1, upon A must always
follow B and not B^1. Necessary connection is believed,
because the principle of identity is believed.

Or, to take a concrete instance: If an ordinary man is
stung by a viper he dies. This has been, we may suppose, tested in experience. Our assertion is that a man
stung by a viper always will die, unless conditions are
(as by the application of antidotes) essentially changed.
Now comes the Paul of the legend in the Acts. He
gathers a bundle of sticks; he lays them on the fire; and
a viper comes out, fastening upon his hand. We are
among the barbarians, and see the event. No visible
antidotes are taken. The conditions under which death
is usually found to follow are believed to be present.
The man must die; he is a murderer, whom vengeance
suffereth not to live. But we look a great while and see
no harm come to him. We change our minds, and say
that he is a god. Why so? Why did we not rather sus-
pect the principle of uniformity? As barbarians we are

not apt to be critical of the facts. Why are we not so
much the more critical of our general principles? Is it
merely an accident of the barbarous consciousness that
we prefer to assume that a god may be shipwrecked and
may have to make fires, instead of assuming that nature
is not uniform, and that vipers may not always be
deadly to men? No indeed, says our present mode of
explanation. Not as barbarians, but as if they were
philosophers, reasoning strictly according to the postulate of identity do these men assume the extra-human
character of Paul. Man is to them a being that among
many other essential qualities possesses this one, that of
dying when stung by a viper. This quality is found to be
absent in Paul, who is nevertheless seen to be moving at
the time under ordinary human conditions. There is
but one conclusion possible from the premises. Paul
cannot be a man. The barbarians were poor observers,
and doubtless ill acquainted with the nature of man.
But they were good reasoners in this case; and their
belief in the uniformity of nature was but an expression of their belief in the identity of the concept "man"
with itself. The whole was a syllogistic process of the
form:

All P is M   All men die when stung by vipers.
No S is M   *This being does not die, though stung.*
∴No S is P   ∴This is no man.

a good syllogism of the form Camestres of the second
figure.

But the obvious implication of the author of the Acts
in writing the story is of the same nature. He wishes us
to conclude, not that Paul was no man, but that he was
under a miraculous care of Providence. The syllogism
that the reader of the Acts will make if he believes the
narrator is:

No man under ordinary conditions escapes death being stung by a viper.

Paul escapes death although stung by a viper.

∴ Paul is no man under ordinary conditions;

i. e. Paul is under miraculous care.

In either case the assumption that like things under like conditions will yield like results, is but an application of the principle of identity. If what seemed to be a like thing under conditions assumed to be like does not yield the like result, we conclude that the seeming has deceived us, and that this is not the same thing. If, however, we assume the thing to be the same, then if the conditions appear to be the same and yet the result does not follow, we again conclude that the seeming is an illusion, and this time say that the conditions must have been different. In short, to quote Mr. Hodgson again (p. 152 of Vol. ii, *Philosophy of Reflection*), "The terms *conditions* and *conditioned* are *relatives* — that is the sum and substance of the axiom of uniformity, and it is a truth of inviolable necessity."

Such is the new effort to reduce the principle of causal nexus to the principle of identity. Mr. Hodgson seems desirous of distinguishing it from the old effort that Kant annihilated both elsewhere and in his famous answer to Eberhard (cf. *Phil. of Refl.*, Vol. ii, p. 110). I have stated this new effort as I understand it (and who can be sure that he understands Mr. Hodgson's *Philosophy of Reflection* when the book was published only two short years since?); and I have illustrated the doctrine as familiarly as I could. Now I ask, is this account a good one? Is the principle of uniformity as thus stated one that accomplishes the true ends of thought in dealing with experience? My answer is that I cannot think that the stated principle does accomplish the ends of thought. By uniformity of nature we mean something more than the identity of everything with itself, or of every class of things with itself, or than the relativity of every condition to its consequences.

The principle of uniformity, as Mr. Hodgson states it, means no more than this: Everything that is, is, and what was, has been, and what is to be, shall be. The principle is no more, so he himself admits, than is implied in the fact of attention, of arrest, as he calls it, *i. e.*, of the conversion of the perceptual order into the conceptual (p. 138; pp. 160 sqq.). Existence is, to use his own illustration, a mosaic, over which a fly walks. Behind the fly is the past, before him the future. He knows not whether there will be or will not be entirely unforeseen experiences awaiting him on the part of the mosaic not yet passed over. But he may be sure of uniformity, *i. e.*, of enduring qualities, at any one point of the mosaic. If looking forward "longitudinally," as Mr. Hodgson says, all appears contingent, looking transversely, that is as the spectator to whom the whole mosaic is visible may be supposed to look, all is fixed and necessary. "Perception gives us what we afterwards call a *flux* of objects; the characteristic element in reasoning, which is expressed by the postulates, consists in arresting one portion of that flux, making it statical, treating it as a *past*, and then going (not forwards from it) but backwards over it again. The question is no longer, what *will be*, but what *has been*. And this holds good whatever the duration of the arrested portion may be, a sudden flash, a half-second, an hour, a day, a year, a million years, the whole course of time — *everything* is *what it is.*" (*Ibid.*, p. 135). According to this, as I understand it, the position of the reasoner is in so far like the position of the supposed spectator of the mosaic, as it is a position in which what to perception was the flow of percepts, becomes the fixed world of concepts, wherein everything has a permanent and necessary relation to everything else. By uniformity of nature we mean no more than this enduring nature of the conceptual order. So at least I understand Mr. Hodgson to mean.

So meagre must be my statement of this marvelously ingenious and suggestive doctrine that I feel ashamed to go on immediately with an effort to show it incomplete. Yet in studying as I do here the purpose of thought, I must investigate whether and why any given statement is incapable of expressing the actual ends of our thinking. Do we seek in thought merely to arrest the stream of our percepts, to conceive the content of each as being such and such, to determine the abiding relations of this percept to all other percepts, and so to be able to sum up all with the statement: "A, being A, has fixed relations to all adjacent and to all remote facts, and is bound up with these relations, and can recur in the stream of consciousness only in so far forth as all its complicated relations recur?" I say, is this process all we mean when we speak of the work of thought and of the belief in the uniformity of nature? Is this what the sciences mean by the uniformity of nature? — "Ah," says some one, interrupting us, "but Mr. Hodgson himself carefully distinguishes the scientific application of the principle of uniformity from the principle itself." In fact, Mr. Hodgson does point out that in science there is an effort to anticipate particular recurrences, special regularities. This anticipation is something more than the axiom. Yet I think that he does not properly lay stress upon the fact that science seeks not merely to note actual past successions, but to predict,

with a probability of some definite degree, future successions. And as Mr. Hodgson says, agreeing in this
with Mr. Bain, with regard to the future recurrence of
any particular sequence, we have "to risk it." Such a
case of future recurrence is not covered by the axiom of
uniformity as he states the same. But is not every such
case an application of the fundamental assumptions of
science? Is not one of the ends of human thought the
gaining of a persuasion that the future will resemble the
past not merely in so far forth as it exemplifies the
principle of identity, but in so far forth as the things
and conditions of the future will grow in definite fashion
out of the things and conditions of the past, so that the
one may conceivably be calculated with exactness when
the other is given and understood? This uniformity of
necessary relation between the content of the part of
the mosaic over which we have passed and the content
of that part of the mosaic over which we have yet to
pass; this likeness of pattern in future and in past: is not
this what we want to find? Suppose that we have heard
a part of some piece of music, say of a theme and variations. We have distinguished in the perceptual order
the theme-melody and its parts, and have, by our act
of attention, transferred them to the conceptual order.
Suppose further that at some point while we are listening and while the melody is recurring, we ask ourselves in
the midst of our attention: Whether or no, is this melody
to be broken off suddenly when half finished, and the
fragment to be followed by a snatch from a street-song?
Now I do not ask, how is this question to be decided?
Of course that will be determined by circumstances? I
ask, what will be the significance of the question? We
want to know whether the first half of the melody M, is
to be followed by the latter half. Is it any answer to

appeal to the axiom of identity and to say thus: "If the
first half of what was before called M is followed not as
before by the last half of M, but by a snatch of a street-
song, then it is plain that this first half is not the first
half of M at all, but something else; since the first half
of a melody is as first half relative to the second half, and
can only be the first half in case the second half follows?" I say, would this account satisfy us? We want
to know not the definition of the whole called M, but
the probability of a disagreeable sensation. Yet I conceive that declaring the uniformity of the course of nature to be nothing but the great fact that a condition
when viewed in relation to its consequent is only this
particular condition in so far forth as it comes to have
this particular consequent, I conceive, I say, that this
account of the uniformity of nature fails as the application of the same principle to the case of the musical
experience would fail. It leaves the one important question unanswered. This question is not: Can we regard
existence past present and future as one vast mosaic, all
of whose parts are in fixed relations? To that question
Mr. Hodgson gives a sufficiently exhaustive answer.
The question is: Can we regard this mosaic as having
such an uniformity of pattern that our guesses as to the
whole can have a fair and definite probability, after we
have noted certain recurring patterns in the parts?

One more example: If we ask, will the theory of gravi-
tation hold true tomorrow? Mr. Hodgson would doubtless answer according to his doctrine of uniformity,
"Yes: if the same matter continues to exist." For
matter that did not follow the present law of gravita-
tion would not be, in the same sense of the term, matter
at all. This is true indeed. Yet I do not see but that it
leaves us just where we were before. We did not ask,

how shall we be forced to alter our logical conceptions of matter in case in the perceptual order there is no more following of the old course of behavior? We asked, what estimate can we form of the probability that the old way of behaving will be followed by the old bodies, or if you like by the new bodies, tomorrow? According to Mr. Hodgson, none at all. We must content ourselves with the thought that pretty nearly everything in this world is perpetually in just that state in which it forever is. Then we declare that we have fixed the flux of percepts, and admire the eternal stability of the world of our thoughts.

But, says an objector, poor as seems this result of philosophic analysis, it is the most we shall ever reach. No one can tell us why the future must resemble the past in any definite way. The task has been tried again and again. The failure has been in every case exemplary. At the end we must admit that we deal with a pure faith. Philosophy can analyze our notions of uniformity, but cannot justify them. Science, in so far as it is more than an application of the principles of identity, is a vast structure resting on a sublime and utterly groundless because fundamental persuasion, the persuasion that the relations and the things of yesterday and today must be essentially like the things and the relations that will exist tomorrow. Nobody can justify, just as nobody can endanger the unreasoning persistent vitality of this boldest of beliefs. All other beliefs, even the wildest, hope in some way to found themselves upon this belief, or at least to be found in agreement with it. Itself, as the ground of all faith, has no foundation, and seeks no allies. Shall we call it probable? No, for what could be meant by a probability that the future as a whole, as a future, will resemble the past? Probability implies existent and recognized conditions, of which some part are abiding and some changing. The combination of these then produces certain results, varying within limits. Within these limits every one of the results is said to be a probable one. How would this definition apply to the future and to its definite similarity with the present or past? To assume that the future must be like the past because the same conditions will continue into the future, is to beg the question in all too shameless a fashion. Let us be honest with ourselves, continues the objector, and admit that there is no way of saying that there is the least definite probability of the likeness between future and past, unless we are already willing to make assumptions as to the future that include all that is meant by the probability to be proven. Recurrences in the past prove nothing whatever about the future simply because the future as such lies completely beyond experience. The nearness or the practical interest of a future event are not qualities that change the case at all. Be an event five seconds in advance or five hundred million years, so long as the event is future we can make no claim to know anything about it which does not include an enormous assumption. That we make the assumption is indubitable. Practically the assumption is indispensable. Logically there is not a particle of positive justification for it. Therefore, concludes the objector, let us not be wroth with Mr. Hodgson for failing to do what cannot be done. Let us leave the assumption to itself, as being far above any reflective justification, and let us return to the business of philosophical analysis.

I have let the objector speak at length, because I recognize the force of the objection. In a cold but delightful style of exposition a contemporary writer, Mr. Balfour, in his *Defence of Philosophic Doubt*, has stated

the sceptic's case so as to make it once more the duty of
everyone to notice the question who wishes to form a
judgment upon the problems involved, in the spirit and
with the caution of modern thought. Surely it is time
that the old talk about the mathematical probability
that the future (conceived in the ordinary way) will resemble the past, a probability based solely upon the
regularity of sequences in the past, should come to an
end. Probability has a definite meaning only in case we
make definite assumptions as to the conditions. The
fallacy of separating such an event as the sunrise from
all other natural phenomena, and of trying to calculate
the probability of the continued occurrence of sunrises while using as a basis only an assumed past number of observed sunrises, is now quite well recognized
(cf. Venn., *Logic of Chance*, second ed., p. 180; Wundt,
Logik, Bd. I, Stuttgart, 1880, p. 394 sq.). Why should
an attempt at estimating the mathematical probability of the general scientific assumption of the uniformity of nature, be regarded as less fallacious?
Assume the existence in the future of certain great
higher laws and conditions, and the probability of particular uniformities can in many cases be estimated.
But what is this but first assuming the uniformity of all
nature, in order that we may estimate in the special
cases the special probability? Never do we escape from
the fatal circle. We were discontented with Professor
Schuppe's account of uniformity, because it seemed not
to express the aims of thought. Let us now admit that
in trying to give a further account of these aims, we
have reached a point where it seems that the aim of
thought can only be expressed in an assumption altogether too sweeping to be regarded with perfect theoretic satisfaction. Still are we driven onwards. What

is the true and final aim of human thought in the assumption of the axiom of uniformity? Must we at last be driven to say, all that is valuable in human thinking rests on a baseless assumption that a perfectly irresponsible experience may at any moment belie? To be sure, even if it turns out that we must admit the fact, no grave practical consequences need be feared. But our theoretical interest in thinking would be in so far disappointed as the result spoken of would apparently be one of universal and hopeless philosophic scepticism. We should simply have to say, the fundamental assumption of thought about experience and the future, is an assumption conceivably untrue and of its nature absolutely beyond proof. Must this conclusion be accepted?

We have studied the axiom of uniformity in two aspects, first as an expression of belief in the tendency of the sequences of experience to recur, and secondly as an expression of belief that the same thing under the same circumstances acts in the same way. In both these aspects we have found that the principle of uniformity expresses an aim of thought that cannot be satisfied either by the axiom that all experience must as experience continue to resemble in some wise our past experience, or by the axiom that all things in so far forth as they continue to be the same things must bear the same relations to adjacent things. If experience must always remain experience, well and good; but we want to know whether the content of experience is not subject to practically unlimited change. If things are defined by their relations to other things, then identity implies likeness of relations to preceding and succeeding phenomena; but we want to know what chances there are of the persistence of the present order of things. The aim of thought seems so far too lofty for the means.

The discrepancy is only to be made up by an arbitrary assumption.

The axiom of uniformity was chosen by us at the outset of this section because it appeared as a typical case of the way in which thought seeks to anticipate experience. The same difficulties would have arisen as to any other of the axioms of experience. The axiom of counting, the geometrical axioms, any other like principles involve similar questions. Why is anything observed in the past necessarily to be anticipated in the future? Always comes the same answer: "We assume the agreement."

But pause a moment. There is one axiom that we have not yet considered at all. It seems not quite like the axiom of uniformity. Perhaps the aim of thought in assuming it is better in accordance with the limitations of thought than in the other cases. Perhaps we shall get some light here. This axiom is the well-known time-axiom, that *facta* cannot become *infecta*, that the past can never be undone. This asserts something of the whole future. In all coming time the inviolability of every moment will be secured as soon as the moment is past. Upon what does this axiom depend? "Upon the principle of identity" would be, as I suppose, the answer of Mr. Hodgson. I partly admit the statement. That the past can never return, is indeed a result of the fact that the past is the past. That the same quality of being irrevocable will accompany all future moments, arises from the nature of time. But why must we suppose time always to have the same nature? Because, if we conceived time as of such a nature that its moments were capable of return, we should be conceiving of it, not as time, but as space. This is true again. But now, to ask the fundamental question, why conceive of any future at all wherein the time-axiom will be verified? Why are we so certain that there will be a future? What is the end of thought in thus assuming that a future will come, and that the time-stream never ceases? Evidently we have here come to a final question which neither admits nor requires an answer. That there will be a future time is an assumption that cannot be based upon any other principle; but no sceptic can formulate any opposition to it. Try to assume a condition of things in which time has ceased, and you introduce a time-element into your assumed condition. Try to conceive an end of experience, and you conceive of your experience as continuing after it has ceased. Therefore, there will be a future, because at the present moment we actively form for ourselves the picture or the notion of a future. The denying of the validity of this fundamental act is the assumption of its validity. For if we try to think away a future, we shall have naught wherewith to fill up the thought-place thus left vacant except a second future.

Therefore, while it is perfectly certain that the present is not a future, and while it is perfectly certain that we are not in the future and that the future is not in our experience, yet it is equally certain that the conception of the future is an absolutely valid conception, and that in our anticipation of the coming of a future our experience can never disappoint us. Here is an anticipation of experience which rests upon an assumption; yet an anticipation to which no sceptical opposition can possibly be formulated. What we mean by a future cannot fail of realization, even though we individuals cease to be. This is the first axiom in which so far in this discussion we have attained perfect confidence.

Now in this axiom, which forms the basis of the time-axiom and of all other anticipations of experience, and in fact of all expressible doubts as to anticipations of experience, an aim of thought immediately coincides with the means of realizing the aim. Thought aims at constructing a notion of a future. The fundamental assumption offers itself, and is instantly made, that the conception of a future is a valid conception. At the moment we aim to believe in a future we do believe in a future. The purpose and its fulfillment are inseparably joined.

Here at last we have found a perfectly certain anticipation of experience. What is meant by future is not an immediately given phenomenon but only a conception of a phenomenon and yet this conception is immediately known to be indubitable. Meaning and justification fall together. To say what a future means is to anticipate a future. Now if we have here an assumption whose validity consists simply in the fact that it is at present made, can we not hope to reduce the axiom of uniformity and the other axioms to such a form that whatever is meant by them is justified in the moment when it is understood? Anticipation of experience will then be the same as the act of constructing the notion of experience. The aim of thought will be to construct for itself in a certain definite wise a conception of the past and future of experience. Then experience will not appear as an independent flux of phenomena, which thought follows without any true power to anticipate the content of the flux; but, on the contrary, whatever notions we have of past and future experience will be seen to be the construction of our own thought, working upon data immediately given in the present. So that what before seemed pure assumption, will now appear as the mere expression of the act of thought in constructing the very notion of the past and future experience concerning which the assumption is made.

I propose then to raise the question whether we cannot regard the notions we have of past and future experience as solely the product of the present activity of thought working upon the data given in the present moment of consciousness. If we can so regard these notions, then the axiom of uniformity will be no baseless assumption as to a course of nature which is entirely independent of our thought, and which will come as it pleases; but the axiom will be the expression of the thought-activity as it actually exists, in its assumptions about an experience which is immediately given in present conception. Then if some one asks us, "how do you know that future experience will continue uniform?" we answer, "how do you know that there will be any future time at all?" If the answer to this is that the conception of future time involves the coming of a future time, for that we define the future only by the conception we now have of it, so that the conception and the validity thereof are one and the same thing, then we shall once more retort that human thought in just the same way conceives of a future experience always as in some fixed relation to present experience. Since then human experience means what we now at this moment conceive to be human experience, this fundamental conception of human experience as of an uniform succession of phenomena can never be disappointed. Disappointment of this thought-assumption can·mean for us now only a failure to make the assumption. Yet we do make the assumption. Therefore by disappointment of our present fundamental notion of a future experience, we can mean nothing that we can now definitely realize. To realize to ourselves that our present assumption of the uniformity of experience should in future be disappointed, could only be to realize that our present definition of future experience as being uniform is not what we mean by future experience. And this would involve a contradiction.

This is the brief statement of the position which suggests itself as a possible solution of our difficulty. If this view turns out to agree with the actual aims of thought, then we have a solution of the great problem different from both the solutions above examined. Professor Schuppe and Mr. Hodgson, with those whose views we let them represent, seem to assume the time-flow, the future, the past, as if they were independent things-in-themselves, before whose manifold possibilities the present moment stands aghast, or ought to, daring only to make the mild assumption that throughout all, each event will be identical with itself, and that all events will belong to the series of conscious states. Since this mild assumption did not express the purpose of thought, we before were discontented with it. Now we advance the view, that past and future and the time-flow are all of them notions expressing something meant by a present thought-activity. They are projections, so to speak, of the present content of consciousness, by an act of thought whose nature must be judged from an immediate perception of its working. As such projections or present constructions in consciousness, both the future and the past are and must be conceived as following certain definite laws in their construction and arrangement of parts. The way in which we conceive of experience determines the nature of experience, because only of the experience of which we have some conception already formed, can we say anything as to whether or no it has or can have any given nature.

The solution of our whole problem will then be at least indicated if we can be sure of the following proposition: *That by future as by past we mean only certain notions we have, that are now and here formed by a present thought-activity dealing with present data of feeling.* Then of course assertions as to the uniformity of nature become mere results of analysis. The course of nature is uniform because by the word nature we mean the complex of experience conceived in the present moment and viewed as uniform. The whole question then will reduce to a simple question of fact. Do we conceive of nature as having a certain uniformity? Then nature has this uniformity. For by nature we mean what we conceive as nature. Do we conceive of the future as in definite connection with the past? Then the future is in definite connection with the past. For by past and future we mean what we now conceive to be past and future. And so our anticipation of experience will become a construction of experience.

This present topic leads us, then, irresistibly to the study of the next.

III

THE AIM OF THOUGHT AS THE CONSTRUCTION OF THE CONCEPTION OF POSSIBLE EXPERIENCE

Here, as I maintain, is found and stated the true theoretic goal of human thought. But some analysis is yet necessary.

Whenever we try to reflect on the process of thought, whether to discover its content or to investigate its methods or to determine its aim, we always find ourselves dealing with a present thought. We can never directly know anything but a present thought. Of this we can study the aim, the quality, the subject-matter.

Past and future, as past and future, are never immediately given. This is a great fact of thought and of conscious life generally.

Now shall we say that since past and future are not immediate data they must be concluded from the present content of consciousness? This is evidently meaningless. What indications shall be regarded as sufficient in the present moment to constitute proof that this present moment has been preceded and will be followed by other conscious moments? Evidently such a proof would depend upon at least a conception of past and of future. And as we have seen before, the conception of past and future is the knowledge of the validity of this conception itself. To think of past and future is to believe that there has been some past and that there will be a future.

If our general conception of a time-relation between a present moment and other moments of experience be valid of necessity, since all that is meant by the time-relation, is involved in the present conception of a time-relation, how is it with the conception of necessary sequence of the present experience from the past experience? Evidently this conception carries its own validity with it in so far as what we at this moment think as past is related to what we this moment think as present, in precisely the way in which we now think the one related to the other. The same holds as to the relation of future to past. At this moment we project our world-picture into an ideal past and an ideal future. The present moment is the builder of both the branches of the conceived time-stream. The rest is pure analysis. Whatever necessary connection we see between the facts of this time-stream, is a necessary connection because we see it as such.

But, says the objector, all this leaves open no place for a difference between truth and error. If by past and future, and by the content of past and future one means only what is conceived as past and future and as the content thereof, then an error in prediction or in history is impossible. And with error disappears whatever is worth calling truth.

The answer is again, what do we mean by a consciousness of error at any moment? We mean, first, that an expectation of experience, possessed by us in the past, has since been disappointed. All other logical meanings of the word error are derived, I apprehend, from this meaning. Now when have we the consciousness of error? When we have the expectation of the experience? No, indeed; the expectation is not a consciousness of its own failure. When then are we conscious of failing? When the expected experience does not come? Not of necessity. At the moment of lacking the experience we do not feel conscious of failure unless we form a conception of the past expectation as a past expectation. When then? We feel, I reply, conscious of error when a present content of experience is found contrasting with and contradicting an expectation now conceived as past. That is, to be conscious of error we must refer the present to a past, and must conceive the present as not satisfying the demands of an ideal past. Now it is a fact, as I conceive, that we often do so regard our present contents of consciousness. We often are conscious of error. Hence this account does not banish the consciousness of error from the world, but only shows that in the consciousness of error, as in all other contents of present moments, we are noting the relation now given between a present experience and a conceived past or future experience.

In like manner as the consciousness of error is possible, is the fear of error also possible, in case we bring a present expectation into relation with a conceived future experience. And with the fear of error are also possible all the forms of definite doubt, of deliberate investigation, and of cautious assertion. A cautious assertion expresses a coincidence not regarded as certain between a conceived future and a present expectation. This is possible in case the future is not definitely conceived, nor the expectation a very strong one.

Now the developed critical or scientific consciousness always has this relation between the present moments and the past or future as conceived in the present: viz., that the conception of past or future is only completed and made quite definite in so far as relates to its general forms, not in so far as relates to its particular content. But the particular content of past and future when conceived at all, is conceived as definitely probable because determined already by the general forms. The forms of past and future are conceived as necessary, the content as contingent but probable. Thus in stating the axiom of uniformity, I am not usually able to state that the relations of particular things tomorrow must certainly take any particular shape that I can designate. The axiom of uniformity is the conception that in the conceived past and future there are throughout realized certain fundamental and absolutely uniform sequences; such, for example, as the sequence expressed in the first law of motion. Now these sequences may not be conceived as known to me; but they are conceived as so certainly existent that I can say: "all that has been or that will be" (meaning the conceived content of the ideal past and future) "is throughout in necessary connection, is made up of causes and effects, joined in neces-

sary union." But as to the particular content which I
conceive as filling past and future, this I conceive or
picture, not as necessary, but as probable. In so far as
I conceive myself to have attained a knowledge of the
absolutely fundamental sequences in nature, I conceive
my present knowledge as extending to a perfectly sure
anticipation of particular past or future facts. In so far,
however, as the particular facts are conceived as not
contained in the general necessity of such uniform sequences as I now know, I view them as probable, and
their probability as definitely measurable in so far as I
can conceive them as resulting from certain general
causes affected by the action of numerous minor and
changing causes. Both the necessity and the contin-
gency are there and are real, because we now conceive
them to be in the ideal past and future which we at the
present moment construct for ourselves.

Present moments may have many contents. Always
however, there is a present feeling, organized in some
form. If the present moment is filled with a thought,
the organized feeling or notion is conceived as standing
in some definite relation to an ideal past and future experience. The relation that is conceived may then take
many forms. The higher and more advanced our
thought, the more are past and future conceived as
wholes, as standing for one World, the more the whole
conception of past and future becomes unified, and the
more definite is found to be the relation of every fact to
the whole conceived time-stream. Furthermore, the
higher our thought rises in the scale of perfection, the
less our conception of past and future appears as a mere
expression of wish, desire, passion, prejudice, or other
individual affection, the more does it appear as a purely
theoretical conception, assumed in order that the

thought of the present may have breadth, fullness, and unity, and in order that present acts may appear not as sufficient unto themselves, but as having an immeasurable import in their relation to a whole universe.

To sum up, from this point of view the end of thought appears to be: That experience past and future, should be conceived as one whole with a necessary connection of parts; that the present and immediately given content of consciousness should be found to be, not alone significant nor enough, but a moment in a world of life; that the relations conceived as necessary for one part of the time-stream should be conceived as necessary for the whole time-stream. And the end of thought is realized in the act of constructing the image of possible experience. For by experience we mean, in addition to what is given, that which is conceived as past and future.

As for the purely possible that is conceived neither as actually past nor as actually future, that is conceived only as a necessary sequence or corollary to the conception of the past and future as such, and needs no special study.

In this wise I would seek to give an account of the problem stated above. That this solution is a good and consistent one, I cannot be sure. For many obvious objections an answer may be attempted at another time. A good deal of reflection has at all events convinced me that no study of thought is complete which does not treat the problems of thought in their teleological aspect, and which does not ask as to every thought assumption: What end does it accomplish? Taking the axiom of uniformity as such an assumption, I have studied it in the foregoing. And my answer is: The end of thought in assuming the axiom of uniformity is the construction of an ideal picture of a world of experience that shall be seen as One.[1]

[1] This argument as to the nature of our knowledge of future and past in some degree resembles the account given by Mr. Hodgson himself of the nature of our knowledge of past time. I refer to his answer to the doctrine that we need "intuitions." to enable us to be sure that memory has any trustworthiness. I have only to remark that my own answer, the result of manifold suggestions derived from reading, is here substantially the same as in the thesis presented to the Johns Hopkins Faculty as a candidate for the Doctor's Degree in the spring of 1878, before I had read, or begun to read, Mr. Hodgson's discussion in the *Philosophy of Reflection*. For that reason only I have not made in the foregoing more special reference to views with which, perhaps, if I understood them better I might agree more perfectly.

GEORGE ELIOT AS A RELIGIOUS TEACHER

[1881]

THE great woman who lately died will no doubt be remembered in the next century chiefly as a literary artist, who knew mankind well, and held an almost perfect mirror up to nature whenever she chose to portray character. And in the minds of many it is an unimportant task to try to piece together from the writings of a great artist anything like a system of general philosophy, or even of ethics. Why should the words of those who spoke so well the rich flexible language of the living human soul be translated into the poor dry speech of metaphysics? If George Eliot, some one may say, ever lost sight of her vocation as artist, and, as in *Daniel Deronda*, filled pages with tedious disquisitions, why should we try to follow her in her wanderings? Her best teachings are her great creations; and from a truly poetic product you may get inspiration, but you must not try to deduce a formula.

Of course, we must not lose sight of the fact that a work of art is always far more than a theory, nor ignore the truth that artists do injustice to their art as soon as they begin to mix abstractions with their concrete creations. But we must also remember that not all art is alike remote from the world of thought. The man who writes an abstract account of the ethical teachings conveyed in the works of some musical composer may indeed keep within the bounds of reason, but he is at least in great danger of talking nonsense. But if one writes a commentary on the doctrines of the Book of Job, the fact that his subject is a work of art, and not merely a treatise, does not render his undertaking less appropriate. Poetry is not always, but yet very often, aptly to be named molten thought, thought freed from the chill of the mountain summits, its crystalline perfection of logical form dissolved, no longer ice, but gathered into tumultuous streams that plunge down in musical song to the green fields and wide deserts of the world where men live, far below. He who follows a streamcourse upward to the glaciers whence it has sprung leaves, indeed, behind him many of the fairest scenes of the lowlands, but he has the satisfaction of assisting at the birth of a river. Mists that have risen from the whole of that great world of the plains — from far beyond, too, in the infinite ocean itself — have come up here to be frozen that they might, by melting again, produce this stream. To suppose that poetry is altogether thought is to see dead forms where one ought to see life; but to refuse altogether to look for the sources in thought whence the stream often comes, is to commit the mistake of the king of Burmah, and to deny that water can ever have been frozen.

George Eliot, furthermore, was by nature quite as much a reflective as a poetical genius, and by training much less a poetical than a reflective writer. We should have supposed beforehand that she would never have produced other than "novels with a purpose." Artist as she actually was, theory was constantly in her mind. The thought of her time governed her. She had occasional glimpses above and beyond it; but if she was Shakespearian in the portrayal of character, she was unlike Shakespeare in her regard for formulas, and no future century will ever be in doubt whether she was Protestant or Catholic. In fine, she certainly wished to teach men, and it is, therefore, our right and duty to attempt the not very arduous task of formulating and of tracing to their chief sources the teachings that she often but thinly veiled beneath the garment of fiction. In doing this we shall not study the loftiest or the most interesting aspect of her work, but our task will not be void of significance.

Let us first sum up what little we as yet know about George Eliot's growth as a thinker. We know that she was an unwearied student of science, of literature, of history, and of philosophy. We know that she sympathized in great measure with what is called modern positivism. We know also, however, that she was well acquainted with the thoughts and beliefs of a class of English men and women, who know and care nothing about modern thought, but who have ideals that she never mentions with contempt, and that she in fact never wholly outgrew. All these elements went together to the making up of her doctrine of life. When her biography is written, we shall know more of their separate growth and of the fashion of their union. But even now, from the facts that are known, we may conjecture much, and the temptation to conjecture about so beloved a teacher is irresistible.

Marian Evans, according to the account of her early life published in the *Pall Mall Gazette*, grew up in an orthodox family, and in the Christian faith. With years she developed remarkable powers of reflection, and the first result of reflection was to make her a very strict Calvinist. The discomfort of this faith urged her to further thought. We do not yet know just what influences made her a free-thinker. At all events, she never rested in the early crude delight of negation, but sought in all directions for more light. In 1850 we find her in London, already in the possession, so Mr. Herbert Spen-

cer tells us, of the wide learning and many-sided thought
that have since made her famous. She was now not far
from thirty years of age. She had as yet made no attempts, at least in public, to write novels. She was
simply a quiet and interesting literary woman, with extraordinary talents and acquirements. Acting under
advice, she translated Strauss's *Leben Jesu*, and Feuerbach's *Essence of Christianity*. She became the sub-
editor of the *Westminster Review*, and buried a great deal
of work in its brief quarterly notices of contemporary
literature. Between 1854 and 1860 she also published
several essays in the same review, whereof the titles
have been given in a late number of the London *Acad-
emy*. These essays all show rather the conscientious
reviewer than the ambitious genius. Nothing but the
style reminds you of *Silas Marner* or of *Romola*. One
becomes almost angry in reading work that must have
cost such a mind so much labor and that yet must of
necessity have but a transient interest. Why wait here,
one says, in this den of book-worms, O great teacher?
Time is flying, the day is far spent, and the words thou
art to speak to all the world are yet but voices in thy
dreams. To thy task, before old age comes! Alas! they
were well spent and yet ill spent years. Happy were
the world if full of such workers. But yet unhappy the
world in which such spirits are confined, even for only
half their lives, to such tasks. George Eliot was nearly
forty years of age when her first tales were published.

But to understand the origin and nature of her later
religious views, we must analyze as well as we are able
the influences that during these years must have been
forming our author's creed. When a strong faith has
left a man, he must do one of two things: either he must
fly to the opposite extreme of pure and scornful negation,

or he must try to find some way in which to save for himself what was essential to the spirit of the old faith, while he rejects its accidental features, such as its ritual, its claim to give power over physical forces, its promises of material good fortune, or its asserted miracles. Now, George Eliot belonged too much to the nineteenth century to fall under the power of the purely negative tendency. She might be an unbeliever, but she never could be a scoffer; and so the search after the essential in the religious consciousness became for her a practical necessity. This search it was, without doubt, that led her to the translation of Strauss and of Feuerbach. To understand the effort that runs all through George Eliot's life-work — the effort to find and to portray the religious consciousness as it exists in men's minds independently of the belief in supernatural agencies — we must glance at the views of these Germans whose thought she first transferred to English soil. They expounded theories that she afterward sought to test by an appeal to living human experience.

Let us speak first of Strauss and of the positive element in religion that this thinker, in the early Hegelian period when the first *Leben Jesu* was written, tried to separate from the supernatural elements of tradition. To understand this matter we must look back a little. German philosophy, ever since Lessing's tract on the *Erziehung des Menschengeschlechts*, had been trying to discover the ultimate significance of religion, natural and revealed. Lessing himself, in the mentioned tractate, saw in revelation the process by which God taught the race from its infancy up. The doctrines of a revelation are, therefore, for him absolute truth, but not all the truth, and by the ignorant race, to whom they are at first revealed, they are only half understood, and, there-

fore, often misunderstood. But the purpose of the revelation is not to reveal what is beyond all human insight.
The purpose of revelation, like the purpose of individual
education, is to hasten and make definite a process of
development that could conceivably have gone on without external aid. "Revelation gives the race nothing
that human reason, left to itself, would not attain; but
it gave and gives to the race the weightiest of these
things earlier than they would otherwise be attained"
(*Erziehung des Menschengeschlechts*, § 4). Therefore, on
the other hand, nothing in revelation is to be free from
the investigations of reason; and the work of reason is to
translate into the language of thought the figurative or
obscure doctrines of revelation. In every such doctrine
reason is to see not a stumbling-block, but a guide; and,
on the other hand, not an incomprehensible mystery,
but an intelligible truth, kindly revealed beforehand
that we may know whither to direct our thought. That
revelation is not all truth, or that it is dark truth, proves
nothing against it, since all teachers give the pupil only
what helps him to work for himself, and do not explain
to him everything. On the other hand, the darkest
truth is revealed that it may in time become clear to
reason. Revelation is given to the end that man may
outgrow it. There will come "the time of completion
when man, however persuaded he is of a better future,
will have no need to borrow of that future motives for
his actions, since he will do good because it is good, not
because arbitrary rewards are offered; for these rewards
were but intended in the foretime to fix and strengthen
his wavering sight to know the inner and better rewards
of goodness. It will come, the time of the new Everlasting Gospel, promised even in the New Testament
books" (*Erziehung des Menschengeschlechts*, §§ 85, 86).

These thoughts of Lessing worked as a ferment in the great philosophic movement of subsequent years. Lessing's own point of view was forsaken for others, but his spirit dominates nearly all later German thought on this subject. Religion, according to one view, is the veiled utterance, the imperfect and poetical grasping of truth that can be and must be otherwise expressed and justified. Religion is, therefore, the necessary path to the higher insight that is to come through philosophy. Or, on the other hand, as Schleiermacher has it, religion is an expression of a feeling, viz., of the sense of dependence, of finite incompleteness, of need of God. This sense, as pure feeling, is the essential element of religion, and the work of philosophical reflection is to find this essential element in all faith, to purify the religious sense from all disturbing doubt, and to prepare the soul to stand alone with God in the undisturbed enjoyment of the satisfaction of its greatest want. These two views — the one for which religion is largely theoretical in content, the expression of an intuitive, uncriticized, impure, or else poetically veiled knowledge; the other for which religion is the effort to express an emotion, a felt need of support, or of something to worship — both contend for the supremacy in modern German religious philosophy. Both have in common, first, the effort to transcend the uncritical faith of unlearned piety, and, secondly, the discontent, with the negations of pure rationalism. The two differ often very widely in the consequences that are drawn from them.

Now Strauss, in the *Leben Jesu*, after applying criticism to the gospel histories, found their content to be throughout, as he held, mythical. His work completed, the question arose, What must we do with the faith whose support seems thus taken away? The answer was,

Religion has not deserted us; only the perishable form in which our thought clothed itself has dissolved. The hidden inner sense is revealed more clearly when we see the mythical element in the popular faith. To determine this inner sense of Christianity, Strauss had recourse to the doctrines of his master, Hegel, which he interpreted — not as Hegel would have done, but as at least one great tendency of the Hegelian philosophy suggested. From the point of view that Strauss adopts,[1] the religious consciousness appears as largely theoretic; viz., as in the intuitive knowledge of the infinite, the recognition in nature, in mind, in history, of the presence of an all pervading, all governing reason, of an absolute spirit in whom are all things. Not as a philosophic theory, but as a purely immediate sense or belief the religious soul makes and accepts this doctrine. But if this is the essence of religious faith, it is not the whole of faith. Unphilosophic as the religious consciousness is, it necessarily embodies its faith in a mythical form. The direct consciousness of the infinite is expressed in the documents of the faith as if it were a particular historical revelation, occurring at some point of time. The presence of the infinite reason in the universe is conceived as the action of a law-giver, working after the fashion of men. The progress of the race, or the growth of the religious consciousness in the individual, is related as if it were a series of miracles. The eternal, in short, is conceived under the form of the transient, the infinite is mythically made to appear finite. So, again, in particular with the Christian doctrines. The knowledge that the human spirit is in essence one with the divine

---

[1] *V.* Pfleiderer, *Religionsphilosophie*, p. 238. Cf., the account in Hausrath, *D. F. Strauss u. d. Theologie Seiner Zeit*, vol. i, the chapter on the first *Leben Jesu*.

spirit, that man is to rise to the actual sense of his unity with God, is veiled under the myth of a historical incarnation. The understanding of the myth is the revealing of its essential content. We do not, reasons Strauss, lose the knowledge of the infinite, nor of our essential unity with it, when we learn the mythical nature of the religious doctrine. This mythical form was an absolute necessity to train men for a knowledge of the truth. We must reject the shell of the dogma, but the kernel of the dogma is our eternal treasure.

It is certain that George Eliot must have been influenced by these views. She looked everywhere for teaching, and we may be sure that she did not translate Strauss merely for the sake of disturbing her countrymen's faith. Of course, she did not accept the Hegelian metaphysic; but just as little is she in her novels willing to express perfect satisfaction with the flat negations of many of the English positivists. Nearer, in some respects, to her actual views, because less given to transcendent speculation than Strauss, may, perhaps, have been Feuerbach, whose *Wesen des Christenthums* she also translated. Feuerbach has, at present, little more than historical interest. What he has concluded as a consequence of his early Hegelianism others have said or thought independently of him. The following account depends upon that in Pfleiderer's late work, *Religionsphilosophie auf Geschichtlicher Grundlage*. Feuerbach's view of religion is intensely skeptical, and yet not wholly unappreciative. He sees in religion the expression of a subjective want, which assumes the deceptive guise of knowledge. See through this disguise, and religion has no truth; and yet the disguise is not the one essential thing in religion, for the want creates the disguise. Man in religion treats his own being as if it were another. Dis-

satisfied with a world that oppresses him, he creates in
his despair a supernatural all-powerful being, enthroned
over the world, and worships this ideal Self as the perfect one. The ideal has no truth, but the indefinite variety of its forms, the strength of the want that creates it,
make its power over life prodigious. In the thought
"there is a God, an image of Me, a perfect, an unlimited
Self, outside of the sphere of change and misery" religion begins. But this thought is not enough. God must
be put in relation to the world. Only as God the Son, as
God appealing to the human heart, knowing our frail-
ties, sympathizing with our needs, hearing our prayers,
does the infinite ideal become truly divine. And it is but
an objectifying of the unhappy world-weary consciousness of disappointed humanity to conceive this God as
himself suffering and overcoming suffering, as the risen
and exalted Self, that has overcome the world.

But in all this Feuerbach finds only a stupendous
phantasm. He will admit nothing in religion as religion
that can endure criticism. Yet see what after all will remain to one who accepts Feuerbach's premises, but regards this purely fantastic exercise of the religious spirit
as after all intensely and eternally significant. Such a
one will say, Men did indeed make to themselves ideals
of God, and these ideals were phantasms; but the spirit
of religion that produced the phantasm is still ours. We
reject the product that made the world seem so sublime
and significant, but we work as if we were in a world
where such things were true. We know ourselves to be
but strangers, who find in the whole real universe
nothing that quite satisfies these our highest longings;
but then, we can and will try to make the world as much
as possible the realization of our longings. Ours it will
be to give life a divine significance, even if no Providence

has already done this for us before our birth. Did George Eliot draw this conclusion herself? We shall have reason to believe that she did.

By training, then, as we may say, our author was at least in part identified with the great characteristic thought-movement of the first half of our century, with the movement that aimed at the understanding and appreciation of the essential elements of religion. This movement was not one of harmony, but of vigorous and often bitter discussion, and no original thinker would be apt to submit himself to the mere formulas of any one of its representatives. Yet in it all there was the one easily appreciated effort to decipher this strange, beautiful language of the pious heart, and to see whether the writing, once deciphered, would furnish any one word that the enlightened mind can accept as eternal truth. With this effort George Eliot was in deep sympathy.

Another influence on George Eliot's religious philosophy must be mentioned, but I see at present no good reason to lay much stress upon it. This is the influence of Comte and of his formulated *Religion of Humanity*. When some one of the most straitest sect of the religious positivists, who is at the same time acquainted with German thought, shall have made clear to us just what, if any, was Comte's original and genuine contribution to the philosophy of religion, beyond his theory of the three stages of the human mind, we shall be able to appreciate the importance of a general sympathy with positivism for the mind of one who knew German religious philosophy so well. Till this information is given I do not see why George Eliot need have been much other than she was had Comte or his later period of thought never existed. She did, as we are told, sympathize with the Positivist sect. But of the ritual and the observances, the fanatical solemnity, and the pharisaical vanity of that sect, she certainly never in her printed works showed any signs. The religion of humanity she did profess, but she exhibits in her writings no tendency to accept the inhuman exclusiveness of any arbitrary dogmatic system of living. If the Positivists were her friends, we may be sure that freedom was a greater friend.

But still another influence remains to be mentioned here, the influence of the study of Spinoza upon George Eliot's life-theory. Of this influence we may be sure; for it has been announced since her death on good authority (in the *Pall Mall Gazette*) that a translation of the whole of the *Ethics* exists in manuscript, prepared by her own hand during this early period of apprenticeship. But just what the influence of Spinoza was it will be her biographer's duty to discover and tell us. Meanwhile there seems to be an inviting field open for philological investigation in the comparison of Spinoza's famous treatise on the passions and their control (*Ethics*, books III–V), with George Eliot's own numerous remarks on the same subject. In reading this part of the *Ethics* one may notice the great likeness of many of the observations in style and in matter to George Eliot. This likeness ought to be examined and tested. Spinoza is, after all, one of the fathers of religious philosophy. His direct influence upon the first religious philosopher that ever wrote great novels would be a problem of no little interest.

Leaving the study of the causes, let us go on to the effects. Not long before the publication of the *Scenes from Clerical Life*, we find in the *Westminster Review* an essay under the title, "Worldliness and Other-worldliness: the Poet Young." This essay is by George Eliot. The poet Young is here reviewed with a good deal of severity. The article has in it something of that dash and boldness in speaking of serious subjects that endeared the *Westminster* of those days to the radical mind, and to young radicals in particular. But the hand is the hand of Marian Evans. Nor do we fail to find in passages her own more moderate tone, such as she used when not in the editorial chair. Young is described in this essay as "a poet whose imagination is alternately fired by the 'Last Day,' and by a creation of peers, who fluctuates between rhapsodic applause of King George and rhapsodic applause of Jehovah." One of Young's "most striking characteristics is," says the essayist, "his radical insincerity as a poetic artist. No writer whose rhetoric was checked by the slightest truthful intention could have said:

> An eye of awe and wonder let me roll,
> And roll forever.

Furthermore, Young wants genuine emotion. "There is hardly a trace of human sympathy, of self-forgetfulness in the joy or sorrow of a fellow-being" in all of the *Night Thoughts* outside of passages in "Philander," "Narcissa," and "Lucia." As a consequence, Young's theory of ethics lacks the element of sympathy, and finds a basis for morality only in the belief in an immorality of rewards and punishments. And here the personal views of the essayist burst forth: "Fear of consequences is only one form of egoism which will hardly stand against half a dozen other forms of egoism bearing down upon it. . . . In proportion as a man would care less for the rights and the welfare of his fellow if he did not believe in a future life, in that proportion is he wanting in the genuine feelings of justice and benevolence, as the musician who would care less to play a sonata of Beethoven's finely in solitude than in public, where he was to be paid for it, is wanting in genuine enthusiasm for music." "Certain elements of virtue, . . . a delicate sense of our neighbor's rights, an active participation in the joys and sorrows of our fellowmen, a magnanimous acceptance of privation or suffering for ourselves when it is the condition of good to others — in a word, the extension and intensification of our sympathetic nature — we think it of some importance to contend that they have no more direct relation to the belief in a future state than the interchange of gases in the lungs has to the plurality of worlds. Nay, to us it is conceivable that in some minds the deep pathos lying in the thought of human mortality — that we are here for a little while and then vanish away, that this earthly life is all that is given to our beloved ones and to our many suffering fellowmen —lies nearer the fountains of moral emotion than the conception of extended existence." The thought of mortality then is favorable to virtue as well as the thought of immortality. "Do writers of sermons and religious novels prefer that men should be vicious in order that there may be a more evident political and social necessity for printed sermons and clerical fictions? Because learned gentlemen are theological, are we to have no more simple honesty and good-will? We can imagine that the proprietors of a patent water supply have a dread of common springs; but for our own part we think there cannot be too great a security against a lack of fresh water or of pure morality. To us it is matter of unmixed rejoicing that this latter necessary of healthful life is independent of theological ink, and that its evolution is insured by the interaction of human souls as certainly as the evolution of science or of art, with which indeed it is but a twin ray, melting into them with undefinable limits." The principal sources of our author's quarrel with Young are thus indicated. But yet more to our present purpose are her criticisms on his conception of religion. "Young has no conception of religion as anything else than egoism turned heavenward; and he does not merely imply this — he insists on it." "He never changes his level so as to see beyond the horizon of mere selfishness." And again: "He sees Virtue sitting on a mount serene, far above the mists and storms of earth. He sees Religion coming down from the skies, with this world in her left hand and the other world in her right. But we never find him dwelling on virtue or religion as it really exists — in the emotions of a man dressed in an ordinary coat, and seated by his fireside of an evening, with his hand resting on the head of his little daughter; in courageous effort for unselfish ends, in the internal triumph of justice and pity over personal resentment, in all the sublime self-renunciation and sweet charities which are found in the details of ordinary life." At the end of the essay Young is contrasted with Cowper, much to the advantage of the latter. "In Young we have the type of that deficient human sympathy, that impiety toward the present and the visible, which flies for its motives, its sanctities, and its religion to the remote, the vague, and the unknown. In Cowper we have the type of that genuine love which cherishes things in proportion to their nearness, and feels its reverence grow in proportion to the intimacy of its knowledge."

The transition in mood is but slight from the last words of this essay to the *Scenes from Clerical Life*. As one reads these one is impressed with the fact that George Eliot has, for the time, resolutely turned away her mind from the learning and speculation with which she is so familiar, and has determined to seek the essential elements of the higher life in the world of simple ignorance, doing penance, as it were, for too much philosophy by refusing at present to portray a character capable of abstract thought, or perhaps, rather seeking rest from the heated war of ideas in a refreshing bath in the secluded, slowly flowing river of commonplace human life. In the *Scenes*, artistic motives seem nevertheless to be struggling still with didactic motives, and the author stops too often to justify herself for thus leaving cultivated life behind her. The born story-teller — such a man as Chaucer, or William Morris, or Paul Heyse, or Turgenieff, or Heinrich von Kleist—never, unless in the absence of the Muse, is guilty of excusing himself for having chosen a given subject, any more than the popular ballad-maker of the Middle Ages thought of explaining why just this tale of all tales must over his lips. In fact, the great curse of George Eliot's art, from *Amos Barton* to *Daniel Deronda*, is her tendency to speak in her own name to the reader for the sake of explaining why she does thus and so. But, apart from their artistic faults, the *Scenes* are full of suggestive thoughts. "These commonplace people," she says (in an often quoted passage in *Amos Barton*, speaking of the mass of the English nation) — "many of them — bear a conscience, and have felt the sublime prompting to do the painful right; they have their unspoken sorrows and their sacred joys; their hearts have perhaps gone out toward their firstborn, and they have mourned over their irreclaimable dead. Nay, is there not a pathos in their very significance — in our comparison of their dim and narrow existence with the glorious possibilities of that human nature which they share?" In the minds of these men, then, we are to find the religious life in its essence exemplified. Here is simple human nature. A religious philosophy that would be universal must bear the test of finding whether these instances fall within the scope of its sounding universal premises.

In *Amos Barton* we meet with a few suggestions bearing directly on this point. A story intended by the pathos of its unromantic events to appeal directly to our sense of the interest of life as life cannot go very deeply into problems. But the author does not avoid giving hints of her doctrines. Thus, for example, after telling of Mrs. Barton's funeral, she speaks of our anguish, when we mourn over our own dead, at the thought that "we can never atone for the little reverence that we showed to that sacred human soul that lived so close to us, and was the divinest thing God had given us to know." What, then, the reader asks, are we to worship those that stand or that have stood nearest us, and is this to be our religion? This, the author seems to say, is the religion death teaches.

But one suspects all teachings that are founded on death alone. The emotions suggested by death, one might reply to George Eliot, are among the highest we know, and yet it is hard to draw any ethical conclusions from them. Quite apart from our beliefs or doubts about immortality, we say when a good man dies, "It is well, his work is nobly done"; and when a bad man dies, "It is well, the world is rid of him." If an old man dies, we say, "The debt of nature is paid, let us not mourn"; if a young maiden, we still say, "Death has saved this fair life from pain and decay, let us cease mourning." Sir Walter Raleigh, in the famous passage at the end of his history, calls death eloquent. One might well rejoin that death is rather the great sophist: argue as we will, he refutes us. He is an evil; but who would live always? a good; but who would forsake life? Death as the seem-

ing end of desire appears at once undesirable, and yet
perfectly satisfying; at once a sacred presence that sanc-
tifies whatever it touches, so that we naturally worship
the memory of the dead, and a horrible nightmare that
pursues the living, so that the free man becomes free
only when, as Spinoza said, he learns to think not at all
of death, but solely of life. What doctrine shall then be
founded on our contemplation of death? Death is the
infinite night, wherein, as the rough-voiced adage had it,
all cows are black. Let us disregard it, and ask our
teacher what she has to tell us about life. What shall we
worship in the world of the living?

In "Janet's Repentance," the third of the *Scenes*, we
are brought face to face with one of the problems that
have most interest for the mind of George Eliot. It is
the problem afterward treated in *Romola*. Suppose a
soul, capable of higher life, but shut out for years from
the thought of it, living in worldliness. Suppose a trouble
that arouses in this soul a sense of wrong, of loneliness,
of the desolation of the universe when there is no object
in it that seems worth our striving. How shall such a
soul become reconciled to life? How shall it attain religious earnestness, and strength, and peace? Janet, a
high-spirited, self-reliant girl, is persistently ill-treated
by her husband. At first she cannot bear to think that
their love should have all come to this. Then she takes
refuge in sullen defiance, broken by passionate out-
bursts. Now and then she upbraids her mother fiercely,
and without reason; but most of the time she tries to
keep silence. She never thinks of religious solace; her
one hope is that in some way her husband may come to
love her again. If he is jovial and good humored for a
day, she is happy. But such times are rare. At last she
falls into the habit of drinking secretly, to forget her

troubles. And so bad becomes worse, until a climax is reached in her husband's temper, and he turns her out of the house at midnight. She takes refuge with a neighbor. The next day her husband drinks enormously, drives alone, meets with a serious accident, and is brought home to his death-bed, raving in *delirium tremens*. Meanwhile, Janet has had time to review her life; her despair is complete; the world is dark, her conscience bad, her future inconceivable. At this point, the day of her husband's fatal drive, she is visited by the new evangelical parson, a hardworking, somewhat fanatical consumptive, who has the ascetic sincerity of a mediaeval saint. Remorse for a youthful crime had driven him into his present life; and his special task is the seeking out of great sinners and of despairing souls of all classes. Janet's husband had been this man's bitterest enemy, and she herself had always before scorned his very name. Now, at the first sight of him, at the first experience of his earnestness and kindness, she feels that here is a new influence. She soon pours out to him her whole heartful of misery and of longing: "I thought that God was cruel, I suppose it is wicked to think so. . . . I feel as if there must be goodness and right above us, but I can't see it; I can't trust in it. And I have gone on that way for years and years. . . . I shall always be doing wrong, and hating myself after; sinking lower and lower, and knowing that I am sinking. Oh, can you tell me of any way of getting strength? Have you ever known any one like me that got peace of mind and power to do right? Can you give me any comfort, any hope?" To answer to this appeal the parson gathers all his strength. He sees in this woman his own old despairing self. He speaks to her out of the fullness of an experience of torture. He uses the conventional terms of orthodoxy, to be sure; but we feel, as we read, that the force is not intended by the author to be in them. Janet accepts the message; but why? Not because of the essential might of the orthodox formula. The devil is not cast out in the name of any power, but by the force of direct present sympathy. Janet feels that here is another, with like nature, tried, tempted, fallen also, but enabled to rise by seeing the vast world of human life about him in which there is so much to be done, in which there is such a mass of suffering and sin, to which his life is but a drop, and for which, as he sees, he must work. "As long," he tells her, "as we live in rebellion against God, desiring to have our own will, seeking happiness in the things of this world, it is as if we shut ourselves up in a crowded, stifling room, where we breathe only poisoned air; but we have only to walk out under the infinite heavens, and we breathe the pure, free air that gives us health, and strength, and gladness. It is so with God's spirit. As soon as we submit ourselves to his will, as soon as we desire to be united to him, and made pure and holy, it is as if the walls had fallen down." This is language that men of a hundred nations and creeds might understand. Wherein lies its force? What is the religious idea at the bottom of it? Hear the author:

Blessed influence of one true loving human soul on another! Not calculable by algebra, not deducible by logic, but mysterious, effective, mighty as the hidden process by which the tiny seed is quickened. . . . Ideas are often poor ghosts. Our sun-filled eyes cannot discern them; they pass athwart us in thin vapor, and cannot make themselves felt. But sometimes they are made flesh. They breathe upon us with warm breath; they touch us with soft, responsive hands; they look at us with sad, sincere eyes, and speak to us in appealing tones; they are clothed in a living human soul, with all its conflicts, its faith, and its love. Then their presence is a power; then they shake us like a passion, and we are drawn after them with gentle compulsion, as flame is drawn to flame.

Religious knowledge and life come to us then, our author teaches, through the influence of individual souls, whose sympathy and counsel awaken us to a new sense of the value of life, and to a new earnestness to work henceforth not for self, but for the Other than self. This Other, as you see, is always at least negatively infinite; it takes in this philosophy the place of the supernatural. You know not its boundaries. This grand ocean of life stretches out before you without discovered shore. You are brought to the strand. Will you embark? To embark and to lose yourself is religion; to wait on the shore is moral starvation. Such seems to be our author's life-doctrine. The infinite is conceived as known only in this world of fellow-beings.

For Janet this new insight means acceptance, and so new life. Her dying husband is to be nursed, and then afterward her neighbors are to be helped. Her religion sustains her. What, then, in her own consciousness, is this religion? A sense of the value and beauty of life, a trust in the parson, a wish to do good, a looking out into the world with trust and resignation. All must be well, for are we not willingly at work? So lambs think, no doubt, as they look up from the tender grass they are cropping. And of such kind, as it seems, George Eliot conceives to be the state of the soul when raised to the plane of this higher life. There is an indefinite sense of worship arising from the depths of a peaceful mind that feels at home in the world, and that, while so feeling, contemplates life. Call this worship by what name you will.

But the process of the religious life is not yet fully described, for one of the hardest problems remains un-

touched. Given the awakened soul, a Janet after her
first conversation with the parson, a Romola when Savonarola has sent her back to her husband and has called
upon her to live for the Florentines even if she cannot
live for her own home, such a soul, as we have seen, is
largely under the influence of the person that has been
the awakener. But this person is only a man, whose
breath is in his nostrils. He may represent, but he is not
humanity. He will die, or worse than that, he will show
weakness or will betray some hidden sinful tendency.
What, then, is to be done for the poor soul that has de-
pended upon this mortal prop? Must the reclaimed fall
whenever the helper stumbles? This problem is more
fully developed in Romola. The heroine here is by nature enthusiastic, but by training a Neopagan, caring
for none of these things. Aroused when in great trouble
and despair to the value of the higher life through the
words of Savonarola, Romola leans spiritually upon
him, makes of him the human deity. What is the result?
It is brought bitterly home to her that her spiritual
father is not perfect, that he is selfish like other men, and
can on occasion, misled by ambition, do her and others
irreparable wrong. Thus the one support is taken away.
There is nothing worth the trouble of life. What is
Florence if its best man is such a man? Romola flees
into the wilderness, caring not what becomes of her.
Coming to the sea, she embarks alone, and the wind
bears her to another shore, where she finds a plague-
stricken village. The sight of suffering arouses the old
fervor. As George Eliot remarks in substance elsewhere,
in presence of pain you need no theories, you have but
to work, and with the work the old faith comes back.
The world needs me, and it is good to be needed. Such
seems Romola's thought; and so the faith in humanity,

the sense that life is significant, is made independent of the trust in the one master who first opened her eyes. He may not be what he seemed or aspired to be; but the light is still there.

The first teacher, the awakener, is therefore often necessary; but the awakened soul must learn to live without this personal presence, in the power of self-sustained enthusiasm. The very faults of the teacher are then seen in a new light, not as disheartening chasms in our way that cannot be overleaped, but as incitements to more earnest work. We are all weak, teachers as well as taught; so much the greater is the demand for unwearied exertion. The process thus indicated reminds one of the well-known Platonic myths in the *Phædrus* and the *Symposium*. The idea of the beautiful, says Plato, is the only one of the eternal ideas that has an earthly representative directly appealing to the senses. At the sight of a beautiful being the soul is awakened from the dreamy life of nature, and a longing for the old home in the heavens is aroused. This longing is human love. Followed upward, love leads to the knowledge of the eternal, of which itself is the beginning. But because love is divine, it does not follow that the love of the one earthly object is enough. No; the object is nothing of itself. As a thing of sense it may not with safety be pursued or possessed. Only as pointing the soul to the eternal, only as arousing us to look beyond itself and to forget what is transient in it and in everything else, is the beloved object of true worth. Just so now in George Eliot the knowledge of the enduring and significant in life comes to us in the words and deeds of perhaps a single human teacher. But we must learn to outgrow the direct influence of the teacher, as Janet outgrows the need of her pastor, as Romola outgrows Savonarola, as

Deronda learns to do without the prophetic voice of Mordecai, or as Gwendolen hopes to do without the personal magnetism of Deronda. We must even learn, as Maggie learns, in *The Mill on the Floss*, to endure when everything forsakes us, and when there is no thought left but that we once did our duty and destroyed our earthly happiness. From the transient we must come to the knowledge of the abiding; from trusting in a teacher we must come to trust in the worth of the higher life. From revering the man we must come to revere the infinity of consciousness whereof he was a representative.

So much, then, for a brief account of the religious consciousness as a process. We come next to speak of this same consciousness as a present fact in the minds of all earnest men and women, whether or no their life has risen or can rise to a very high conscious plane. Silas Marner, the weaver, crushed by early disappointment, loses all faith, almost forgets religion, and becomes a miser. His gold is stolen, but the child is found on his hearth, the little girl whose mother had been frozen in the snow. In bringing up this child the weaver learns to live again; she means for him his religion. Now again, with time, he becomes known to his fellowmen and awakened to the memory of what he was. Life as a problem rises before his unlearned mind, and with it the old puzzles of destiny. Why was it that I was thus tried and tortured? What did Providence, if there is any, mean with me? Hear, then, the weaver reasoning high with Dolly Winthrop, a village matron whose religion is a matter of faith only, and sometimes of wavering faith, too. "It al'ays," she says, "comes into my head when I am sorry for folks, and feel as I can't do a power to help 'em, not if I was to get up i' the middle o' the night — it comes into my head as Them above has got a deal tend'rer

heart nor what I've got — for I can't be any better nor
Them as made me; and if anything looks hard to me, it's
because there's things I don't know on; and for the
matter o' that, there may be plenty o' things I don't
know on, for it's little as I know — that it is. And so,
while I was thinking o' that, you come into my mind,
Master Marner, and it all came pouring in; if *I* felt i' my
inside what was the right and just thing by you, isn't
there Them as was at the making on us and knows better and has a better will? And that's all as ever I can be
sure on, and everything else is a big puzzle to me when I
think on it. For there was the fever come and took off
them as were full-growed, and left the helpless children,
and there's the breaking o' limbs. . . . Eh, there's
trouble i' this world, and there's things as we can niver
make out the rights on. And all as we've got to do is to
trusten, Master Marner — to do the right thing as fur
as we know, and to trusten. For if us as knows so little
can see a bit o' good and rights, we may be sure as
there's a good and rights bigger nor what we can know
— I feel it i' my own inside as it must be so. And if you
could but ha' gone on trustening, Master Marner, you
wouldn't ha' run away from your fellow-creatures, and
been so lone."

"You're i' the right," is Marner's answer. "There's
good i' this world — I've a feeling o' that now; and it
makes a man feel as there's a good more nor he can see,
i' spite o' the trouble and the wickedness. The drawing
o' the lots is dark: but the child was sent to me: there's
dealings with us — there's dealings." Here then, is the
elementary philosophy of religion, the knowledge that
in all the obscurity and mystery of the universe the confidence in the supreme value of duty and of love remains
to us. Dolly Winthrop in working for the suffering, Silas

Marner in caressing the little girl's golden hair, have they not both of them found a crude elementary religion, wherein there is nothing of sentimentality, but merely a plain, matter-of-fact, everyday recognition of the true object of life? One's mind is borne by the strange contrast of subjects to the words of Ernst Renan, in his London lecture on Marcus Aurelius: "The religion of Marcus Aurelius is the absolute religion, that which results from the simple fact of a high moral consciousness brought face to face with the universe. The religion is of no race, nor of any country. No revolution, no change, no discovery will be able to change it." Is not this, one asks, the religion of Dolly Winthrop as well as of the Roman emperor?

But we cannot wait to give more examples. I have tried to show that George Eliot's effort to express the religious consciousness in terms of natural, not of supernatural, facts is, in part, a sequence from the philosophical movement of her age, the movement that began with Lessing and is not yet ended. But our investigation has led us to see certain peculiarities of George Eliot's own mind and method in viewing these things. She was an appreciative student of many systems, but she let none of them rule her. She heard what they had to say, and then she went to actual human life to see whether the theory held good. In studying the life the theory was not permitted to interfere; unless, to be sure, we must make exception of the unhealthy predominance of analysis, of reflection, and of preconceived opinion over emotion and art in *Daniel Deronda*, or in some of those insufferable dissections of human weakness that fill the first part of *Theophrastus Such*. On the whole, we must see throughout in George Eliot's works an intense earnestness, and a conscientious effort to comprehend the real-ities of the human heart. She feels what she tells, and to her the religious consciousness whereof she writes is a fact of her own heart. The sermons of Dinah in *Adam Bede* were, as she said in a private letter published since her death, written in hot tears, were the outcome of personal experience, and not, as some have supposed, merely a cold study from observation. Thus in her writings the best power of analytic vision is joined with depth of emotion. She is, then, the best possible witness to her own doctrines. She has seen and felt what she describes as the true religious life. When Deronda says to Gwendolen, "The refuge you are needing from personal trouble is the higher, the religious life, which holds an enthusiasm for something more than our own appetites and vanities," he speaks less from his own experience (for he has not yet had the interviews with Mordecai) than from the author's experience.

George Eliot never finished an abstract statement of doctrine, partly because she was at her best an artist, not a philosophic systematizer, and partly because she was too intensely skeptical to accept easily any one formula. In *Theophrastus* there is a chapter of conversation with an evolution philosopher on the probable practical consequences of indefinite progress, which shows how critical our author remained, to the very last, of even the most familiar doctrines of the school with which she was affiliated. And this skeptical element is one of the most significant features in her works. Nothing has done more harm in the history of religion than the dead formula, held to notwithstanding its failure as an expression of life. And even the successful formula, the true expression of life, is dangerous as soon as we try to substitute it for the life, or to imagine that salvation can come through preaching alone. The destruction of the letter is the great purpose of skepticism. The skeptical spirit is the Mephistopheles of the religious consciousness, the companion that this Faust "no more can do without." And so we welcome the spirit that could look with the Germans for the abiding element in religious life, without cramping poetical freedom from the very beginning by an acceptance of some cut-and-dried system. If ever we have a religious philosophy, the poets on the one hand, the merciless skeptics on the other, will have helped the speculator at every step in his search for a theory. Without them speculation is a tale told by an idiot, full of sound and fury, yet signifying nothing. George Eliot is at once speculative, skeptical, and poetic. Whatever she has done best, depends upon the successful union of these three faculties. When the speculative tendency triumphs she becomes mystical and wearisome; when the skeptical triumphs she becomes wearisome and excessively analytic; while the poetical tendency may be said never, in her writings, to free itself, for more than a moment at a time, from the influence of the other tendencies. And so, the constant presence of self-criticism makes us more confident of whatever we find in our author in the way of positive result.

And now, to leave the work of simple exposition, and to estimate our author's accomplishment in the direction of an understanding of religion, what is the one fact of human nature that is brought into prominence in all these particular instances? It is, as we may make sure upon reflection, the fact of the self-surrendering, of the submissive moment in the action of free human beings when they are brought face to face with the world of life. Man, especially the higher man, is not even by original nature altogether selfish. Before all training he is prone to submission whenever he meets another being whom he regards as higher, better, more admirable than himself. Training makes definite and potent this original tendency. The soul into which has come the wealth of knowledge that springs from feeling ourselves to be but atoms in a great stream of life, is aroused to an essentially new existence. The main-spring of such a nature is conscious submission to the demands of the world of sentient existence. This motive needs no supernatural faith, but may express itself in the language of a hundred faiths. The spirit involved in it is neither optimism nor pessimism, but simply earnestness, determination to make the world significant. It is a fact, we see, that such consciousness is, and can be. Call this spirit what you will. A sound religious philosophy, such as Lessing dreamed of in *Nathan*, such as our century has been struggling to attain, will, we need not doubt, see in this spirit the essential element of that greatest of higher human agencies, Religion.

NATURAL RIGHTS AND SPINOZA'S ESSAY ON LIBERTY[1]

[1880]

IT is known that one of the earliest statements of the doctrines of religious and political toleration is to be found in the *Tractatus Theologico-Politicus* of the great Jewish thinker Spinoza. Spinoza's story has often been told, and the most important part of his thought is not contained in the Tractate. Yet we shall doubtless find a sufficient reward for our labor if we devote a little time to a study of this work in its connection with the author's life and time. Originality in statement we cannot seek. The material facts are well known, and into the abstruse questions of the Spinoza philologists we shall not try to enter.

The seventeenth century is noted in the history of political and moral science as the age when a number of efforts were made, by men of no small ability, to construct philosophical theories of law and ethics on a purely rational basis, without reference to theology. The speculative idea or principle on which these theories were founded was that of the so-called "Law of Nature." The purpose of the authors was to determine the universal and eternal elements in human institutions by means of an analysis of man's character and place in the world. "Nature," as was assumed, has made man with certain powers, desires, rights and duties. By introspection, or by some general study of human destiny, these "natural" characteristics may be discovered and

[1] Condensation of a lecture still extant on "Spinoza's Theory of Religious Liberty in the State," read before the Historico-Political Club, March 1, 1878.

formulated. Knowing these, we may possibly deduce with mathematical accuracy all the particular rules and conventions about rights and duties in so far as these rules are of enduring worth for humanity. The result of our investigation would be a complete code of "natural" polity, embracing the features that ought to be found in every organized society, and so laying down the law to the law-givers themselves.

This doctrine of "Natural Law" is now out of favor. Nevertheless many elements of it are still retained in our modern social doctrines and speculations. Its fault lay in the arbitrary and subjective character of its method. One wishes to find out the Law of Nature. What then is Nature? Do we mean by natural duties or rights or sentiments those that are in fact common to all men? Then our list will be limited to certain ethically unimportant qualities that do indeed distinguish men from beasts, but do not serve as guides to proper action. It is natural for all men to eat, but what is it natural for them to eat? As a fact some eat oil and tallow, others fruits and worms, and others bread and beef. Nature is here no guide unless we analyze her data very carefully. But do we mean by Nature those human tendencies only that are praiseworthy or generally useful? Then what is our criterion of praiseworthiness? Is this criterion to be found by a study of what men everywhere regard as good? Then we shall be as we were before, swamped in a stormy sea of conflicting traditions. Or are we to question our own minds for some intuitive test of excellence? Then in fact, our minds will probably advise us in strict accordance with just the traditions in which we happen to have been brought up.

But these objections to the method of analysis as the seventeenth century philosophers practised it, do not

make their work of any less historical importance. Their
theories were an important step forward. As speculative
masterpieces they will always remain of interest. As
expressing the revolt against ecclesiastical tradition
they have made possible all that has been done in political science since their day. And, for the rest, that
word Nature has in our time by no means lost its power.
The theory of evolution seems to give it new life and
meaning. At all events the word suggests a very ancient
puzzle. The Greeks first brought it into prominence,
and they made the natural an ideal for conduct. Aristotle elevated the term Nature to a well defined place in
speculation; and the Stoics made Nature their god. The
Neoplatonic philosophy, however, brought the natural
into disrepute, and Medieval Christianity condemned
it outright as a rival of the divine. With the Renascence
the old concept revived; and in view of its fortunes ever
since we might well call the idea of Nature the "Wandering Jew" of Philosophy. Nobody knows precisely
what it means; yet few thinkers can avoid it altogether.
It is old, hoary, unhappy. The thinker has not yet
arisen who can solve the problems it suggests; nor the
day of judgment come when the wanderer can be sent
to rest.

It may help us in understanding Spinoza's statement
of the doctrine of natural right in its application to the
questions of liberty and toleration, if we first summarize
the doctrine upon the same point set forth by Hobbes,
in the *Leviathan*, a work with which Spinoza may possibly have been acquainted. The contrast between the
two views will appear further on.

For Hobbes, natural law has its basis in the fact of the
complete and undiluted selfishness of the natural man.
Because of this complete selfishness of human beings,

the state of nature is one of perpetual war. For men's selfish interests are always apt to interfere with one another. Government being thus not an immediate result of the natural condition, must be the result of a social contract, whereby men have agreed to restrict their individual liberty for the sake of avoiding the perpetual warfare, and of thus better satisfying their own selfishness. In the original condition all were at war with all. If one alone grew weary and stopped, the others would kill him. You could not in such a case hope to correct men's selfishness; for to try to change men would be to make a new appeal to their selfishness. The only way out would be a general agreement to submit the wills of all to the will of one sovereign. This once done, the business of the sovereign will be the enforcing of such laws as shall in the nature of things tend to check the outbreak of disorder and injustice. All other members of society must obey the sovereign. They will obey because to resist would be to meet destruction. And such resistance would mean destruction because the resistance will be either unsuccessful, or successful. And in the first case punishment follows; while, in the second case, with the overthrow of the sovereign there would be a general return to the state of nature and the most destructive of all tyrannies, the universal warfare, would begin again. The sovereign may be the popular majority, or the majority in a legislative body, or a single man. The last mentioned way is the best, thinks Hobbes, because a single man best knows his own will, and takes the most immediate selfish interest in the success of his own government. The great danger is that we may have a weak or irresolute government; and legislative bodies are subject to bribery and instability. The sovereign will indeed be selfish, but, if a single per-

294 NATURAL RIGHTS AND

son, his selfishness will be enlisted in favor of society; since the welfare of the state is the glory of its ruler. The sovereign's authority must be in all cases supreme and final. And thus through absolutism we may escape some of the calamities of selfishness.

The doctrine of Hobbes is so lucidly and cogently stated, and so plausibly deduced from first principles, that in reading the *Leviathan* we are strongly tempted to overlook the author's gloomy and severe view of human nature while enjoying the sober beauty and architectural elegance of his reasoning; insomuch that we at times almost wish this splendid myth more like the reality. For if it were the truth, political science would be comparable in exactness to mathematics. But in fact the view is as one-sided as the reasoning is rigid; while the idea of the world embodied in it is as dispiriting, not to say terrible, as the presentation is noble. Hobbes saw only one aspect of human nature.

It is Spinoza who sees the other aspect. But before speaking especially of the *Tractatus*, let us glance hastily at the life and character of the author. Spinoza was by early training neither philosopher nor student of politics, but a Hebrew scholar. In Rabbinical literature he found, perhaps, the most important of the suggestions that led him finally to the composition of the *Tractatus*.[1] Certain it is that the theological views set forth in this work belong to the first period of his independent

[1] In a series of monographs Joel, a specialist in Rabbinical literature, has tried to show that in very many of his philosophic views, and especially in the theological parts of the *Tractatus Theolog. Pol.*, Spinoza is a pretty close follower of the rationalistic philosophers among the Jews, *e. g.*, Maimonides and Gersonides. See the summary of Joel's views in H. Ginsberg's introduction to his edition of the *Tractatus*. But Joel has been contradicted.

thought, and that they are the ones that led to his expulsion from the synagogue. But perhaps study of the philosophic commentators among his own people would have made him only a speculative rationalist; it was his life after he was cut off from Israel that made him the author of a more practical work on religious toleration and political freedom. For after his own people had declared him accursed (as they did formally in the year 1656 when he was twenty-four years of age) Spinoza lived much alone, always a keen observer of what went on in the world about him, always a good patriot and a great lover of mankind. One thing he saw during this unprejudiced study of the world, viz., that one of the saddest of things is the strife of religious sects. As he himself explains in the preface to the *Tractatus Theologico-Politicus*, he notices that the fundamental principles of virtue, such as charity and piety, were taught by all sects alike, and violated by all in their treatment of one another. And the cause for this singular agreement in diversity Spinoza found to be the tendency of the sects to lay stress not upon the really fundamental virtues, but upon certain peculiar doctrines that each claimed to have received from some obscure and supernatural source. This tendency resulted in the fashion of each sect to find in the Scriptures just what pleased itself, and to accuse everyone else of spiritual blindness for not finding the same thing. Reflecting upon this matter, Spinoza was led to think that a strife so dangerous to the public welfare might be rendered less violent if people could be brought to see, first that Scripture ought not to be interpreted in the ordinary manner of the sects, and then that no sect ought to be allowed to intrude its peculiar creed, as furnishing any rule for law-givers, into the affairs of government. In consequence of these considerations, Spinoza projected a treatise in two parts, whereof the first should discuss the true nature of religion in its relation to morality, while the second should treat of the proper behavior of the state towards the various religious sects and towards individual expressions of faith. The outcome of the plan was the *Tractatus Theologico-Politicus*. The first or theological part was the one that was based no doubt very largely upon our philosopher's early Rabbinical studies. For the second part he was indebted to his later study of political philosophy,[1] in which he was at least somewhat influenced by the reading of Hobbes.

In elegance of expression the clear-witted and learned Englishman far surpasses the profound and, perhaps, slightly uncouth Hebrew. But in insight the political parts of the *Tractatus Theologico-Politicus*, brief as they are, outweigh the ingenious constructions of even the *Leviathan*. To Spinoza as to Hobbes, man is by nature a selfish animal. In Spinoza's theory, as in the other, each being has an original right to all he can get. But while Hobbes has only the way of absolutism, whereby to escape from this labyrinth of individual desires, Spinoza finds that individual sacrifice is necessary and natural, not merely in case of the supreme act of the social contract, but in the whole conduct of life. For Spinoza selfishness is only the starting point. Because of the continual inner conflict of the selfish desires the wise man ultimately seeks to rise above desire and to be

[1] Hobbes' *Leviathan* could not have been read by Spinoza, so say the scholars, before its appearance in Latin at Amsterdam in 1668 not long before the first publication of the Tractate. Cf. Ginsberg's Introduction to the *Trac. Theol.-Polit.* Yet one need not suppose Spinoza to have been wholly dependent upon Hobbes for his knowledge of political philosophy.

free from self in the contemplation of enduring truth. Such is the doctrine of the *Ethics*, and of the *Tractatus de Deo*. On its political side this doctrine becomes one of a conservative republicanism; a belief that every man's welfare is best helped by granting the greatest possible freedom of development to his neighbor, and that a certain degree of unselfishness is not only useful but natural to men. With Hobbes the State is the last desperate resort of war-weary savages; with Spinoza it is the expression of the higher consciousness of mankind. The truly useful State is therefore for Spinoza the one whose laws are founded on mutual charity, freedom and justice. If every man begins by desiring first of all his own preservation, every man must come in the end to desire his neighbor's preservation quite as much as his own.

As to the forms and duties of government, Spinoza holds with Hobbes that the first requisite is stability; but unlike Hobbes he prefers the republican form, since in it is best expressed and secured that mutual interest of man in man which, according to his view, government is chiefly to express. Hobbes had objected to the republican form of government that the people will quarrel, and that they will be at the mercy of demagogues. Spinoza finds that the people will know best what satisfies them, and that the majority will be trained into such respect for the minority as not to make immoderate laws. Like Hobbes again, however, Spinoza holds that revolutions are injurious; and that the form of the government should not be changed, as had been attempted in the English Rebellion. But Hobbes gave as a reason the necessary return to a state of nature which would result from revolution in the commonwealth. Spinoza appeals merely to the fact that men's habits are not easily changed; and regards the form of government as a habit of the public mind.

In particular, Hobbes had held that the sovereign can make the most arbitrary decisions as to special laws, religion and the forms of social life. Spinoza maintains that a government which does not recognize the wishes of the public it governs is in the highest degree dangerous, both to its own interests and to the general peace. It must use force indeed, but only in cases where this force can be employed in the name of the mass of the people. Theoretically, the government is the fountain of all law, and can, therefore, change every law at pleasure. Practically it is to make and change laws only for the promotion of peace and harmony. Theoretically it has complete right over the person and property of the subject; but practically it has not a particle of control over the thoughts of the subject, and so must respect these thoughts. For if the subjects do not think favorably of the government, the government will not long exist to maintain its rights, theoretical or practical. In a single sentence the sum of the whole is: It is not the ultimate purpose of government to rule, nor to put men under the restraint of fear, nor to subject them to external authority; but on the contrary to free everyone from fear, and to secure him his life, his natural right to existence, and that apart from any hurt to himself or to another. This is the sum of the whole, I say, as given by Spinoza himself, and there is something of a truly fascinating boldness in the way he utters his final paradox, *finem reipublicae non esse dominari*. Why, what, we ask then, may be the use of sovereignty if not to hold the mastery over the subject? What indeed, retorts Spinoza, unless to give the subject liberty?

Such are the outlines of Spinoza's theory of political

liberty. How he applies these principles to the case of religion we cannot expound at length, because the theological discussions of the *Tractatus* are beyond our present scope. It is enough to say that Spinoza tries to show that there is in Scripture only this element of authoritative and divine doctrine, *viz.*, the teaching that there is a power rewarding in some way virtue, and punishing in some way vice. Any sect recognizing these doctrines is to be tolerated, and must in turn tolerate others. And in consequence the State ought never to restrict the liberty of the subject to think about all religious questions whatever he chooses, and to say what he thinks.

To sum up, Spinoza's *Tractate* is an example of the highest results that could be reached in political philosophy by those who based their theories on the abstract assumptions about Nature and Right that were current in the seventeenth century. In his views about toleration, liberty, and the functions of government, he anticipates ideas now often regarded as axiomatic, but then so far ahead of the times that even in the free Dutch Republic the book was condemned by authority, while its author did not during his life time dare to undertake or to permit a translation of it into the vulgar tongue. And the theological speculations of the work anticipate much of the later efforts of scholars to bring about an historical understanding of the Hebrew Literature. On the whole, neither the great author himself, nor this the most immediately practical of his books ought in our studies to be neglected.

THE DECAY OF EARNESTNESS[1]

[1881]

EVERY animal, when not frightened, shows in its
own way a certain quiet self-complacency, a confidence in the supreme worth of its individual
existence, an exalted egotism, which is often not a little
amusing if we reflect on the shortness, the insignificance,
and the misery of most creatures' lives. This animal
self-complacency characterizes, also, as we know, all
naturally-minded men. We know, too, that most men
are nearly as much in error as the beasts, in the degree
of importance that they attach to their lives. But what
I have just now most in mind is that the same kind of
blunder is frequently found in the judgment that any
one age passes upon itself and its own work. Every
active period of history thinks its activity of prodigious
importance, and its advance beyond its predecessors
very admirable. So the eighteenth century thought that
the English poetry of past times had been far surpassed
in form and in matter by the poetry of the age of Dryden
and of Pope. Long since the blindness of the eighteenth
century upon this point has been fully exposed. The
Neoplatonic philosophy, the Crusades, the First French
Empire, are familiar instances from the multitudes of
cases where men utterly failed to perform the permanent work which they were very earnestly trying to do,
and where they were, at most, doing for the world that
which they least of all wished or expected to do. Like
individuals, then, whole eras of history go by, sublimely
confident in their own significance, yet often unable to

[1] There exists among the author's MSS. a revised and enlarged version of this essay, but in unfinished form. — *Ed.*

make their claims even interesting in the sight of posterity.

The same lesson may be drawn both here and in the case of individuals. The man is vain; so is the age. The man ought to correct his vanity first by negative criticism; so ought the time. But the disillusioning process is a cruel one in both cases. It is hard for the man to bear the thought that, perhaps, after all, he is a useless enthusiast. So it is hard for an age to bear the thought that its dearest worship may be only idolatry, and its best work only a fighting of shadows. But for both the lesson is the same. Let them find some higher aim than this merely natural one of self-satisfaction. Let their work be done, not that it may seem grand to them alone, but so that it must have an element of grandeur in it, whatever be the success of its particular purposes. Grandeur does not depend upon success alone, nor need illusions always be devoid of a higher truth. The problem is to find out what is the right spirit, and to work in that. If the matter of the work is bad, that must perish, but the spirit need not.

Now, in our age we are especially engaged upon certain problems of thought. We discuss the origin of the present forms of things in the physical and in the moral universe. Evolution is our watchword; "everything grew," is the interpretation. Our method of inquiry is the historical. We want to see how, out of certain simple elements, the most complex structures about us were built up. Now, in the enormous thought-activity thus involved, two things especially strike one who pauses to watch. The first is, that in studying Evolution men have come to neglect other important matters that used to be a good deal talked about. The true end of life, the nature and grounds of human certitude, the problems of Goethe's *Faust* and of Kant's *Critique* — these disappear from the view of many representative men. The age finds room to talk about these things, but not to enter upon them with a whole-souled enthusiasm. Yet these are eternally valuable matters of thought. The age for which they are not in the very front rank of problems is a one-sided age, destined to be severely criticized within a century. The other fact that strikes us in this age is that the result of our one-sidedness is an unhappy division, productive of no little misery, between the demands of modern thought and the demands of the whole indivisible nature of man. The ethical finds not enough room in the philosophy of the time. The world is studied, but not the active human will, without whose interference the world is wholly void of human significance. The matter of thinking overwhelms us; we forget to study the form, and so we accept, with a blank wonder, the results of our thinking as if they were self-existent entities that had walked into our souls of themselves. For example, we make molecules by reasoning about facts of sensation, and by grouping these facts in the simplest and easiest fashion possible; then we fall into a fear lest the molecules have, after all, made us, and we write countless volumes on a stupid theme called materialism. This unreflective fashion of regarding the products of our thought as the conditions and source of our thought, is largely responsible for the strife between the ethical and the scientific tendencies of the time. The scientific tendency stops in one direction at a certain point, content with having made a theory of evolution, and fearing, or, at any rate, neglecting, any further analysis of fundamental ideas. The ethical tendency, on the other hand, rests on a rooted feeling that, after all, conscious life is of more worth than anything else in the universe. But this is, nowadays, commonly a mere feeling, which, finding nothing to justify it in current scientific opinion, becomes morose, and results in books against science. The books are wrong, but the feeling, when not morose, is right. The world is of importance only because of the conscious life in it, and the Evolution theory is one-sided because of the subordinate place it gives to consciousness. But the cure is not in writing books against science, but solely in such a broad philosophy as shall correct the narrowness of the day, and bring back to the first rank of interest once more the problems of Goethe's *Faust* and of Kant's *Critique*. We want not less talk about evolution, but more study of human life and destiny, of the nature of men's thought, and the true goal of men's actions. Send us the thinker that can show us just what in life is most worthy of our toil, just what makes men's destiny more than poor and comic, just what is the ideal that we ought to serve; let such a thinker point out to us plainly that ideal, and then say, in a voice that we must hear, "Work, work for that; it is the highest" — then such a thinker will have saved our age from one-sidedness, and have given it eternal significance. Now, to talk about those problems of thought which concern the destiny, the significance, and the conduct of human life, is to talk about what I have termed "the ethical aspect of thought." Some study we must give to these things if we are not to remain, once for all, hopelessly one-sided.

In looking for the view of the world which shall restore unity to our divided age, we must first not forget the fact that very lately all these now neglected matters have been much talked about. It is the theory of Evolution that, with its magnificent triumphs, its wonderful ingenuity and insight, has put them out of sight. Only within twenty years has there been a general inattention to the study of the purposes and the hopes of human life — a study that, embodied in German Idealism, or in American Transcendentalism, in Goethe, in Schiller, in Fichte, in Wordsworth, in Shelley, in Carlyle, in Emerson, had been filling men's thoughts since the outset of the great Revolution. But since the end of the period referred to our knowledge of the origin of the forms of life has driven from popular thought the matters of the worth and of the conduct of life, so that one might grow up nowadays well taught in the learning of the age, and when asked, "Hast thou as yet received into thy heart any Ideal?" might respond very truthfully, "I have not heard so much as whether there be any Ideal."

Yet, I repeat, the fault in our time is negative rather than positive. We have to enlarge, not to condemn. Evolution is a great truth, but it is not all truth. We need more, not less, of science. We need a more thorough-going, a more searching — yes, a more critical and skeptical — thought than any now current. For current thought is, in fact, naïf and dogmatic, accepting without criticism a whole army of ideas because they happen to be useful as bases for scientific work. We need, then, in the interests of higher thought, an addition to our present philosophy — an addition that makes use of the neglected thought of the last three generations. But as preliminary to all this, it becomes us to inquire: Why was modern thought so suddenly turned from the contemplation of the ethical aspect of reality to this present absorbing study of the material side of the world? How came we to break with Transcendentalism, and to begin this search after the laws of the redistribution of matter and of force? To this question I want to devote the rest of the present study; for just here is the whole problem in a nut shell. Transcendentalism, the distinctly ethical thought-movement of the century, failed to keep a strong hold on the life of the century. Why? In the answer to this question lies at once the relative justification, and at the same time the understanding, of the incompleteness of our present mode of thinking.

By Transcendentalism, I mean a movement that began in Germany in the last thirty years of the eighteenth century, and that afterward spread, in one form or another, all over Europe, and even into our own country — a movement that answered in the moral and mental world to the French Revolution in the political world. Everywhere this movement expressed, through a multitude of forms, a single great idea: the idea that in the free growth and expression of the highest and strongest emotions of the civilized man might be found the true solution of the problem of life. Herein was embodied a reaction against the characteristic notions of the eighteenth century. In the conventional, in submission to the external forms of government, religion, and society, joined with a total indifference to the spiritual, and with a general tendency to free but shallow speculation, the average popular thought of the last century had sought to attain repose, rather than perfection. The great thinkers rose far above this level; but, on the whole, we look to the age of the rationalists rather for ingenuity than for profundity, rather for good sense than for grand ideas. The prophetic, the emotional, the sublime, are absent from the typical eighteenth century mind-life. Instead, we find cultivation, criticism, skepticism, and at times, as a sort of relief, a mild sentimentality. The Transcendental movement expressed a rebound from this state of things. With the so-called

Storm and Stress Period of German literature the protest against conventionality and in favor of a higher life
began. Love, enthusiasm, devotion, the affection for
humanity, the search after the ideal, the faith in a spiritual life — these became objects of the first interest.
A grand new era of history seemed opening. Men felt
themselves on the verge of great discoveries. The highest hopes were formed. A movement was begun that
lasted through three generations, and far into a fourth.
It was, to be sure, in nature a young men's movement;
but as the men of one generation lost their early enthusiasm, others arose to follow in their footsteps — blun-
deringly, perhaps, but earnestly. When Goethe had
outgrown his youthful extravagances, behold there were
the young Romanticists to undertake the old work once
more. When they crystallized with time, and lost hold
on the German national life, there came Heine and the
Young Germany to pursue with new vigor the old path.
In England, Wordsworth grows very sober with age,
when there come Byron and Shelley; Coleridge fails, and
Carlyle is sent; Shelley and Bryon pass away, but Tennyson arises. And with us in America Emerson and his
helpers renew the spirit of a half century before their
time. This movement now seems a thing of the past.
There is no Emerson among the younger men, no Tennyson among the new school of poets, no Heine in Germany
— much less, then, a Fichte or a Schiller. Not merely is
genius lacking, but the general public interest, the soil
from which a genius draws nourishment, is unfavorable.
The literary taste of the age is represented by George
Eliot's later novels, where everything is made subordinate to analysis, by the poetry of several skillful masters
of melody, by the cold critical work of the authors of the
series on "English Men of Letters." Men of wonderful

power there are among our writers — men like William
Morris in poetry, or Matthew Arnold in both criticism
and poetry; but their work is chiefly esoteric, appealing
to a limited class. Widely popular writers we have upon
many subjects; but they are either great men of abstract
thought, like Spencer and Huxley; or else, alas! mere
superficial scribblers like Mr. Mallock, or rhetoricians
like Rev. Joseph Cook. The moral leader, the seer, the
man to awaken deep interest in human life as human life,
no longer belongs to the active soldiers of the army of
today; and, what is worse, the public mind no longer in-
quires after such a leader. There must surely be a cause
for this state of public sentiment. Neglect of such vital
questions must have sprung from some error in their
treatment. Let us look in history for that error.

The Storm and Stress Period in Germany began with
the simplest and most unaffected desire possible to get
back from conventionality and from shallow thought to
the purity and richness of natural emotion. There was
at first no set philosophy or creed about the universe
common to those engaged in the movement. The young
poets worshipped genius, and desired to feel intensely
and to express emotion worthily. To this end they dis-
carded the traditions as to form which they found embodied in French poetry and in learned textbooks.
Lessing had furnished them critical authority. He had
shown the need of appealing to Nature for instruction,
both in the matter and in the manner of poetry. Popular
ballads suggested to some of the young school their
models. Their own overflowing hearts, their warm, ideal
friendships with one another, their passion for freedom,
their full personal experiences, gave them material. Together they broke down conventions, and opened a new
era in literary life, as the French Revolution, twenty

years later, did in national life. Every one knows that Goethe's famous *Werther* is the result of this time of ferment. Now, if one reads *Werther* attentively, and with an effort (for it needs an effort) to sympathize with the mood that produced and enjoyed it, one will see in it the characteristic idea that the aim of life is to have as remarkable and exalted emotional experiences as possible, and those of a purely personal character; that is, not the emotion that men feel in common when they engage in great causes, not the devotion to sublime impersonal objects, not surrender to unworldly ideals, but simply the overwhelming sense of the magnitude and worth of one's own loves and longings, of one's own precious soul-experiences — this, and not the other, is to be sought. Werther cannot resist the fate that drives him to load his heart down with emotion until it breaks. He feels how far asunder from the rest of mankind all this drives him. But he insists upon despising mankind, and upon reveling in the dangerous wealth of his inspiration. Now surely such a state of mind as this must injure men if they remain long in it. Men need work in life, and so long as they undertake to dig into their own bowels for the wonderful inner experiences that they may find by digging, so long must their lives be bad dreams. The purpose of these young men was the highest, but only those of them who, following this purpose, passed far beyond the simplicity of their youth, did work of lasting merit. The others stayed in a state of passionate formlessness, or died early. The result of remaining long in this region, where nothing was of worth but a violent emotion or an incredible deed, one sees in such a man as Klinger, who lived long enough to reap what he had sown, but did not progress sufficiently to succeed in sowing anything but the wind. I remember once spending an idle hour on one of his later romances, written years after the time of Storm and Stress had passed by, which well expresses the state of mind, the sort of *katzenjammer* resulting from a long life of literary dissipation. It is Klinger's *Faustus* — the same subject as Goethe's masterpiece, but how differently treated! Faustus is a man desperately anxious to act. He wants to reform the world, to be sure, but that only by the way. His main object is to satisfy a vague, restless craving for tremendous excitement. The contract with the devil once made, he plunges into a course of reckless adventure. Where he undertakes to do good he only makes bad worse. Admirable about him is merely the magnitude of his projects, the vigor of his actions, the desperate courage wherewith he defies the universe. Brought to hell at last, he ends his career by cursing all things that are with such fearless and shocking plainness of speech that the devils themselves are horrified. Satan has to invent a new place of torment for him. He is banished, if I remember rightly, into horrible darkness, where he is to pass eternity perfectly alone. Thus terribly the poet expresses the despair in which ends for him, as for all, this self-adoration of the man whose highest object is violent emotional experiences, enjoyed merely because they are his own, not because by having them one serves the Ideal. As a mere beginning, then, the Storm and Stress Period expressed a great awakening of the world to new life. But an abiding place in this state of mind there was none. What then followed?

The two masters of German literature who passed through and rose above this period of beginnings, and created the great works of the classical period, were Goethe and Schiller. As poets, we are not now specially concerned with them. As moral teachers, what have they to tell us about the conduct and the worth of life? The answer is, they bear not altogether the same message. There is a striking contrast, well recognized by themselves and by all subsequent critics, between their views of life. Both aim at the highest, but seek in different paths. Goethe's mature ideal seems to be a man of finely appreciative powers, who follows his life-calling quietly and with such diligence as to gain for himself independence and leisure, who so cultivates his mind that it is open to receive all noble impressions, and who then waits with a sublime resignation, gained through years of self-discipline, for such experiences of what is grand in life and in the universe as the Spirit of Nature sees fit to grant to him. Wilhelm Meister, who works eagerly for success in a direction where success is impossible, and who afterward finds bliss where he least expected to find it, seems to teach this lesson. Faust, at first eagerly demanding indefinite breadth and grandeur of life, and then coming to see what the limitations of human nature are, "that to man nothing perfect is given," and so at last finding the highest good of life in the thought that he and posterity must daily earn anew freedom, never be done with progressing, seems to illustrate the same thought. Do not go beyond or behind Nature, Goethe always teaches. Live submissively the highest that it is given you to live, and neither cease quietly working, nor despair, nor rebel, but be open to every new and worthy experience. For Goethe this was a perfect solution of the problem of life. He needed no fixed system of dogmas to content him. In the divine serenity of one of the most perfect of minds, Goethe put in practice this maxim: Live thy life out to the full, earnestly but submissively, demanding what attainment thy nature makes possible, but not pining for more.

Now, this of course is a selfish maxim. If the highest life is to be unselfish, Goethe cannot have given us the final solution to the problem. His selfishness was not of a low order. It was like the selfishness in the face of the Apollo Belvedere, the simple consciousness of vast personal worth. But it was selfishness for all that. We see how it grew for him out of his early enthusiasm. The Storm and Stress Period had been full of the thought that there is something grand in the emotional nature of man, and that this something must be cultivated. Now, Goethe, absorbed in the faith of the time — himself, in fact, its high priest — learned after a while that all these much sought treasures of emotion were there already, in his own being, and that they needed no long search, no storming at all. He had but to be still and watch them. He needed no anxious brooding to find ideals; he went about quietly, meeting the ideal everywhere. The object of search thus attained, in so far as any mortal could attain it, Goethe the poet was in perfect harmony with the Goethe of practical life; and so was formed the creed of the greatest man of the century. But it was a creed of little more than personal significance. For us the grand example remains, but the attainment of like perfection is impossible, and we must look for another rule of living. For those sensitive and earnest people who learn, as many learn while yet mere school boys or school girls, that there is a great wealth of splendid emotional life, of affection and aspiration and devotion, shut up in their own hearts; for those who, feeling this, want to develop this inner nature, to enjoy these high gifts, to order their lives accordingly, to avoid shams and shows, and to possess the real light of life — for such natural Transcendentalists, what shall Goethe's precept avail? Alas! their little lives are not Olympian, like his. They can-

not meet the Ideal everywhere. Poetry does not come
to express their every feeling. No Grand Duke calls
them to his court. No hosts of followers worship them.
Of all this they are not worthy. Yet they ought to find
some path, be it never so steep a one, to a truly higher
life. Resignation may be the best mood, but Goethe's
reason for resignation such souls have not.

Perhaps Schiller's creed may have more meaning for
men in general. In fact, Schiller, though no common
man, had much more in him that common men may,
without trouble, appreciate. His origin was humble,
and the way up steep and rough. In his earlier writings
the Storm and Stress tendency takes a simpler and
cruder form than that of Werther. What Schiller accomplished was for a long time the result of very hard
work, done in the midst of great doubt and perplexity.
Schiller's ideal is, therefore, to use his own figure, the
laborious, oppressed, and finally victorious Hercules —
i. e., the man who fears no toil in the service of the highest, who knows that there is something of the divine in
him, who restlessly strives to fulfill his destiny, and who
at last ascends to the sight and knowledge of the truly
perfect. Schiller's maxim, therefore, is: Toil ceaselessly
to give thy natural powers their full development, knowing that nothing is worth having but a full consciousness
of all that thou hast of good, now latent and unknown
within thee. Resignation, therefore, though it is the
title of one of Schiller's poems, is never his normal active
mood. He retains to the end a good deal of the old
Storm and Stress. He is always a sentimental poet, to
use the epithet in his own sense; that is, he is always
toiling for the ideal, never quite sure that he is possessed
of it. He dreams sometimes, that he soon will know the
perfect state of mind; but he never does attain, nor does

he seem, like Goethe, content with the eternal progress. There is an under-current of complaint and despair in Schiller, which only the splendid enthusiasm of the man keeps, for the most part, out of sight. Some of his poems are largely under its influence.

Now, this creed, in so far as it is earnest and full of faith in the ideal, appeals very much more immediately than does Goethe's creed to the average sensitive mind. Given a soul that is awake to the higher emotions, and if you tell such a one to work earnestly and without rest to develop this better self, you will help him more than if you bid him contemplate the grand attainment of a Goethe, and be resigned to his own experiences as Goethe was to his. For most of us the higher life is to be gained only through weary labor, if at all. But what seems to be lacking in Schiller's creed is a sufficiently concrete definition of the ideal that he seeks. Any attentive reader of *Faust* feels strongly, if vaguely, what it is that Faust is looking for. But one may read Schiller's "Das Ideal und das Leben" a good many times without really seeing what it is that the poor Hercules, or his earthly representative, is seeking. Schiller is no doubt, on the whole, the simpler poet, yet I must say that if I wanted to give any one his first idea of what perfection of mind and character is most worthy of search, I should send such a one to Goethe rather than to Schiller. Schiller talks nobly about the way to perfection, but he defines perfection quite abstractly. Goethe is not very practical in his directions about the road, but surely no higher or clearer ideals of what is good in emotion and action can be put into our minds than those he suggests in almost any passage you please, if he is in a serious mood, and is talking about good and evil at all.

But neither of the classical poets satisfied his readers

merely as a moral teacher. As poets, they remain what they always seemed — classics, indeed; but as thinkers they did little more than state a problem. Here is a higher life, and they tell us about it. But wherein consists its significance, how it is to be preached to the race, how sought by each one of us — these questions remain still open.

And open they are, the constant theme for eager discussion and for song all through the early part of the nineteenth century. Close upon the classical period followed the German Romantic school. Young men again, full of earnestness and of glorious experience! On they come, confident that they at least are called to be apostles, determined to reform life and poetry — the one through the other. Surely they will solve the problem, and tell us how to cultivate this all important higher nature. Fichte, the great idealist, whose words set men's hearts afire, or else, alas! make men laugh at him; young Friedrich Schlegel, versatile, liberal in conduct even beyond the bounds that may not safely be passed, bold in spirit even to insolence; the wonderful Novalis, so profound, and yet so unaffected and childlike, so tender in emotion and yet so daring in speculation; Schelling, full of vast philosophic projects; Tieck, skillful weaver of romantic fancies; Schleiermacher, gifted theologian and yet disciple of Spinoza; surely, these are the men to complete the work that will be left unfinished when Schiller dies and Goethe grows older. So at least, they thought and their friends. Never were young men more confident; and yet never did learned and really talented men, to the most of whom was granted long life with vigor, more completely fail to accomplish anything of permanent value in the direction of their early efforts. As mature men, some of them were very influential and useful, but not in the way in which they first sought to be useful. There is to my mind a great and sad fascination in studying the lives and thoughts of this school, in whose fate seems to be exemplified the tragedy of our century. Such aspirations, such talents, and such a failure! Fragments of inspired verse and prose, splendid plans, earnest private letters to friends, prophetic visions and nothing more of enduring worth. Further and further goes the movement, in its worship of the emotional, away from the actual needs of human life. Dramatic art, the test of the poet that has a deep insight into the problems of our nature, is tried, with almost complete failure. The greatest dramatic poet of the new era, one that, if he had lived, might have rivaled Schiller, was Heinrich von Kleist, author of the *Prinz von Homburg*. Driven to despair by unsolved problems and by loneliness, this poet shot himself before his life-work was more than fairly begun. There remain a few dramas, hardly finished, a few powerful tales, and a bundle of fragments to tell us what he was. His fate is typical of the work of the younger school between the years 1805 and 1815. There was a keen sense of the worth of emotional experience, and an inability to come into unity with one's aspirations. Life and poetry, as the critics have it, were at variance.

Now, in all this, these men were not merely fighting shadows. What they sought to do is eternally valuable. They felt, and felt nobly, as all generous-minded, warm-hearted youths and maidens at some time do feel. They were not looking for fame alone; they wanted to be and to produce the highest that mortals may. It is a pity that we have not just now more like them. Yet their efforts failed. What problems Goethe and Schiller, men of genius and of good fortune, had solved for themselves alone, men of lesser genius or of less happy lives could only puzzle over. The poetry of the next following age is largely the poetry of melancholy. The emotional movement spread all over Europe; men everywhere strove to make life richer and worthier; and most men grew sad at their little success. Alfred de Musset, in a well known book, has told in the gloomiest strain the story of the unrest, the despair, the impotency of the youth of the Restoration.

Wordsworth and Shelley represent in very much contrasted ways the efforts of English poets to carry on the work of Transcendentalism, and these men succeeded, in this respect, better than their fellows. Wordsworth is full of a sense of the deep meaning of little things and of the most common life. Healthy men, that work like heroes, that have lungs full of mountain air, and that yet retain the simplicity of shepherd life, or children, whose eyes and words teach purity and depth of feeling, are to him the most direct suggestions of the ideal. Life is, for Wordsworth, everywhere an effort to be at once simple and full of meaning; in harmony with nature, and yet not barbarous. But Wordsworth, if he has very much to teach us, seems to lack the persuasive enthusiasm of the poetic leader of men. At all events, his appeal has reached, so far, only a class. He can be all in all to them, his followers, but he did not reform the world. Shelley, is, perhaps, the one of all English poets in this century to whom was given the purest ideal delight in the higher affections. If you want to be eager to act out the best that is in you, read Shelley. If you want to cultivate a sense for the best in the feelings of all human hearts, read Shelley. He has taught very many to long for a worthy life and for purity of spirit. But, alas! Shelley, again, knows not how to teach the way to the acquirement of the end that he so enthusiastically describes. If you can feel with him, he does you good. If you fail to understand him, he is no systematic teacher. At best, he will arouse a longing. He can never wholly satisfy it. Shelley wanted to be no mere writer. He had in him a desire to reform the world. But when he speaks of reform one sees how vague an idea he had of the means. Prometheus, the Titan, who represents in Shelley's poem oppressed humanity, is bound on the mountain. The poem is to tell us of his deliverance. But how is this accomplished? Why, simply when a certain fated hour comes, foreordained, but by nobody in particular, up comes Demogorgon, the spirit of eternity, stalks before the throne of Jupiter, the tyrant, and orders him out into the abyss; and thereupon Prometheus is unchained, and the earth is happy. Why did not all this happen before? Apparently, because Demogorgon did not sooner leave the under-world. What a motive is this for an allegoric account of the deliverance of humanity! Mere accident rules everything, and yet apparently, there is a coming triumph to work for. The poet of lofty emotions is but an eager child when he is to advise us to act.

The melancholy side of the literary era that extends from 1815 to 1840 is represented especially by two poets, Byron and Heine. Both treat the same great problem, What is this life, and what in it is of most worth? Both recognize the need there is for something more than mere existence. Both know the value of emotion, and both would wish to lead men to an understanding of this value, if only they thought that men could be led. Despairing themselves, of ever attaining an ideal peace of mind, they give themselves over to melancholy. Despairing of raising men even to their own level, they become scornful, and spend far too much time in merely negative criticism. The contrast between them is not a little instructive. Byron is too often viewed by superficial readers merely in the light of his early sentimental poems. Those, for our present purpose, may be disregarded. It is the Byron of *Manfred* and *Cain* that I now have in mind. As for Heine, Matthew Arnold long since said the highest in praise of his ethical significance that we may dare to say. Surely both men have great defects. They are one-sided, and often insincere. But they are children of the ideal. Byron has, I think, the greater force of character, but the gift of seeing well what is beautiful and pathetic in life fell to the lot of Heine. The one is great in spirit, the other in experience. Byron is, by nature, combative, a hater of wrong, one often searching for the highest truth; but his experience is petty and heart-sickening, his real world is miserably unworthy of his ideal world, and he seems driven on into the darkness like his own Cain and Manfred. Heine has more the faculty of vision. The perfect delight in a moment of emotion is given to him as it has seldom been given to any man since the unknown makers of the popular ballads. Hence, his frequent use of ballad forms and incidents. Surely, Byron could never have given us that picture of Edith of the Swan's Neck searching for the dead King Harold on the field of Hastings, which Heine has painted in one of the ballads of the *Romancero*. But, on the other hand, Heine lacks the force to put into active life the meaning and beauty that he can so well appreciate. He sees in dreams, but he cannot create in the world the ideal of perfection. So he is bitter and despairing. He takes a cruel delight in pointing out the shams of the actual world. Naturally romantic, he attacks romantic tendencies, ever fresh with hate and scorn. In brief, to live the higher life, and to teach others to live it also, one would have to be heroic in action, like Byron, and gifted with the power to see, as Heine saw, what is precious, and, in all its simplicity, noble, about human experience. The union of Byron and Heine would have been a new, and, I think, a higher, sort of Goethe.

Since these have passed away we have had our Emerson, our Carlyle, our Tennyson. Upon these men we cannot dwell now. I pass to the result of the whole long struggle. Humanity was seeking, in these its chosen representative men, to attain to a fuller emotional life. A conflict resulted with the petty and ignoble in human nature, and with the dead resistance of material forces. Men grew old and died in this conflict, did wonderful things, and — did not conquer. And now, at last, Europe gave up the whole effort, and fell to thinking about physical science and about great national movements. The men of the last age are gone, or are fast going, and we are left face to face with a dangerous practical materialism. The time is one of unrest, but not of great moral leaders. Action is called for, and, vigorous as we are, spiritual activity is not one of the specialties of the modern world.

So much, then, for the reasons why what I have for brevity's sake called Transcendentalism lost its hold on the life of the century. The reasons were briefly these: First, the ideal sought by the men of the age of which we have spoken was too selfish, not broad and human enough. Goethe might save himself, but he could not teach us the road. Secondly, men did not strive long and earnestly enough. Surely, if the problems of human conduct are to be solved, if life is to be made full of emotion, strong, heroic, and yet not cold, we must all unite, men, women, and children, in the common cause of living ourselves as best we can, and of helping others, by spoken and by written word, to do the same. We lack perseverance and leaders. Thirdly, the splendid successes of certain modern investigations have led away men's minds from the study of the conduct of life to a study of the evolution of life. I respect the latter study, but I do not believe it fills the place of the former. I wish there were time in our hurried modern life, for both. I know there must be found time, and that right quickly, for the study of the old problems of the Faust of Goethe.

With this conclusion, the present study arrives at the goal set at the beginning. How we are to renew these old discussions, what solution of them we are to hope for, whether we shall ever finally solve them, what the true ideal of life is — of all such matters I would not presume to write further at this present. But let us not forget that if our Evolution textbooks contain much of solid — yes, of inspiring — truth, they do not contain all the knowledge that is essential to a perfect life or to the needs of humanity. A philosophy made possible by the deliberate neglect of that thought-movement, whose literary expression was the poetry of our century, cannot itself be broad enough and deep enough finally to do away with the needs embodied in that thought-movement. Let one, knowing this fact, be therefore, earnest in the search for whatever may make human life more truly worth living. Let him read again, if he has read before, or begin to read, if he has never read, our Emerson, our Carlyle, our Tennyson, or the men of years ago, who so aroused the ardent souls of the best among our fathers. Let him study Goethe, Schiller, Heine, Wordsworth, anything and everything that can arouse in him a sense of our true spiritual needs. And having read, let him work in the search after the ideal — work not for praise, but for the good of his time.

And then, perhaps, some day a new and a mightier Transcendental Movement may begin — a great river, that shall not run to waste and be lost in the deserts of sentimental melancholy.

DOUBTING AND WORKING[1]

[1881]

THERE is a well known speculation of Dr. Holmes as to the number of people who really are concerned in a conversation between any two men. Each one of these men has a real and true character — is what he is. Each one of the men has a notion of the other's character, and probably thinks his notion a very fair one. And each one has a still more distinct and fixed idea as to his own character. Now, the words of each man are determined by what he himself really is, by what he thinks of himself, and by what he holds of the other. So that in fact six people, two real and four imaginary — to wit, the two real men, their ideas of themselves and their ideas of each other — take part in this simplest form of human society. How complicated then, must be the state of things when a whole group of people are concerned, each one speaking forth his own true nature, but affected in his words by what he supposes his own nature to be, and by the way in which he fancies his sayings will impress the ghostly images that are what he takes to be his real companions.

This speculation suggests a like one as to the number of partly imaginary worlds that form subjects of study and amusement for the myriads of human beings in the one actual world. It is a commonplace that in some sense every man may be said to move in a world of his own. Yet the consequences of this commonplace are not always considered. Think of them a moment. Here is an ordinary person before us, taken as a type of hu-

[1] Revision of an earlier essay on "The Work of the Truth-Seeker," read before the Literary Society.

manity. His view of the world might be taken as an example, so it would seem, of the way in which the people of this planet know and appreciate the universe. Yet, no. Could you look into his soul for a minute it is probable that you would find very much in his consciousness that would be strange to you and to other men. Think first of his senses themselves. Experience has shown that common men can go through the world for a very long time without suspecting or showing that they have some very important defect of the senses. Cross-eyed men, I have heard, sometimes by a painless process lose the sight of one eye, and yet go for years without finding out their defect until chance or necessity brings them under the skilled examination of an oculist. Late statistics make a basis for the claim that as many as one in every twenty-five male persons will be found to be color blind. Yet only by careful tests are color-blind people to be distinguished from people with normal vision. It is probable that there are often somewhat similar defects in the sense of hearing which go unnoticed for a long time. Yet more, the researches of men like Helmholtz have proved that there are many optical illusions common to most or to all of us, which are unnoticed or unconsciously corrected our lives long, and which never could become known without skillful experiment. And if all this is true, how can we ever feel sure that in the field that lies beyond the reach of possible experiment, in the field of each man's own primary sensations themselves, there are not entirely mysterious sources of variety, so that the ultimate sensations of one person may be of their nature not comparable at all with the ultimate sensations of his neighbor? Thus, then, our normal man may be in fact a creature of entirely peculiar constitution; yet we may not know the fact. His

world may be one that would be inconceivably strange
to us. Yet we talk with him in common fashion day
after day. But, leaving the field of conjecture and coming back to the point where it is possible to judge and
compare, I say that we may very probably find upon
examination that there are peculiarities in the mind of
the person we are considering which may make the
simplest operation of his thought such as we can neither
imitate nor easily understand. Take, for example, his
memory.[1] There seem to be two somewhat different
kinds of memories in the world. I suppose that there are
all the gradations between the two extremes, but at the
extremes the contrast is very marked. One kind of
memory is that which is especially helped by images,
which is in fact largely a reimaging in the mind of
things past, so that they appear much as they actually
seemed when they were presented to the outward senses,
only fainter. The other is a memory moving less in distinct and vivid images than in faint and broken incomplete mind-symbols that come up one after another, as
association or volition calls them into consciousness.
How, for example, do you remember that seven multiplied by seven equals forty-nine? If you have the image-
memory, you may picture well before you a bit of the
multiplication table, as you once saw it, with figures of
some definite color, on a ground of some definite color.
Clearly stand out the images in your mind as soon as you
think of the numbers. You simply read off the result.
If you have the other kind of memory, probably there
arises a confused and faint form of the figures, curiously
mingled with a memory somewhat more well defined, of

[1] See concerning the following: The communications of Mr.
Francis Galton to the journal, *Nature*, at various times within
the past two years, and his article in *Mind* for July, 1880.

the sound of the names of these numbers. The imaging is so obscure that you doubtless are inclined to say that you know not how you do remember at all, but merely know that you remember. Plainer becomes the contrast between the two kinds of memory when we come to speak of what happened to us at any time. The images of past scenes that arise in our various minds differ much as to completeness of detail and as to definiteness of outline. For one, forms are clear in memory; for another, colors. One remembers the positions of things, another faces and expressions. One knows when a passage in some book is referred to or quoted whether he saw that passage printed on the right or on the left side of the open page of the book where he read it. Such a one will remember on what shelf of a library he found a certain work. To another all these things are vague, but he can remember nearly a whole play, passage after passage, after witnessing the play twice on the stage, or a whole piece of music, after one or two performances. Yet, perhaps, such a one could not remember the demonstration of a theorem in geometry long enough to repeat it in a class-room. Now, if you reflect what a great part memory plays in our actual consciousness, I think you must readily admit that when memories differ so much, not merely in power, but in nature, the thoughts of men, their ideas of the world about them, their whole conscious lives, must differ very much also.

I have mentioned differences in men's views of the world as thus exemplified in the more elementary activities of mental life. What shall we say when we come to the more complicated structures of the human mind, to those vague forms of consciousness in which are expressed our sense of the value of life and of the world, and to our opinions? Who shall serve for our

normal specimen man here? How vastly we differ in all
these things. How hard it is for us to come to an understanding. How the delights of one man appear as the
most hateful of things to another, and the ideals of one
party seem inventions of the devil to their opponents.
All this illustrates the fact that we live in worlds differing far more from one another than we commonly like to
think. Our normal man would surely be hard to choose.
If we choose him, we should hardly comprehend him. To
be more particular in our study, let us glance briefly at
the wide range of what I may call purely general impressions, such as we in some wise get of life and of the
universe, and which we so keep without analyzing or
being well able to analyze them, although such impressions influence all our acts.

Every one has, I suppose, some ideal, some notion of
what he anticipates and desires in his life and in the
world about him. To every one this world appears as an
excellent or as an evil place, and every one has some
highest good which he seeks here in life, though he may
never have formulated his aim. Now, it is certain that
any man's creed, and the extent of the knowledge he is
to acquire (and so what we have called above this man's
world), will depend on the way in which this general
view of the aims and conditions of life leads him. Against
the fundamental prejudices of a man you will argue in
vain. Time may change them; you cannot. And these
prejudices make for him his world. To a man who defined poetry as "misrepresentation in verse," and to the
poet Shelley, how was it possible to look on this universe
of forms and colors, of lights and shadows, of land and
water and infinite space, and to see in it the same world?
To the one it must be a complex of determinate relations; to the other a scene of grand conflicts, of divine

life, and of supernatural beauty. The difference between Mr. Herbert Spencer and Cardinal Newman, or between Professor Huxley and Mr. Ruskin, or between Hegel and Heinrich Heine — shall we call it merely a difference in the interpretation of the recorded facts of experience? No; evidently there are here different kinds of experience concerned, actually different worlds, different orders of truth. These men cannot come to a good understanding, because they have qualitatively different minds, irreconcilably various mental visions. Each of two such individuals may be inclined to regard the other as perverse. Both are, in fact, shut up within the narrow bounds of a poor individual experience. They will never understand one another so long as they remain what they are — finite minds full of fallacy and self-confidence, and of a darkness that is broken only here and there by flashes of light.

If the world's leaders are thus such narrow men, what are we who follow? How poor and narrow and uncertain must our world-pictures be. Glance inward at your own experience for a moment. You often say that a color, or odor, or melody, or place, or person is associated in your minds with some event, or feeling, or idea. You cannot think of one without the other.

Now, a study of mental life convinces us that these vague associations of which you speak tend to combine and multiply in manifold wise. When an association is itself forgotten, the effect of it lives on in the form of some liking, or aversion, or mental prejudgment. By combination these associations form foundations on which yet higher structures can be built. All go to make up your picture of the universe. Yet many such associations are purely personal. You can but ill describe them. Still more, you inherit from your ancestors not merely the general mass of common tendencies that belongs to humanity as a whole, but you also inherit certain peculiar tendencies, associations, and feelings that influence your whole life, and that make you in a sense incomprehensible to those whose disposition is different from your own. If we could see one another's minds open before us, and study them at our leisure, how many singular phenomena we should witness. No museum of curiosities could approach in variety and oddness a museum in which some hundred minds were preserved and bottled up, or dissected and laid out for inspection under glass cases; or, better still, left alive behind bars, and allowed to exhibit their whole action for our benefit. As it is, the study of the inner workings of men's individual minds is obscured by the complexity of each, by the lack of the virtue of frankness, by the impossibility of finding in most cases a skilled observer. Every one has nooks and corners in his own mind to which he is himself more or less a stranger. Every man is an enigma to every other. And this variety in our minds, what does it mean but vagueness and uncertainty and obscurity in all our opinions?

But, now (coming to the study of the opinions themselves), every one of these many minds sets itself up as a measure of truth. Distorted by the heterogeneous medium into which the light falls, the images given by experience must still serve, poor as they are, to fill up for us the picture of our world. Exposed to the largest errors of observation, to the greatest defects of memory, to the incalculable interference of passion and prejudice, to the disadvantage of being surrounded by numberless obscure associations, we, the thinking beings, live in this amusing chaos of our fleeting conscious states and spend our time in making assertions about the universe.

What does this fool-hardiness mean? What right have we to hold opinions at all? Why must we not be perfect skeptics? What in a short life of mistake and conjecture can we be supposed to learn about the nature of things? What can be the truth, that we should look for it?

To this problem we are led then, irresistibly. Here is a chaos of various minds whose simpler ideas seem to vary enormously, whose feelings grow so far asunder that each man becomes a mystery to his neighbor, whose conflicting opinions in consequence are all the results largely of accident, and certainly of narrowness of view. Yet it seems to be thought an excellent thing for each one of them to form fixed opinions about at least some matters, a sane undertaking for them to look for some sort of abiding truth, and a grand act to suffer loss, or even death, for the sake of the strongest and highest at least among one's beliefs. Why should this be the case? What is the use of truth-seeking when so little truth will ever be found on this planet? What is the worth of remaining true to one's opinions when everything tends to make them fleeting? These questions must, I think, come into the mind of every active person at some time during his life. I have not in the foregoing stated the skeptic's case nearly as strongly as I could state it. The more you consider human knowledge, the more you will see that some of its dearest pretenses are found upon examination to be only pretenses. And when you see this, you are, if of vigorous mental constitution, once for all aroused from what a great philosopher called the "dogmatic slumber," and sent out upon a new search. The questions you then propose to yourself can thus be stated: What kind of truth may I hope to discover? In what spirit ought I to search for truth? Am I to hope for much success? Am I to bear myself as one to whom truth will certainly be revealed, if he but work for it? Or shall I, in a humbler spirit, say that I am probably to remain in doubt so long as I live? Or, finally, shall I, neither confident of success nor resigned to defeat, rise with all my strength and declare that, whether finding or baffled, whether a wanderer forever, or one who at last is to reach a secure harbor of faith, I will, through confidence and through doubt, through good and through evil report, search earnestly for truth, though I never find anything that it is worth my while to call abiding? Some suggestions about the answer to this whole series of questions form my subject in the rest of this paper. And, first, what is the spirit in which we should search for the truth that now, from this skeptical point of view, seems so far away from us?

The first answer to this question seems an obvious one. We must begin our undertaking in a spirit of self-distrust. For our former confidence in our chance opinions we must substitute complete skepticism. We must doubt every belief that we possess until we have proved it. This answer, I say, seems the obvious one after the foregoing discussion. Is it a good one?

Note just here, if you please, that the precept, begin to look for truth by doubting all you formerly believed, does not imply irreverence or mere rashness. On the contrary, this doubt means simply modesty, self-distrust, and is founded not on a whim, but on a persuasion that all one's former beliefs have been largely the result of accident. The precept says such and such a belief that you have may indeed be very dear and sacred, and may have to do with very high and holy things. But consider — it is your opinion, is it not? Yes. The question is not the loftiness, or the sacredness, or the dearness of

the objects about which your faith concerned itself, but
the worth of that particular belief you have about these
objects. When we say question your belief, we do not
mean that this or that subject that seemed to you holy
ground before shall not seem holy ground now. Not in
the least is it desired to affect your emotions as emotions.
We are talking of your individual opinions. If this
ground is holy, so much the better reason that you
should not profane it with your narrow-mindedness and
mistakes. Better that you should say, "Here is a subject of awful and sacred import, but I know very little
about it," than that you should proudly affirm, "Of this
sacred theme my mind is so full that I know whole volumes of truth about it" — should affirm this and yet
should really be in gross error about the theme. The
loftier, the more worthy of reverence the subject of your
belief, the more necessary it is that you examine skepti-
cally the faith in which you by accident have grown up,
lest where the highest interests are concerned your mind
should be farthest away from harmony with reality. If
you understand the precept in this way, as a precept to
doubt yourself and all beliefs that have grown up in you
uncriticized, then I am sure that you will not find the
precept in its nature irreverent or over-hasty.

Yet this precept itself has often been called in doubt.
In answer to the arguments just urged, it has been set
forth that truth-seeking never ought to begin with a
doubt universal — that doubting is dangerous when it
touches upon certain sacred matters, and that such
truth-seeking as I have described is only fit for those
who, like Nihilists, undertake to upset the whole existing order of things, in law, in morality, and in religious
belief. This counter-argument, to the effect that unlimited doubting is idle and often wicked, I ought to

mention and to consider. Let us be careful, when we
speak of truth-seeking itself, against taking too much of
any kind of assertions for granted. I examine then forthwith the precept given above.

The object of your universal doubt, says one, is, as
you declare, to lead you to a knowledge of the truth.
You doubt because you desire to learn. Your doubting
is to be a transition stage. You must assert then that
truth is an end sufficiently valuable to be worth attaining through all the pain and toil of your search. The
truth then, would be something very well worth knowing. Is it not so? To complete your own individual
narrow world-picture, and so to get the only proper
world-picture, this you hold would be a great end gained.
All this seems certain enough.

Now, continues the objector, how can you know that
it would be a good thing to be possessed of the truth, in
case you do not know whether the world you live in is a
good world, and whether the life you live in it is one that
is worth living? In other words, earnest truth-seeking
implies a persuasion that the truth, if known, would be
not disheartening, dreadful, inhuman, but inspiring,
lovely — of a nature to satisfy the best cravings of the
human heart. If this is so, the objector goes on — if, in
order to make the search for truth a worthy quest, we
must assume that the world of truth is a world of excellence — where shall we then first of all look for an ideal
picture of this world, such that, by contemplating the
ideal picture of what truth must be, we shall be inspired
to search for what truth is? The answer is, we must
search in that system of belief which expresses in the
clearest form to our minds the highest cravings of our
hearts. If that system of belief is substantially true, then
the search for more truth is well founded. If we must,

however, begin by doubting the truth of this system along with all our other beliefs, then we must begin to search for truth by doubting that it is worth while to search for truth at all. What will become of our earnestness? In short, says the objector, either the foundations of my religious belief are sure beyond a doubt, or else it is not worth while to make any extended search for truth beyond the bounds of this faith. For either my faith agrees with reality — and then why doubt it? — or this faith, wherein are embodied the highest longings and ideals of my nature, is at variance with the reality. Then the world is a hopeless maze to me. Nothing is worth the trouble of living at all. Still less is it worth my while to enter upon any ardent quest, to search for a far off and difficult truth, that will be, when found, simply intolerable. I decline to seek truth, and prefer to remain where I am.

Such is, in brief, the case of those who hold that seeking for truth must be begun in a spirit of faith, and not in a spirit of doubt; that we must first hold fast that which is plainly good, and then prove all else. Yet I cannot feel satisfied, that I have stated this case strongly enough. Because I am myself inclined to the opinion that the truth-seeker must begin by doubting all his old beliefs, and must then follow his thought wherever research leads him, I may have failed in justice in the statement of a view which has the sanction of many of the world's ablest minds. Let me translate, therefore, the words of a noted German thinker of our day, Hermann Lotze, a philosopher who among his great qualities has certainly not omitted the virtue of ceaseless self-criticism, but who yet holds fast by the faith that we study the world because we believe it to be a good world. Lotze says in the preface to his book, called the *Mikro-*

kosmos (I translate with some omissions and condensations):

The growing self-consciousness of science, which, after centuries of wavering, sees indubitable laws reigning in some at least of the classes of phenomena, threatens to distort the true relation between the heart and the intellect. We are no longer content to postpone the questions with which our dreams and hopes disturb us when we set about our investigations. We deny our duty to pay any attention to these questions at all. We say that science is a pure service of truth for the sake of truth, and need not care whether the truth satisfies or wounds the selfish wishes of the heart. And so here, as elsewhere, the human spirit changes its tone from hesitation to defiance, and after it has once felt the pride of independent investigation, throws itself into the arms of that false heroism which takes credit for having renounced what never ought to be renounced; and thus the mind estimates the amount of truth in its new belief according to the degree of hostility with which this belief offends everything that appears to the living emotional nature of man outside of science, too sacred to be touched. This worship of truth seems to me unjust. Could it be the only concern of human research to picture in the mind the precise state of things in the outer world, what would then be the worth of this whole trouble, which would end only in an empty repetition, so that what was before outside the soul now would be found again imaged in the soul? What significance would there be in the empty play of this duplication, what necessity that the thinking mind should be a mirror for whatever is unthinking, in case the discovery of truth were not always at the same time the creation of some good thing, that would justify the trouble of winning it? Individual seekers may, absorbed in their toil, forget the great fact that all their efforts have in the end only this significance, that, in company with the efforts of numberless others, they may draw such a picture of the world as shall tell us what we have to reverence as the true end of existence, what we have to do, and what we have to hope. As often as a revolution in science drives out old fashions of opinion, the new organization of belief will have to justify itself by the enduring or growing satisfaction that it offers to the invincible demands of our emotional nature.

So far, then, for the opinion of those who hold that truth is sought not for its own sake, but for the sake of the good it carries to mankind — and carries not merely because it is truth, but because the world of which it is the truth is a good world. Such persons must conclude that all earnest and considerate search for truth is based on the postulate that our world is a good world. If we shall accept this view, we will always carry with us our religious faith whenever we set about an investigation of nature's mysteries. But is this view, with its objections to the precept wherewith we set out, a true view? For my part, I am inclined to hold fast by my former precept. I admit that looking for truth implies a postulate that truth is worth the looking for, and a postulate that the world is such that it would be a good thing to know the nature of the world. Yet I still cling to my rule, and say, begin to search for truth by doubting all that you have without criticism come to hold as true. If you fail to doubt everything, doubt all you can. Doubt not because doubting is a good end, but because it is a good beginning. Doubt not for amusement, but as a matter of duty. Doubt not superficially, but with thoroughness. Doubt not flippantly, but with the deepest — it may be with the saddest — earnestness. Doubt as you would undergo a surgical operation, because it is necessary to thought-health. So only can you hope to attain convictions that are worth having. If you do not wish to think, then I have nothing to say. Then, indeed, you need not doubt at all, but take all you please for granted. But who then cares at all what you happen to fancy about the world?

Why do I persist in this terrible precept, with all the objections before me? Why, if doubting is dangerous and almost certainly transient, and very probably agonizing, should I still be determined to doubt and to coun-sel doubting of every uncriticized and unproved opinion? Let me tell you.

If one says I must begin my thought by clinging fast to my faith, because only that gives me assurance that there is anything in the world worth seeking, then we reply: to what faith? What is the one persuasion that gives to human life a worthy aim? Is it the faith of Confucius, or of Buddha, or of Plato, or of St. Paul, or of Savonarola, or of Loyola, or of Luther, or of Calvin, or of Wesley, or of Lessing, or of Kant, or of Fichte, or of Emerson, or of Schopenhauer, or of Spencer, or of Cardinal Newman, or of Auguste Comte? These names stand, some indeed, near together, but others not for small differences of opinion, but for widely distinct mountain peaks of human faith, separated sometimes by dreadful abysses of doubt. Which shall you ascend? Merely the one at whose base you happen to have been born? Where shall you find an abiding place? If you say, but some of these leaders are in close agreement, some are disciples of others, I reply well and good, but some are so far from the others that there is no understanding, almost no tolerance possible. Surely, there are some great highest beliefs that are worthy of intelligent following on the part of all men. But what are those beliefs? How do you know what they are till you examine, and examine not with a foregone conclusion awaiting you smilingly at the other end of a course of reasoning upon which you start already convinced, but with genuine skepticism that refuses to be satisfied with anything short of reasoned conviction.

I have touched upon something that really involves the whole nature of this work of truth-seeking. I have said that there is incongruity in accepting a faith as true

simply because you happen to feel it agreeable or satisfying to even your highest interests, for other men have
felt other opposing faiths equally satisfying. What faith
is there that is not regarded as cold and dreary, as opposed to the highest nature of man, by one who fails to
sympathize with it? What earnest and conscientious
faith is there that may not seem inspiring to the one who
has formed or accepted it? There are limits no doubt.
There are earnest faiths that are unable to give comfort
to the possessors. But that fact of itself is no test of
truth. For what was our object in setting out to search
for truth at all? Our starting point, you remember, was
the fact of the narrowness of all men, of their powerless-
ness to see beyond a very limited range. The narrowness
resulted in strife. This strife of opinion meant discontent. Now, what would be the abiding and satisfactory
truth if we found it? Evidently, this truth would have
one great characteristic. It would be of a nature to demand acceptance from all men. It would be the one
faith opposed to the many opinions, and certain to conquer them. It would be the one reality that could wait
for ages for a discoverer. So, at least, we suppose. That
is our ideal of truth. What, then, is the practical aim in
seeking for truth? Evidently, the practical aim is to
harmonize the conflicting opinions of men, to substitute
for the narrowness and instability of personal views the
broadness of view that should characterize the free man.
And so we come to the real core of the matter. You may
not, you dare not, if it is your vocation, to think at all —
you dare not accept a faith simply for the satisfaction it
gives you. You dare not, I say, because as a thinker
your true aim is not to please yourself, but to work for
the harmonizing of the views of mankind, to do your
part in a perfectly unselfish task. This is the one great

argument against all uncritical faith. If you accept an opinion because it seems pleasing to you before criticism, then you choose rather your selfish satisfaction than the good of mankind. You ought to work not to increase the variety of human opinions, to render closer the limits of personal experience, but to extend the field of harmony and to unite men, so that they may cease their endless warfare and have a common experience. The sight, I say, of the mass of conflicting opinions of men in the world ought to nerve one to do his best in a task that interests all men, that needs the combined efforts of millions, and that needs above all the sacrifice of personal comfort. Your faith seems agreeable to you — well and good. Other men's faith seems agreeable to them. Is this lack of sympathy, this strife of opinions, with all the intolerance that springs from it, a good thing? No, indeed! Then, ought you to increase it by simply staying blindly shut up in your own narrow faith? No, this is selfish. For your own comfort you will then sacrifice the good you might do to the world by joining the great company of the honest doubters, whose end is to reach a universal and abiding human creed.

But, you say, is it not true that all opinions are finally accepted because they are satisfying to some mental want? Yes, and this is the real meaning of the doctrine that we seek for truth, because we believe truth to be good. Our highest object of search is no doubt some state of consciousness. Our universal creed, if ever reached, will be universally acceptable to the real intellectual needs of all men educated up to its level. But this does not mean that what is acceptable to my intellectual needs must be the truth. My needs are narrow and changing. It is humanity in its highest development to which the truth will be acceptable. I must give up my desires that the unity of all human spirits may be sooner attained. For the sake of perfect tolerance, I must be perfectly critical of myself. I must doubt, in order that by doubting and working I may bring, perhaps, not myself to certainty, but mankind a little nearer to the truth.

But this assumption we still are making that truth is a good thing, what is the sense of that? Must we not assume at the outset something as already certain about the world we live in? Must we not assume that the world is a good world, and the truth by nature so satisfying that it is worth while for each and all to make great sacrifice therefor? And is this not a creed, a faith somewhat vague, but very intense? How can we say that we are to begin by doubting everything when we do not doubt that it is worth while to search for truth? I reply, at the outset we are not certain that it will turn out worth while to search for truth. We doubt that as well as everything else. But consider: Our condition is not this, that being possessed of a good in itself satisfactory, we leave this good without knowing whether we are to reach anything better. If that were what we did, we might be wrong. On the contrary, what we do is to flee from an evil condition in which we are. We know that difference of opinion, and narrowness of view, and intolerance are bad. We know that even if we individually are content with our creed, the mass of mankind, being of different creed, is in a pitiable condition of error or doubt. In the service of humanity, then, we must seek to get rid of this evil, and our only way of being certain that we are doing the best work of which we are capable is to begin with universal and genuine doubt. Now, indeed, we cannot be sure that by taking this, the only right course, we shall be successful. The search for truth, though prosecuted earnestly and in the best spirit known to us, may be a fruitless search. But our object is good. We do not seek that profitless duplication of the world by a copy in our own souls of which Lotze spoke. Against that kind of truth-seeking his argument is conclusive. No; in seeking truth we want to make human life better, because we see that men want large-mindedness and peace, while error means narrow-mindedness and war. Since our object is good, we have not first to ask whether we are certain of getting it. Our business is to do what we can, and fail if we must. Truth-seeking is merely like the rest of life — a search after ideal goods that are perhaps unattainable, a conflict in which victory is never secure so long as life itself lasts. Therefore, without contradiction we can say that we set out on the search for truth, doubting even whether our search will turn out profitable, but feeling sure that it is morally required. We determine that there shall be significant truth. We are not sure *a priori* that there is any attainable.

But, you say, then at the outset we at least know that we ought to do what is right — that we ought, for example, to serve mankind as best we can by our thoughts as by our actions. I reply, you cannot be said to know at the outset that it is well to do right and to serve mankind. I suppose only that you feel that it is excellent or desirable to do right and to serve mankind. If you choose to be selfish, and to do your thinking solely for your own amusement, I cannot prove to you, at least at the beginning, that you ought not to be selfish. It is your choice; you are judges. If you want to do good by your opinions, then the best way to do good is to question and criticize these opinions unsparingly, to hold none of them as opinions sacred. That you should think it a desirable thing to do good to mankind, how am I, how is any one else, to bring you to this point by argument? Your moral judgments belong to you in particular, and are not convictions about the world, but expressions of your own character.

In what spirit we should search for truth has been at some length discussed. It remains for us to consider very briefly the immediate consequences of truth-seeking. They have been indicated in what has been already said. First, we have seen that the purpose of truth-seeking is the aiding in the great process of emancipating men's minds from those states of narrowness, intolerance and instability which are so painful to all concerned. I think it wrong to say that in seeking for truth we desire, first of all, to duplicate in our own minds the things and relations that are outside us. Lotze's argument is here sufficient. The thinking mind ought not to have as its sole object conformity to things that do not think. That is not our highest aim. Mistake and disagreement and cruel intolerance and superstition are evil states of mind. They may content or please this or that man for a while. They mean injury and anguish to the mass of mankind. Therefore the desire for ideal harmony of belief. Therefore the unselfish eagerness to be at one with all men by making all men at one with what we hold to be true. If this is the purpose of our truth-seeking, an evident consequence is that we ought in fact to reverence the business of truth-seeking as we reverence all toil for the good of mankind. We ought to regard truth-seeking as a sacred task. Perhaps it is our calling to do good in other ways than by truth-seeking. Let us, however, in that case see in the truth-seeker, a fellow-worker, and honor an earnest and thorough-going doubter as we honor any one who undertakes a painful task for the good of his fellows. For honest and thorough-going doubters are much rarer than you might suppose.

Another consequence is this, that we must be content to take a very subordinate place in the great work of human thought, and to concentrate our attention on a small part only of the field of truth. As millions of brains must toil doubtless for centuries before any amount of ideal agreement among men is attained or even approximated, we must be content if we do very little and work very hard. We can be tolerably certain that in a world where so much is dark nearly the whole of our labor will be wasted. But this is natural. There is the delight of activity in truth-seeking; but when you compare your hopes and claims with the shadowy and doubtful results that you will probably reach, or with the exact but very modest conclusions to which, if you are a successful scientific investigator, you may in time be led, the comparison cannot seem otherwise than melancholy. Through the failures of millions of devoted servants, the humanity of the future may possibly (we cannot know that it will certainly) be led to a grand success. This far-off divine event to which, for all we know, the whole creation may be moving, but which at any rate we regard with longing and delight, constitutes the whole end and aim of our action. It is good to strive.

But I must conclude this imperfect study of a great subject. We began with the fact that every individual is a creature of peculiar constitution, with possibly indefinitely great idiosyncrasies of senses and feeling. We have been led from this on to think of ideal truth as it would appear in the mind of one who was not bound by accidents of sense and emotion to a narrow range of conflicting opinions. To approach this perfect individual, I have said that we must begin our efforts with conscientious and thorough-going doubt of all that we find uncriticized and yet claiming authority in our minds. I have tried to justify this doubting by showing that it is not merely a privilege, but a duty, of any one who proposes to do the least bit of genuine thinking for the good of his fellow-creatures.

I have stated at length the argument according to which at least our religious persuasions, as the expressions of the highest needs of our minds, must be exempted from even provisional doubts. In answer to this argument, I have tried to show that in so far as one's own comfort is concerned, truth-seeking ought not to regard personal comfort at all, and that in so far as humanity is concerned, religious beliefs can be made in the highest sense useful only when they have stood the test of doubt and study. As my discussion is purely general, I would not be understood as bringing the least material argument to bear against the particular convictions of anybody. If you have reasoned fairly and earnestly, have criticized conscientiously, and still retain your religious belief, you have no doubt a glorious possession, worth far more than it ever could have been worth to you if you had not reasoned about it. Perhaps you are still in error. Perhaps the highest truth is already within your grasp, and you have solved in your own person the puzzles of ages. If so, you are to be congratulated. Your treasure is worth more to you than all the wealth in the world would be. But remember, no man liveth to himself. Remember your duty to mankind. Remember that your personal satisfaction with your creed is nothing, your desire to bring all mankind to the truth everything. Never rest quiet with your belief, therefore, until every means has been taken by you to purify it from all taint of your own narrow-mindedness. If any one of us has so purified his belief, he is, I am persuaded, the greatest genius that the world ever saw. If he has not, it is his duty in the service of humanity to be in so far skeptical. If he has attained the perfect belief, then he must never rest in his efforts to teach it to others. I should fear as a general thing to have power given me to ordain for other human beings what their lives should be. But I wish that just for this moment it were given me to summon every man to a calling that should remain his calling for life, and to which he should willingly devote himself. I should summon every one to a life of unswerving devotion to this one end — the making of human life broader, fuller, more harmonious, better possessed of abiding belief. As it is, I can only recommend that you be ceaselessly active for this great end. And as for the end itself, I know not if it will ever be attained in any great measure, but I know that if it ever is attained it will be by the self-sacrifice of countless millions, who, through their own failures, shall secure the success of those that come after them.

HOW BELIEFS ARE MADE

[1882]

A PERSON for whose opinions I have much respect once said to me, that he disclaimed all responsibility for the beliefs that he held on certain
very important matters.

"I try," said he, "to conquer prejudice; but having
done this, I can do no more. My belief, whatever it is,
forms itself in me. I look on. My will has nothing to do
with the matter. I can will to walk or eat; but I cannot
will to believe. I might as well will that my blood should
circulate."

Now, as I admire not a little some of the beliefs of the
person mentioned, I was disappointed to find him not
responsible for them. It seemed a pity to regard his
faith as no more creditable to him than the strong
boughs are creditable to the oak that they adorn. But
upon this matter I did not agree with my friend. Despite
his disclaimer, I thought, and yet think, that he has
made his beliefs very much for himself, and that these
beliefs do him honor, as the statue does honor to the
artist that chiseled it. To be sure, my friend did not
hew out his beliefs from a wholly passive material, as the
sculptor hews from marble. But his beliefs, as I think,
resulted from a sort of struggle between him and the
surrounding world. The world tried sometimes to check
his thought, and to confine it to one channel; sometimes
to confuse his thought, and to scatter it into spray before the quick heavy blows of innumerable disconnected
sense apparitions. But my friend was a man of energy,
and controlled the current of his thought. He fought
hard, now for freedom from oppressive narrowness of

thought, now for wholeness and unity of thought; and he has in so far conquered as to be the master of a very manly and many-sided system of doctrine. I think him responsible for this system; and I think that neither he nor any other person having the least influence with younger truth-seekers ought to think or speak slightingly of the personal factor that has so large a power in forming every man's creed. As a man is, so he thinks. The only absolute truth of which we mortals seem to have any clear notion would be found in a perfect agreement of all rational beings with one another; and this agreement would simply express the fact that we were all in perfect moral harmony. Our beliefs are, therefore, in part the expression of our own will; and nobody can justly disclaim responsibility for his creed. He must be judged by the earnestness, the aim, the success of the efforts that he has made in struggling with his own experience to produce this creed.

Setting out with such a notion about the nature of belief, one is forthwith confronted by the objector who calls for the "facts." Are our beliefs actually formed through our interference? Does our will, our personal activity, have any large share in building our faith? And is such interference, where it exists, justified?

May the reader pardon our boldness in asking him to consider with us these matters, until we have shown him some of the ways in which our own personal activity is constantly interfering to form or to modify our simplest as well as our most complicated beliefs. The importance of the matter may excuse us for troubling the reader just now, and we promise to confine our attention to simple illustrations, saying in this article as little as possible about the deeper metaphysical aspect of our problem. Our purpose is a practical one. We wish to suggest the responsibility that a man has for his creed as well as for his conduct. We shall do this by pointing out that the formation of a creed is a part of conduct. And this we shall show by illustrating the way in which, whether one directs the process or not, one is at all times reacting upon what experience puts into his mind, so as to build for himself what mere experience could never give. If this is true, then it follows that we are in duty bound to direct this natural process in the way that seems to us morally best.

Every one recognizes that at least our more abstract knowledge depends largely upon our own mental activity. Knowing is not mere passive reception of facts or of truths. Learning is not solely an affair of the memory. The man who without reflection commits things to memory is justly compared to a parrot, and might yet more justly be compared to the sponge of Hamlet's figure: "It is but squeezing you, and sponge, you shall be dry again." No knowledge, then, without active hospitality in the mind that receives the knowledge. But as soon as we recognize in mental life this our power to modify our knowledge by means of our own activity, just so soon do all the old comparisons of the mind to a wax tablet, to a sheet of paper, or to other like passive subjects of impression lose for us their meaning. Mental life becomes for us, in view of these facts, a field of constant activity. The commonest processes of knowledge acquire a new significance.

Let us begin our study of this activity with a distinction. Two kinds of activity are concerned in the attainment of knowledge. One kind consists in simply receiving impressions from without, such as sensations, or, on a higher plane, statements of truth, the other consists in modifying and in organizing these impressions.

First, then, the receptive activity is partly a physical activity, since the one who receives information must use his eyes and ears, must keep awake, must at times move about; and this receptive activity is also partly made up of the mechanical processes of the memory. Association by contiguity, or learning by rote, is in the main a receptive process, though this process of reception requires some active effort on the part of the receiver. Committing words and sentences to memory is often hard labor, as we all of us learned when we first were tortured with ill-wrought geographies and grammars, or with merciless Latin declensions and conjugations. But of the whole of this receptive activity I shall make no further mention in this essay. Simply receiving, keeping your mind in a submissive attitude, directing your eyes in the proper direction, using your ears, writing down your notes, memorizing whatever needs memorizing — all this is essential to knowledge, but has no reactive effect, does not modify the form or the matter of your knowledge. Secondly, however, knowledge is determined for each of us by his own reaction upon what he receives; and this second mentioned kind of mental activity, that which forms the subject of the present paper, consists in a modification as well as in an organization of what we have received from without. All processes of reasoning, and so all original discoveries in science and in philosophy, all speculations, theories, dogmas, controversies, and not only these complex processes, but, as we shall see, even simple judgments, commonplace beliefs, momentary acts of attention — involve such independent reaction upon the material furnished to us from without. The nature of this reaction we are to examine.

Let us begin with simpler forms of knowledge. Sense-impressions constantly suggest to us thoughts; in fact, we have few thoughts that are not either immediately suggested by sense-impressions, or else sustained in their course by a continuous stream of suitable sense-impressions.

To carry on a train of even the most abstract reasoning, I must keep my eye on some diagram, or on a formula; or, perhaps, closing my eyes, I must look steadfastly with the mental eye at imaginary forms and colors, or must listen to imagined words. Thus, either the present sense-impression, or the memory of a sense-impression, is something essential to the keeping up of a train of thought. But now, how does the sense-impression go to form knowledge? What transforms it into knowledge?

The answer is, first of all, attention, an active mental process. The sense-impression is itself not yet knowledge. A sense-impression to which we give no attention slips through consciousness as a man's hand through water. Nothing grasps and retains it. No effect is produced by it. It is unknown. You cannot even tell what it is. For to know what such an unnoticed impression is, would be to pay attention to it. But let us now consider some familiar examples of the working of attention. A simple instance will bring home to us how the boundaries of our consciousness are crowded with unknown impressions — unknown, because not attended to; but yet in some inexplicable way a part of our consciousness, since an effort of attention serves to bring them, any one of them, clearly into mental vision. At this instant you are looking at something. Now without moving your eyes, try, by merely attending to your visual impressions to say what is now in the field of vision, and where is the boundary line of the field of vision. The experiment is a little hard, because our eyes, condensed embodiments as they are of tireless curiosity, are always restless, and rebel when you try to hold them fast. But conquer them for an instant, and watch the result. As your attention roams about the artificially fixed visual field, you will at first, indeed, be confused by the vagueness of all but the center; but soon you will find, to your surprise, that there are more different impressions in the field than you at first can distinguish. One after another, many various impressions will appear. But notice: you can keep your attention fixed on only a portion of the field at a time. The rest of the field is always lost in a dim haze. You must be receiving impressions all the time from all points of the field. But all of these, except the few to which you pay attention, nearly or quite disappear in the dim thickets that seem to surround the little forest-clearing made by our attentive consciousness. A like experiment can be tried with the sense of hearing, when you are in a large room full of people who are talking all around you in many independent groups. A mass of sound comes to your ear. Consciousness interferes to make you pick out one or another of the series of sounds, an act which is indeed made possible by the natural analytic tendency of the human auditory sense, but which does not take place without a noticeable effort of attention. When you are learning a foreign language, and are for a while much among those who speak it, there comes a time when your ear and mind are well enough trained to follow and understand ordinary speakers with only a little effort of attention; but yet, at this stage, you are able, by simply withdrawing your attention a mere trifle, to let very common phrases run through your sense without your understanding them one whit. You can thus, by a slight change of attention, convert the foreign language from a jargon into a familiar speech, and back again into a jargon; just as, in the fixed visual field, you can make yourself see an object pretty plainly, or lose it altogether by ceasing to give attention.

All these instances, which could be indefinitely multiplied, prove, first, that what we call attention modifies the knowledge that we at any moment get; and secondly that this modification, through attention, may take place without any change in the impressions that at any moment come from without. The first stage in getting knowledge from bare sense-impressions is, therefore, the modification of sense by attention — a process belonging wholly to the subjective side; *i. e.*, to our own minds.

But what is attention? and how does it modify sensation? Apparently, attention in the previous instances has been merely a power to increase or to diminish the intensity of impressions. But is this all that attention does? No: there are many cases in which attention directly affects the quality, at least of our complex impressions. This direct modification is commonly attended by some alteration of our emotional state. It is a familiar fact, that in listening to a series of regular and even beats, such as the strokes of an engine, or of a pendulum, or the ticking of a watch, we have a tendency to modify the impressions by introducing into their series the more elaborate regularity of rhythm. In paying attention to them, we increase, at our pleasure, the intensity of every third or fourth beat as heard, and so make a rhythm, or series of measures, out of the actually monotonous impressions. Now, attention, which here first acts by modifying the intensity of impressions, soon produces the effect of qualitatively modifying our total impression of the whole series. If I have taken the fancy to listen to the even strokes in quadruple time, intensifying by my own act every fourth stroke, the character of the series is changed for me. The impressions are less monotonous, and they arouse new associations. They seem to be caused by some force that rhythmically increases and decreases. Perhaps a melody, or some phrase of a few words, arises in my mind, and persists in associating itself with the strokes. Probably some vague feeling, as of rhythmic motion through the air, or of pleasure or of displeasure in the presence of some rhythmically moving living being, is awakened. Qualitatively, my consciousness is thus altered through my attention. I seem to be experiencing something that, as an objective reality, I do not experience. More striking becomes this qualitative alteration of experience through attention, in case you bring together two watches of different beat, or a watch and a clock, and listen to both at once at the distance of a few inches, first, perhaps, stopping one ear to avoid confusion. Here, by attention, you make or try to make a compound rhythm and this effort alters a good deal the total impression that you derive from the sound. If the two series are such that a simple small multiple of the interval of one gives you a simple small multiple of the other's interval, you can combine the two series into one rhythm, and then there is an immediate impression as if the two series were really but the complex ticking of one source of sound. But if the series will not agree, there is an odd sense of something wrong, a disappointed effort to combine, joined, as I think I have noticed, with a tendency to hasten one of the series, so as to make it agree with the other. Another case where attention alters the quality of total impressions, and not merely the intensity of any part, appears in certain psychological laboratory experiments, described by Wundt in his *Physiologische Psychologie*. Here, for the sake of determining the actual time taken by an act of attention, an observer is to make an electric signal as soon as he becomes conscious of a certain impression, while the impression itself is produced by an assistant at a time exactly determined. The source of the impression is the ringing of a bell, the flash of an electric spark, or something of the kind, agreed upon at the outset. To distinguish from one another the various causes of the delay of the signal, the conditions of experiment are variously modified. In one set of experiments, the observer does not know beforehand whether he is to experience a flash of light, or a sound, or some sensation of touch, nor how intense the sensation will be, nor when it will come; but he knows that he is to be on the lookout for one of the three kinds of sensation. He waits, with attention all aroused. In this case, it always takes him longer to signal than if he knew beforehand the kind and the strength of the coming sensation. Moreover, his attention now makes him uneasy; the coming sensation is expected, with signs of excitement, and is often received with a start. Here the feeling of effort that accompanies attention affects by its strength the character of the impression received.

Moreover, in many of these experiments there appear phenomena that show that attention alters our perception of time, not merely as to length, but also as to sequence; so that, under circumstances, an impression that really preceded another can appear in consciousness as succeeding it. Yet more: attention sometimes serves to combine two sets of simultaneous impressions, and to make them seem as if proceeding from one source. So much for the influence of attention alone. But what is attention? We reply, evidently an active process.

When impressions are modified by attention, they are actively modified. And if you ask about the nature of this active process, the reply is, attention, in its most elementary forms, is the same activity that, in a more developed shape, we commonly call will. We attend to one thing rather than to another, because we will to do so, and our will is here the elementary impulse to know. Our attention leads us at times into error. But this error is merely an accompaniment, the result of our will activity. We want to intensify an impression, to bring it within the sphere of knowledge. But in carrying out our impulse, we do more than we meant. We not only bring something into clearer consciousness that was before out of clear consciousness, but we qualitatively modify this thing in attending to it. I want to observe a series of beats, and in observing it, I make one beat in three or four seem heavier than the others, or I even alter the apparent length of one interval in three or four, by making it seem longer than the others. I observe a series of visual impressions, and at the same time a series of auditory impressions; if there is a certain agreement between them, I irresistibly unite these two series by my act of attention into one series, and refer them to a common cause. In this way, for example, part of the laughable illusion in the sport known as dumb orator is produced, where the two series of impressions must have some sort of agreement in order to produce the illusion. And so in the other cases. Attention seems to defeat, in part, its own object. Bringing something into the field of knowledge seems to be a modifying, if not a transforming, process.

We all know how this same law works on a higher plane. Giving our whole attention for a time to a particular subject seems necessary for the growth of our knowledge. Yet such attention, if long kept up, always modifies our power to know, affects our whole mental condition, and thus injures our power to appreciate the relations between the subject of our study and the other things in the world. Constant attention to one thing narrows our minds, until we fail to see the very thing we are looking at. Our lives are thus really passed in a constant flitting from one more or less partial and distorted view of things to another, from this one-sided judgment to that. Change the book you are reading, and your whole notion of the universe suffers some momentary change also. Think this week in the fashion of Carlyle, attending to things as he brings them to your attention, and human life — in fact, the whole world of being as you thought of it last week, when you were following some other guide — becomes momentarily clouded. This truth seems out of relation to that. Your change of attention qualitatively alters your apprehension of truth. Attending now even to the same things, you view them in new lights. The alteration of mental attitude becomes confusing to yourself. But refuse to make any such changes, settle down steadfastly to some one way of regarding all things, and your world becomes yet more misty. You see only a few things, and those in such a bad light that you are in danger of utter darkness. Frequent change of mental view (I, of course, do not mean constant change of creed or of occupation, but only frequent alteration of the direction of our thought) is essential to mental health. Yet this alteration implies at least some temporary change in our knowing powers, and so some change in our appreciation of truth.

Before going on to speak of the effect of our own activity upon our knowledge, when attention is combined with active recognition of impressions, I want to formulate the law that governs this action upon sense-impressions of attention when viewed alone. This law seems pretty well established by experience, and is, at all events, quite simple. It is this: Any act of attention tends, first, to strengthen the particular set of impressions to which it is at the moment adapted; and secondly to modify those impressions in such a way as shall make the total impression derived from them all as simple an impression as possible. These two statements could be reduced to one, thus: Attention constantly tends to make our consciousness more definite and less complex; that is, less confused, and more united. More definite, less confused, attention tends to make consciousness; since, out of many vague impressions, attention fixes upon one or a few, and helps them to crowd out the others. Less complex and more united or integrated attention makes the impressions attended to; as when, for the indefinite multiplicity of the successive even beats of a watch or of an engine, attention substitutes the simpler form of a rising and falling rhythm of more and less emphatic beats; or, as when two parallel series of impressions are reduced to one, by combination. If impressions are so complex and so imperative in their demands as to impede greatly the simplifying and clarifying efforts of attention, the result is a disagreeable feeling of confusion, that may increase to violent pain.

This law, that our consciousness constantly tends to the minimum of complexity and to the maximum of definiteness, is of great importance for all our knowledge. Here we have a limitation that cannot be overleaped. Whatever we come to know, whatever opinions we come to hold, our attention it is that makes all our knowing and all our believing possible; and the laws followed by this, our own activity of attention will thus determine what we are to know and what we are to believe. If things have more than a certain complexity, not only will our limited powers of attention forbid us to unravel this complexity, but we shall strongly desire to believe the things actually much simpler than they are. For our thoughts about them will have a constant tendency to become as simple and definite as possible. Put a man in a perfect chaos of phenomena, sights, sounds, feelings; and if the man continued to exist, and to be rational at all, his attention would doubtless soon find for him a way to make up some kind of rhythmic regularity, which he would impute to the things about him, so as to imagine that he had discovered some law of sequence in this mad new world. And thus, in every case where we fancy ourselves sure of a simple law of Nature, we must remember that a good deal of the fancied simplicity may be due, not to Nature, but to the ineradicable prejudice of our own minds in favor of regularity and simplicity. All our thought is determined, in great measure, by this law of least effort, as it is found exemplified in our activity of attention.

But attention is not the only influence that goes to transform sense-impressions into knowledge. Attention never works alone, but always in company with the active process of recognizing the present as in some way familiar, and of constructing in the present ideas of what is not present. At these two other active processes we must very briefly glance.

Recognition is involved in all knowledge. Recognition does not always mean a definite memory of a particular past experience that resembles a present one. On the contrary, recognition is essentially only a sense of familiarity with something now present, coupled with a more or less distinct applying of some predicate to this present thing. I recognize a horse, a landscape, a star, a friend, a piece of music, a book, when I feel more or less familiar with the impression of the object in question, and when, at the same time, I predicate more or less distinctly something of it. This, I say, is my friend, or the north star, or Webster's Dictionary, or Smith's horse. Or, perhaps, in recognizing, I recognize, not merely the whole object, but one of its qualities, or of its relations to other things. Then I say, this is large or small, good or bad, equal or unequal to another thing, and so on. In all these cases, recognition involves a lively reaction of my mind upon external impressions. Recognition is not found apart from attention, though attention may exist more or less completely without recognition. Recognition completes what attention begins. The attentive man wants to know, the recognizing man knows, or thinks he knows. Recognition implies accompanying attention. Attention without recognition implies wonder, curiosity, perplexity, perhaps terror. But what is the law of this process of recognition? Does the process affect the impressions themselves that are the basis of the recognition? The answer is: Very distinctly, recognition does affect the impressions. The activity involved in recognition alters the data of sense, and that in almost every case. Two of the ways in which this alteration occurs are these: (1) In recognizing, we complete present data by remembered past data, and so seem to experience more than is actually given to our senses. Thus, then, in reading, we read over misprints (even against our own will), thinking that we see words when we do not see them, or when we see only parts of them. Again: in listening to an indistinct speaker we often supply what is lacking in the sounds he makes, and seem to hear whole words when we really hear but fragments of words. Or, merely whistling a few notes, we recall to ourselves, and seem to have present, the complex instrumental harmony of some music that we have heard played. Or, in dim twilight, we imagine the form of a man, and seem to see it plainly in detail, when, in fact, a mass of shrubbery, or a coat on a chair, is the one source of our impressions. In all these cases, the activity of recognition alters the data of sense, by adding to them, by filling out the sketch made by them. (2) However, even the qualities of sense-impressions are altered according to the way in which we recognize their objects. The colors of a landscape are dimmer, and less significant as colors, so long as we recognize the objects in the landscape. Look under your arm, with head inverted, and the colors flash out with unwonted brilliancy. For when you so look, you lose sight of the objects as such, and give your attention solely to the colors. Mistake a few brown leaves in some dark corner of a garden for some little animal, and the leaves take on for the moment the distinctive familiar color of the animal; and when you discover your blunder, you can catch the colors in the very act of fading into their dull, dry-leaf insignificance. Many facts of this sort are recorded by psychologists and by artists, and can be observed by any of us if we choose. To separate a sensation from its modifications that are produced by recognition is not a little difficult.

Now, in both these kinds of alteration a law is observed, very similar to the one previously noted. The alteration of the data of sense in the moment of recognition are alterations in the direction of simplicity and definiteness of consciousness. The present is assimilated to the past; the new is made to seem as familiar as possible. This reaction of the mind upon new impressions is easily seen in our thoughts and words in the first moment of great surprise or fright. When Macbeth turns from his door to the table, and sees the ghost of Banquo in his chair, his first words are not the "*Avaunt, and quit my sight!*" wherewith he greets the second appearance of the ghost, nor yet even the "*Which of you have done this?*" that he utters as soon as he recovers himself. No: his first conscious reaction, in presence of the horrible impression, is a quiet remark, "*The table's full.*" And when they tell him that there is a place reserved, he persists with a "*Where?*" In this scene, Shakespeare's instinct is perfectly accurate. Our effort always is to make the new as familiar as possible, even when this new is inconceivably strange. It takes us some time to realize, as we say, a great change of any sort. Recognition, however, is yet further modified by the interest with which we at any moment attend to things. But when we speak of interest, we are led, to the third kind of active modification by which our minds determine for us what we know.

At every moment we are not merely receiving, attending, and recognizing, but we are constructing. Out of what from moment to moment comes to us, we are building up our ideas of past and future, and of the world of reality. Mere dead impressions are given. We turn them by our own act into symbols of a real universe. We thus constantly react upon what is given, and not only modify it, but even give it whatever significance it comes to possess. Now this reaction takes a multitude of forms, and cannot be fully discussed without far more than our present space. But we can name one or two prominent modes of reaction of mind upon sense-data in this province of mental life.

1. Definite memory is possible only through present

active construction from the data of feeling. Nothing
can come to us certifying for itself that it formed a part
of our previous experience. When we know a thing as
past, we actively project our idea of it into a conceived
past time. Without this active interference of our own
minds, everything would be but a present, and there
would be no time for us, only fleeting life from moment
to moment.

2. Definite belief in external reality is possible only
through this active addition of something of our own to
the impressions that are actually given to us. No external reality is given to us in the mere sense-impressions. What is outside of us cannot be at the same time
within us. But out of what is in us, we construct an idea
of an external world; and we ourselves give to this idea
all the validity that for us it can ever have.

3. All abstract ideas, all general truths, all knowledge
of necessary laws, all acceptance of doctrines, are, in like
fashion, an active process coming from within. Change
the fashions of our mental activity, and nobody can tell
how radically you would change our whole conception
of the universe.

4. All this active construction from sense-impressions expresses certain fundamental interests that our
human spirit takes in reality. We want to have a world
of a particular character; and so, from sense-impressions, we are constantly trying to build up such a world.
We are prejudiced in favor of regularity, necessity, and
simplicity in the world; and so we continually manipu-
late the data of sense for the sake of building up a notion
of a regular, necessary, and simple universe. And so,
though it is true that our knowledge of the world is determined by what is given to our senses, it is equally
true that our idea of the world is determined quite as

much by our own active combination, completion, anticipation of sense-experience. Thus all knowing is, in a very deep sense, acting: it is, in fact, reacting and creation. The most insignificant knowledge is in some sense an original product of the man who knows. In it is expressed his disposition, his power of attention, his skill in recognition, his interest in reality, his creative might. Exact knowledge is, in fact, only possible in cases where we ourselves make what we know. So only is mathematical knowledge possible; for mathematical ideas are all products of a constructive imagination. And so it is in all other thought-life. Mentally produce, and thou shalt know thy product. But remember, for what we produce, we are in some sense morally responsible; and thus, as we said at the outset, in discussing the nature of knowledge, we are trespassing on the borderland of ethics.

We said, at the beginning of our study, that our purpose is a practical one. We wish to point out the importance of the active personal factor in the formation of belief, and to draw from the facts a moral lesson. And what is this lesson? Plainly, since active inner processes are forever modifying and building our ideas; since our interest in what we wish to find does so much to determine what we do find; since we could not if we would reduce ourselves to mere registering machines, but remain always builders of our own little worlds — it becomes us to consider well, and to choose the spirit in which we shall examine our experience. Every one is certain to be prejudiced, simply because he does not merely receive experience, but himself acts, himself makes experience. The great question for every truth-seeker is, In what sense, to what degree, with what motive, for what end, may I and should I be prejudiced?

Most of us get our prejudices wholly from the fashions of other men. This is cowardly. We are responsible for our own creed, and must make it by our own hard work. Therefore, the deepest and most important of all questions is the one, "*For what art thou at work?*" It is useless to reply, "*I am merely noting down what I find in the world. I am not responsible for the facts.*" The answer is, "A mere note-book thou art not, but a man. These are never simply notes; thy thoughts are always transformed reality, never mere copies of reality. For thy transforming activity, as well as for thy skill in copying, thou art answerable."

A NEGLECTED STUDY

[1890]

WE students of philosophy have an old fashion of pointing out defects in other men's knowledge, and of assigning tasks for our fellows to perform. The fashion is old, I say; for it was set by our master, Socrates, whose wisdom lay in his well-known confession of ignorance, and the equally well-known cross-questioning whereby he made plain to his opponents in dialogue their own unwisdom and their need of sound doctrine. Ever since, philosophical students, not always indeed with the Socratic modesty of self-confession, have loved to point out this or that gap in human knowledge, this or that needed and unaccomplished task, which the presumably wider outlook of their own professional studies, has, as they pretend, enabled them to see in the province of some special pursuit. If in this little paper I venture afresh on such a thankless task as this, I can only plead the time-honored privilege of my trade. It is a privilege not at all free, of course, from its off-setting disadvantages. The philosophical student, when he accuses any of his fellows in some sister art of having left a ripe harvest of truth here or there ungarnered, stands himself at the mercy of whosoever chooses to retort that philosophy, with all its disorganized multitude of opinions and of researches, has so far dishearteningly few sheaves of ripe grain to show for its toil. A doctrine that consists, so to speak, mainly of unaccomplished tasks, may thus appear in an evil light when it pretends to criticize the omissions of its fellows. But, after all, not recrimination but mutual exhortation is the true purpose of students when they discourse about the needs and the defects of their various branches of research; and it is the privilege of philosophy to have acquired, in its long experience of unfulfilled hopes, a peculiarly keen sense of what constitutes unfulfillment in human intellectual efforts.

The unfulfilled task, the neglected branch of study, which this paper wants to point out for the benefit of young students who may be wondering what to do with their wits, lies at a certain place in the wide field of modern Literary Research. In our own language, namely, as we shall find, the books that endeavor to deal with just this task, in any well-equipped fashion, are still surprisingly few. The young students who understand the importance of the matter are very hard to find. A curious popular prejudice concerning the nature and the possibilities of literary research stands meanwhile stubbornly in the way of the prosperity of the branch of investigation to which I refer. But because in any case the study that I mean can be more easily defined by its spirit and by its purpose than through the naming of any list of books, I may as well begin with a suggestion, by analogy, of the region of Literary Research where our neglected study lies. Many scholars, indeed, know of this study; some scholars even in our midst are lovers of it, and a few may rank as masters in its service; but these are indeed few. The multitude pass it by without any real comprehension.

Yet analogy, as I have just said, will suggest at once our needed study. Classical Philology, in the time from the Renaissance to the beginning of our present century, used to consist, as everybody knows, of two main branches: one the literary study of classical masterpieces for the sake of their beauty and of their wisdom; the other, grammatical research into the structure of the classical languages as such. Each of these main branches of erudition had its subordinate branches. Text-criticism, of the older school, served for instance as handmaid to the grammarian. The infant science, Archæology, supplemented in a measure the work of the student of pure literature. But such subordinate branches of study were not only imperfectly developed; their very significance and their true aim was not yet understood. Only when, at the close of the last century and at the beginning of this, the modern historical method began that wonderful development which in our day has at last borne fruit in the doctrine of evolution — only then was it possible for Philology to get the definition which, for scholars like Boeckh, ere long became characteristic. Philology, for such men, meant the study of the whole life, of the entire thought and civilization of classical antiquity. How fruitful this idea of the philologist's task hâs become for classical study in modern times I may leave for wiser men to describe. It is enough for me at present to suggest how much the value of those older branches of learning themselves, namely, the purely linguistic study of Greek and Latin, and the purely æsthetic appreciation of the literary masterpieces of antiquity, has in fact gained, in recent times, through this high ideal of philological scholarship to which our century has given birth. The grammarian used to be a person whose learned devotion to details only his fellows could prize. He seemed to have some mysterious passion for particles, for moods and tenses, and the rest, purely for their own abstract sakes. This passion was his life. It was an end in itself to him.

> So with the throttling hands of Death at strife,
>   Ground he at grammar;

> Still thro' the rattle parts of speech were rife.
> While he could stammer
> He settled *Hoti's* business — let it be!
> Properly based *Oun* —
> Gave us the doctrine of the enclitic *De*,
> Dead from the waist down.

Thus his learning, as Browning's well-known lines suggest, was throughout a determined separation of himself from life.

> "Time to taste life," another would have said
> "Up with the curtain!"
> This man said rather, "Actual life comes next?
> Patience a moment!
> Grant I have mastered learning's crabbed text,
> Still there's the comment."

Well, the modern classical scholar, on the contrary, when he is true to the spirit of his age, seems, as far as I have had any chance to observe him, to love no less his enclitics, but to love their living meaning more. His linguistic study is not an end in itself, so much as a contribution towards the fair appreciation of that wonderful live thing called the Greek mind — that most remarkable of the spontaneous variations to which the human type has given birth. The modern classical scholar is in fact a biologist, who is studying the variety of man called ancient Greek, and the other variety called Roman. His interests are essentially the biological, and in particular the psychological interests. When he studies grammar, he is simply learning about the habits of thought which characterized the men whose life he tries to read. And when he examines literary masterpieces, his scientific aim is still the same. He does not abstract the æsthetic from the other vitally significant aspects of literature. Such abstraction would in his eyes be an absurdity. And yet the men who in former centuries enjoyed the "elegance" of their Horace, and the "nobility" of their Sophocles (as of course they had every right to do), used too often to make just such an absurd abstraction. They used to conceive that you read Horace or Sophocles *either* for "polite" enjoyment, or *else* for grammatical exercise. The two thus narrowly defined aims hindered each other. That true literary enjoyment is heightened, not hindered, by a deeper comprehension of the temperament whose products you are enjoying; and that grammatical rules are merely a means of getting at the habits of the language-using animal to whom belonged this temperament — all this the older scholars, so far as I understand their point of view, used too often to forget. In short, then, the ideal of modern classical philology is, I apprehend, something of this kind: — The remarkable variety of the *homo sapiens* whose habits of doing and of thinking were embodied in the monuments of classical antiquity, needs to be comprehended, just as any other animal needs to be comprehended, by studying his temperament and his peculiar vital processes. Only, just this variety of live creature chances to have been peculiarly thoughtful, significant, productive. So fine a tone of brain-cortex functioning has never elsewhere appeared on our planet. Therefore it is that all the characteristic habits of the Greek are worthy of so much study. Therefore it is that his *oun's* and his *de's*, and his *an's*, his optatives, his subjunctives, and his composite words, deserve such elaborate scrutiny. Linguistic study is justified by its place among the biological sciences. The reflexes of the Hellenic speech centers are very highly noteworthy phenomena in human psychology. And, even so, the products of Greek literary art, the wonderful masterpieces themselves, must be examined with a truly scholarly seriousness and minuteness. The genuine literary student is no man of "polite" leisure, who merely glances about him and gracefully estimates this or that. He, too, is a psychologist. His calling is one with that of the true grammarian. They are both equally philologists, because they are both equally engaged in a psychological study of the life of antiquity. Literary enjoyment is, or ought to be *res severa*. You enjoy only what you comprehend. You comprehend only what you grasp in its relations, see as a symptom of the life whereof it formed part, lovingly and minutely scrutinize, patiently follow into all its windings and its intricacies. To be sure, where the task is so vast there has to be division of labor. One philologist gets his revelations concerning ancient life rather from *an* and the optative; another is devoted to choral metres and to verse translations; a third is an archæologist; a fourth drinks in his literary knowledge in long draughts of continuous reading, and seems fitted to be rather the general historian than the linguist. But all know that their "division" must not mean real separation, that each depends on his fellows, that they are at work upon a common task, and that this common task is the one called Philological Research.

Our analogy is thus before us. I must apologize to the classical philologists, should any of them glance at this paper, for my layman's effort to describe their spirit. I aim only to cite their very instructive example. And now for our neglected study. What I miss in recent scholarship in this country, as well as in England, is a sufficiently serious and thorough-going effort to study modern literature, and, above all, English Literature itself, in this truly philological spirit. Ask a young student of today what is meant by English Philology, and he too often answers, "Anglo-Saxon and Early English studied in a purely linguistic fashion." Now I am far from venturing, or from even faintly wishing, to make light of two such important branches of philological study as Anglo-Saxon and Early English. Only if I asked any one to point out to me a horse, and he insisted upon showing me the horse's hind legs, and upon assuring me that they were the only true animal, I should be puzzled. And to my mind it is not any disparagement of the hind legs to insist that a knowledge of their anatomy is but a small part of the composition of the true horse, necessary part though it be. English Philology, I apprehend, is an organic science, whose purpose is the study of the English mind in its wholeness. Like Classical Philology, this is one of the biological sciences, and in particular it is a branch of psychology. Its task, like that of any other biological science, is one of endless wealth and variety, demands therefore, endless division of labor, and specialization of studious functions. But complete separation of studies is never the aim of science. Differentiation must not mean isolation. And what I complain of in many of our younger students of English "Philology" is not that their linguistic work is unimportant, but that they themselves fail to realize its importance, because they have so little comprehension of the unity of philology as a whole. These young linguists sometimes (I speak now of the youth only) pride themselves upon their entire separation from the superficial persons who are "only literary students," or who are "light literary critics" — to use a phrase that a certain linguistic specialist in England once, in an unhappy moment of wrath and chagrin, applied to Mr. Lowell himself. Ah, this idea of the "lightness" of literary criticism — what mischief has it not caused! Is life so very "light" an affair? And whose task is weightier than is that of the man who undertakes to gauge the very issues of life themselves, and the works that embody these issues? In any case, however, nothing is more degrading to the true dignity of the linguist's task than this self-imposed separation of his interests from the "purely literary" interests. As if, I repeat, the laws of language were anything but a record of the habits of the speaking animal, and as if such records were anything but one means more of comprehending that very humanity whose vital passions produce literature, and give to it its worth. Meanwhile, of course, the "purely literary students" often suffer equally from their acceptance of this separation. They fancy that scholarship in these matters means only crabbed linguistic study. Their own pursuits become fragmentary, inorganic, unworthy of serious men. If the young linguists confine themselves to the anatomy of the horse's hind legs, after he is dead, the "purely literary students" content themselves with admiring his contour, and betting on his wind and his speed, so long as he is alive. This constitutes their "literary criticism." Meanwhile nobody amongst them all, young "linguists" or young "critics" really loves the horse well enough to desire to study his whole structure, his vital processes, his reflexes, his instincts, his habits, his ancestry, and his evolution, with anything of the biologist's comprehensiveness and devotion. And so our horse remains essentially an unknown creature.

"But surely," one may retort to all this, "it does not need an article like the present one to point out, even to young men, the importance of a true study of the English mind in its wholeness. All our greater critics, all our

more ambitious historians in recent times, have they
not pointed out to us in a hundred ways that history
deals with human evolution, that literary history is a
part of this general study of evolution, and that English
literature, if only any one man could learn the whole
truth about it, ought to be capable of furnishing important contributions to such a study? Who, indeed,
that lives in the great Age of Evolution, should fail to
appreciate this fact?" The trouble, it will be said, lies
then, in the complexity of the subject itself. A man
must specialize; and one man loves his Anglo-Saxon, another his Lake Poets. Nobody can contribute very
much to so vast a task. Let each do what he can.

I answer, what I am pleading for is a spirit of study,
not the learning of any one group of facts. And what I
point out is that, despite frequent and varied and authoritative insistance upon just the truths upon which I
here insist, the particular spirit which I advocate still
remains unknown to a great part of our studious American public. How much is yet to be done in the way of a
genuine history of the life and thought of the English
people! How little does a student who, like myself,
occasionally needs for professional purposes special instruction as to the history of the great English Moral
Ideas and Ideals, find to aid him in our libraries! Essays
of fragmentary and capricious literary criticism, ambitious failures like the magnificently planned and hopelessly unsuccessful book of Taine, numberless biographical sketches, of every degree of power and skill, large
collections of raw material, and finally elaborate para-
sitical growths such as the mass of literary industry that
has grown up at Shakespeare's expense: such are the
treasures of wisdom that offer themselves to whoever
seeks for light as to the evolution of English Literature

in its wholeness. I do not want to speak ill of this colossal mass of material. But what I do often want to find in it is guidance — guidance as to the meaning, the causation, the relationships of English thought and passion. And such guidance I in great measure miss, because so few even of our best literary critics, and even of our wisest scholars, have clearly conceived of such a thing as Modern Philology, whose ideal should be formed after the analogy of the ideal of Classical Philology whereof I spoke above. I do not demand the impossible. I do not hope that anybody can as yet succeed in accomplishing the task which Taine set himself, the task of writing a Philosophy of the History of English Literature. For the conquest of so vast a field the time is not yet come, nor can it soon come. But what I wish is that the true spirit of modern philological research should prosper amongst a large body of our young students, and that this false and lamentable and absurd opposition which nowadays keeps asunder the men who are devoted to what they call English Philology, and the men who are "purely literary students," should give place to a cordial coöperation in the one task of comprehending the English mind as it has existed in all its successive periods.

That I long to see similar methods applied to the whole study of modern literature, I have already suggested. I think that a failure to understand the one duty of the philologist, which, is, through *both* "linquistic" and "literary" study, to come nearer to a comprehension of Mind, is responsible in large part for the condition of public opinion which, in our day and country, encourages the "light literary critic" to accept the supposed limitations of his calling, and to become rather a *doctrinaire* than a sincere and laborious student of human nature. The literary critic is, forsooth, not to be a "scholar." A "scholar" is a grammarian who knows about Greek particles, or about Anglo-Saxon, or about Ulfilas. As of course there can be nothing thus "scholarly" about novel reading or about a knowledge of Browning or of Shelley, the "purely literary man" must needs do something else than be learned. He must rather be "authoritative," *i. e.*, self-confident, dogmatic. He must "lead a movement," or at any rate follow one. Hence, the public wants to know to what "school" he belongs. Is he a pessimist, or a follower of Tolstoi, or a believer in Ibsen, or a hater of the realistic novel writers? Best of all, if he is a "literary man" and still wants to seem a very serious person, a "leader" in the imposing sense — best of all is it for him nowadays to concern himself with some burning "social question." He must be a socialist, or organize a reform society of some sort, or write on the New South. Anything will do, if so be only that it is *not* an effect to comprehend the life of man through studious literary research (for there is no studious literary research but that of the linguist!). The "purely literary man" must inflict his whims, his prejudices, on the world, unless indeed he is able to get the world to read his poems, when he will become a productive artist and pass to a higher plane. So long as he remains a "critic" he has nothing to do but to be either "light," or "prophetic," and in any and every case to be whimsical rather than scholarly. In consequence he too often sees little, because he is so anxious to become independently luminous on his own account. His office is not to be one of discernment, but of a sort of phosphorescent literary glowing whereby attention shall be attracted to himself.

It is this glow-worm life, to which, in the absence of

scholarly ideals, many, especially of our younger literary critics, are nowadays condemned, that is responsible for the "crazes" which at the moment are the curse of our American literary life. The "craze" that makes Browning or Ibsen or any other literary man a solitary idol, is a symptom of a condition of intelligence for which literature in its true sense is as good as non-existent. For the solitary idol is no organic part of literature; nor is he studied with any truly psychological concern. To your "Browningite," Browning is not a live creature, splendid in vigor, and with all the finely stubborn and obvious defects of a very manly and original temperament — a live creature, to be first studied with all a naturalists' devotion and *then* criticized, precisely as he used to criticize others, with a healthy man's freedom of reaction. No, Browning is a sublime sort of person, called a seer, and this, in the minds of the average Browningites, who have no idea of psychological types, and who would not know a live seer from a handsaw if they met one — this means that Browning stands for a creed, a doctrine, an elaborate system, a revelation. This creed you first accept with awe. Then you proceed to find out what it is. Browning's mysteries dawn upon you slowly. The actual behavior in verse of the man Browning, passionate, whimsical, romantic, humane, capricious, wise, and exasperating, as he was — this you are not concerned to study, as he studied his *Men and Women*, namely with a loving eye for their very crudities and narrownesses as well as for their heroic qualities. For the true philologist would indeed look upon Browning much as Browning looked upon his fellowmen; namely with a keen scrutiny and an unsparing but humane estimate of faults. As for Browning himself, few men have as it were, more frankly confessed their literary faults to the world, have more pressed them upon the reader's notice. Browning's greatest fault was his capriciousness; and this he is constantly confessing. His creed meanwhile is an extremely short and simple one, which needs no clubs to expound it. Few men have had a more childlike depth and clearness of faith. His verse is obscure mainly because he chose to amuse himself by making it so. Nobody could write simpler and warmer lyrics than he; nobody of his rank has ever chosen to torment his readers with as many caprices. This capricious temperament of Browning's is, however, for this very reason, so much the more fascinating in its paradoxes to the lover of original types. Would that we had more such lovers amongst us. As it is, the question: "How do you view Browning?" means to most minds: "Do you or do you not accept the mysterious, profound, and obscure thing called the Teaching of Browning?" What the question ought to mean would be "Have you yet found time to become acquainted with the type called Browning?" — a splendid, manly, modern type, whereof God found room for only one example; while nobody need wish, in a world full of fascinating types and of exasperating puzzles, for more than one.

But of the literary "crazes" I had no wish to speak at length. What I wish to insist upon is this crying need for a scholarly study of modern, and especially of English Literature, in the spirit in which Boeckh studied Classical Philology. The history of politics, of ethics, of morals, of society, of all civilization, is dependent for its progress upon the true and philological comprehension of the history of language and of literature. There is not *one* scholarly task called linguistic science, and *another*, but an *un*scholarly task, giving rise to endless creeds, dogmas, and "crazes" and called "merely literary study," or "light literary criticism." There is in fact but *One* Philology, and its purpose is the comprehension of human life as recorded in the monuments of language. To this task linguists and literary critics can alike contribute. The neglect of such study it is that gives especial impetus to those "crazes" wherein a vague sense of the greatness of literature joins itself with a Philistine dogmatism and an indolent unwillingness to study life as it actually is in the living creatures. The true philologist studies his authors as living souls, and tries to comprehend their place in a national life. He does not merely speculate; nor does he merely study grammar. He is essentially a naturalist in his concerns and methods. And his is the study that, as I think, is nowadays too much neglected.

THE PROBLEM OF PARACELSUS

[1893]

THE collection of poems belonging to what may be called the "Faust-cycle," in the literature of the present century, contains no extended work whose machinery of plot and of incident is, when externally regarded, simpler than that of Browning's "Paracelsus." [1] The relations of hero and tempter are nowhere freer from external complication than when the hero is explicitly the deceiver of his own soul. With Paracelsus this is actually the case.

For classing "Paracelsus" with the Faust-cycle in this way there are many grounds. The real Paracelsus was a contemporary of the historic prototype of Faust. The two figures were, as a fact, closely linked in Goethe's mind, as they must have been in Browning's. Such a classification in no wise detracts from the sort of originality which the poem possesses, while it aids us in finding our way when we consider its problem. The absence of an external tempter in no wise excludes the poem from the Faust-cycle; for the tempter in most such creations is but the hero's other self, given a magical and plastic outer reality, as with Manfred. As regards the positive aspects of the analogy, the typical hero of a poem of the Faust-cycle is a man of the Renaissance, to whom the church is no authority, and to whom the world is magically full either of God's or of Satan's presence, or of both. This hero risks his soul in a quest for some abso-

[1] This paper was read before the Boston Browning Society, November 26, 1893. [Printed in Boston Browning Society Papers, 1886–97, published by The Macmillan Company, New York, 1897. — Ed.]

lute fulfillment of pleasure, power, wisdom or peace.
Thus staking everything, he gets, like an early voyager
to the New World, either the doom of the outlaw,
or the glories of the conquistador; but meanwhile he
comes near, if he does not meet, an evil end in the
abyss.

Thus regarded, the problem of Paracelsus readily defines itself. We are to study the career of a spiritual
relative of Faust. Accordingly, we have to consider his
original quest, and the strong Satanic delusion to which
he fell prey. In such a light we may hope to express the
sense of his tragedy.

1. Browning has told us several times, in the course
of the poem, where to look for the heart of the mystery.
Paracelsus made it his early ideal "to know." Failing
in this undertaking, conceived as it was in a spirit of
ideal youthful extravagance, the maturer Paracelsus
learns from the poet Aprile, in the scene at the Greek
conjurer's house, that the goal of life ought to be "to
love" as well as "to know." He endeavors, in consequence, to reform his life according to the new insight;
but the attempt comes too late. The "love" that the
great alchemist tries to cultivate in his heart turns
rather to hate. He flees from his office as professor at
Basel, wanders, wastes years fruitlessly, and dies, seeing
indeed at last his true defect, and explaining it in the
wonderful closing speech of the poem.

The whole tragedy thus turns explicitly upon this
poetic antithesis between "loving" and "knowing."
But these words are among the most manifold in meaning of all the words of human language; from the nature
of the case they have to be so. In this poem, then, just
as in daily usage, they will mean whatever the whole
context of the action shows. Browning portrays, as

usual, a "mood" (the word is his own, used in the preface to the first edition of the poem). He leaves us to draw for ourselves the conclusions from the situation before us. His choice in this regard but embodies the natural privilege of the dramatic poet; the critical problem that results for us is one of the most legitimate sort. A tragic conflict has occurred through the interplay of two of the most universal and Protean of human interests. How these interests are here colored and defined and why they thus conflict, we are, as readers, to determine. Such questions of interpretation are necessary in case of every serious dramatic issue.

The very simplicity of seeming of the two familiar words "love" and "knowledge" has, however, blinded many readers to the actual complications of the poem. Of the critics some, like Mr. Arthur Symons, find the tragic error of Paracelsus in the fact that he is "one whose ambition transcends all earthly limits, and exhausts itself in the thirst of the impossible." This is of course true in a measure of any hero of the type of Faust; but one thus defines, as it were, only the genus, not the species, of this particular flower from the fields of tragedy. Of the antithesis between "love" and "knowledge" itself, other critics, notably Mr. Berdoe, together with far too large a number of readers, appear to make little more than would be expressed by the comparatively shallow and abstract platitude that the intellect without the affections is a vain guide in life. I doubt not that Browning most potently believed this platitude. Who of us does not? But with such abstractions one gets but a little way, and creates no tragic issues. As a fact, nobody who has a nature on the human level, ever lives by either the intellect alone or the affections alone. Every rational being both "knows" and "loves," if by

these words be meant only the bare abstractions called
the "pure intellect" and the "affections." One might
"love" Hebrew roots, or "know" the art of love-
making. In either case, in actual life, one would combine the two functions of loving and knowing, whatever
one did. But the problem of life is always what to know
and what to love. Apart from specific objects, the two
tendencies have no true antithesis. If, then, Browning's
contrast means anything, these two words must be used,
as St. Paul used them, or as common sense always uses
them, in a pregnant sense, and with an implied reference to particular objects known or loved.

Browning cannot mean to ascribe his hero's failure to
the fact that he is a "pure intellectualist," in the sense
in which that term is often applied to a man who is exclusively in love with the study of some one abstract
science. Such a devotee of pure science Browning actually sketched for us later in the "Grammarian's Fun-
neral." The poet, fond as he is of strenuousness, has no
word of blame for the ideal of such a student, whose
one-sidedness he finds not tragic, but glorifying.

> Let a man contend, with his utmost might,
> For his life's best prize, be it what it may.

That is Browning's creed, from first to last. I can conceive, then, no error more hopeless than to suppose that
the pregnant words which name the ideals of "love"
and "knowledge," here tragically and sharply opposed
to each other, are merely names for the intellectual and
the affectionate sides of human nature, or that the poem
is merely a sentimental protest on the part of a young
poet against the too exclusive devotion of a thoughtful
hero to his life's chosen business. Were that the case, it
would be the solitary instance in all Browning's works

where a hero suffers in the poet's estimation because of a too sincere devotion to his chosen ideal.

As a fact, such an estimate of our poem would here contradict the most obvious facts of the text. The man Paracelsus, at his coldest, never even tries to appear in this poem as a partisan either of a pure intellectualism of any sort, or of what we nowadays should call the "scientific spirit." He is no abstract reasoner, but a man of intuitions; no admirer of the so-called "cold intellect," but a passionate mystic; no steadily progressive student, busied with continuous systematic researches, but a restless wanderer; no being of clear-cut ideas, but a dreamer. The attentive reader cannot miss these altogether fundamental considerations. Unless we bear in mind these characteristics — the dreaminess, the ardor, the mysticism, the unsteadiness, and the essential unreasonableness of Browning's Paracelsus — the man and his fortunes will remain a sealed book. No interpretation that forgets these facts in defining what "knowledge" meant for Paracelsus, and how it was opposed to the "love" of the poet Aprile, will be able even to approach a comprehension of the text, or to see wherein Paracelsus was deceived.

I may observe in passing that Browning was fond of using the words "love," "knowledge," and "power" in a pregnant sense. All three are so used not only in this poem but also down to the latest period of the poet's work. The use of familiar words in a pregnant sense, to be defined by the context, is the poet's substitute for technical terms. In "Reverie" in "Asolando," precisely the same antithesis as that upon which the tragedy of "Paracelsus" is based is treated, not in its relation to a hero's character, but in a general and meditative fashion, with the use of the words "love" and "power" as the terms. In fact the problem of "Paracelsus" involves one of Browning's most frequent and favorite topics of reflection.

2. In the case of a tragedy of Browning's creation, one can do little with the ideas, unless one first understands the hero's personality. How ideal are the aspirations which Browning attributes to his hero, every reader knows. What many readers neglect is that other and far less ideal disposition which, with a characteristic respect for the complexities of human nature, he attributes to what one may call his hero's lower self. Browning has affixed to the poem certain prose notes, meant to help us in understanding the author's attitude. Read by themselves, these tend to make us think of Paracelsus and his fortunes in anything but an ideal light. The excesses, the charlatanry, the other marks of degradation — the roughness of speech of this rugged being, when once he is angered, his pettiness of motive when once he is involved in difficulties — to all these the notes deliberately attract attention. All are fully reflected in the poem itself. Browning is not the slavish admirer of his own hero, but the true dramatic poet, who takes interest in the struggle of a great but burdened and in some respects degraded soul for the far-off light. Until the very end we must not expect to find Paracelsus wholly or even very largely an enlightened being. He has to work aspiringly in the dark.

As a creature of flesh and blood, Browning's Paracelsus is, first of all, rather a dreamer than a thinker. He is extremely intelligent, but essentially a creature of flashes of insight. He is of indomitable courage and of restless temper, impatient of restraint, and extremely fond, like many other professional men, of the sound of his own voice. He is very unconscious meanwhile of a certain curiously sentimental fondness for his intimate friends which lurks in the background of his rugged temperament, and which, especially in the third and fourth acts, gets very noteworthy expressions. Unable to bring this sentimental motive either to form or to consciousness, he is driven to search ceaselessly for exciting experiences, to the end that a heart which can never be satisfied may be kept constantly stimulated. So long as life is new, he indeed is able to refrain absolutely from all meaner indulgences; but he is somewhat coarse-fibred, and when higher excitements fail, he takes a certain rude delight in more ignoble sport, and meanwhile despises himself therefor. He is overwhelmingly proud, and is by nature condemned to a profound loneliness of experience.

In order to comprehend what sort of "knowledge" is in question in the poem, let us observe something suggested by the relation of our hero to the real Paracelsus. Browning says: "The liberties I have taken with my subject are very trifling; and the reader may slip the foregoing scenes between the leaves of any memoir of Paracelsus he pleases, by way of commentary." Browning was twenty-two years old when he thus wrote. His previous reading had been varied and industrious. From first to last he was fond of what is called mystical literature. Mrs. Sutherland Orr mentions among the books read in the poet's boyhood an old treatise on astrology. For the poem itself he read during a few months very extensively. There is no evidence, however, that he considered it his task, as poet, to trouble himself much concerning the technical aspect of the opinions which distinguish the actual Paracelsus from other thinkers of a similar intellectual type. It is fairly plain, however, that Browning had interested himself to collect from such sources as he used a number of illustrations of the characteristic speeches and the personal attitudes of his hero. The special doctrines of the thinker had less concern for him. Their spirit, and the deeper nature of the man, he sought authentically to portray.

Especially authentic as characterizing the real Paracelsus and especially important, also, for understanding the poetic antithesis of "love" and "knowledge," as here developed, is an intellectual trait which Browning makes prominent in his hero throughout the poem — the curious union of a very great confidence in private intuitions, in the inner light, as such, with a very great respect for what Paracelsus regards as the right sort of external experience of the facts of nature. Here is a man to whom "knowledge" means his own private, immediate and intuitive apprehension of truth through the inner light; but to whom this inner light means nothing except in relation to the details of outer experience, as he himself has verified them; a dark-lantern sort of spirit who has to shine alone apart from other lights, and whose spiritual insight forever flashes its brilliant beams now on this, now on that chance fact of the passing moment. To understand the significance of this tendency we must give the matter still closer scrutiny.

3. Browning well read in the real Paracelsus the just-mentioned fundamental and noteworthy feature of his mental processes. Some men believe in the intuitions, in the inner light, of either the reason or the heart; and, therefore, they find these intuitions so satisfying that they neglect or even abhor the baser revelations of the senses. Such men go into their closet and shut the door, or, as Schiller has it, they "flee from life's stress to the holy inner temples." Here they can be alone with God, with the truth, with their love, or with all their noble

sentiments. Such men may be abstract thinkers, serene
and deep, like Spinoza. If they are more emotionally
disposed, they become, in various untechnical and de-
vout fashions, contemplative mystics, quietists, seers of
divine and incommunicably beautiful dreams. On the
other hand there are men who stand in sharp contrast to
the former; these believe, as they say, only " in the hard
facts of experience." Accordingly, they mistrust all intuitions, whether rational or emotional. Men of this
type we call pure empiricists or positivists.

But these two sharply contrasted types do not any-
where nearly exhaust the possibilities. Many men there
are who join, in one way or another, intuition and experience. Of these latter there are not a few — even
among the patient students of natural science, still more,
among the students of the moral world — who look to
see the divine law illustrated and incarnated in the facts
of experience, vivifying either the whole, or some luminous part thereof, with its own grace and significance.
In the classification of these mixed types we must appeal
to a very ancient and familiar distinction — that between the world of our physical and the world of our
moral experiences. Upon this distinction the problem of
our whole poem turns.

Granted, then, that one may expect a divine order,
such as the higher intuitions have seemed to reveal to
the mystics, to be more or less obviously embodied and
exemplified in some type of the concrete facts of our experience, there still remains the question, Is it Nature,
or is it Spirit; is it the physical world, or the moral
world; is it the outer order of natural events, or is it the
conscious life of mankind in their social, their moral,
their emotional relations; is it the world as the student
of natural wonders, or the world as the lover of human

life, the artist, the portrayer of passion, comprehends it; in fine, is it the world of the "powers" of nature, or the world of the heart of man, that is the most likely and adequate to furnish facts capable of illustrating and embodying the divine purpose? This question is one of the oldest in the history of the higher problems of human thought. The vision of Elijah at Horeb is an ancient comment on this topic. Is God in the wonders of nature — in the storm, the thunder, the earthquake? No, answers the story, He is not in these. He is in the "still small voice." The antithesis is thus an extremely familiar one; it was a favorite topic of consideration with Browning. His own personal view agrees with that of the narrator of the vision of Elijah.

Many men (for instance, the modern followers of the ethical idealism that resulted from Kant's teachings) have learned to be very skeptical about finding any revelation of the divine will, or of any absolute truth, in the world of the facts of physical nature. These facts they find, like Browning in "Reverie," too complex, too deep, too full of apparent evil, too dark, to show us the divine will. God may be behind them, but they merely hide Him. Our insight into external nature is essentially limited. We vainly strive, in the present life, to peer into such mysteries. The world of physical experiences is, as Kant declared, but the world of our limitations. It is the moral world, then, and not the physical world, that can show the divine. In "Reverie" Browning states the issue and its possible solution substantially thus: If one looks outwards, one sees a world which Browning calls the world of "power," that is, the physical universe. It is a world of rigid law, and in the observer it begets a state called knowledge, that is, in the language of this poem, an outward-looking and

helplessly submissive acceptance of what one finds
there: —

"In a beginning God
Made heaven and earth." Forth flashed
Knowledge: from star to clod
Men knew things: doubt abashed
Closed its long period.

"Knowledge obtained, Power praise," continues the
poet; but he observes that what knowledge has thus revealed is everything and anything but a manifestly
divine order. This world of natural knowledge shows
itself full of strife, evil, death, decay. Can one hope,
then, for a solution here? No, but there is another world,
the moral world, the world of love, and of conscious and
ideal activity. This is the world that to the hopeful lover
of the good shows, amidst all its incompleteness, genuine traces of the divine will. The poet contrasts this, the
moral world, as being, despite its mixture of tendencies,
rather the world of "Love," with the other world —
that of "Power."

The world of "knowledge," whose facts come from
without and simply mould the passive mind to accept
and submit in the presence of an undivine destiny, is
still further contrasted with the facts revealed in the
"leap of man's quickened heart," in the "stings of his
soul which dart through the barrier of flesh," and in all
that striving upwards, that moral idealism, which is for
Browning, somewhat as for Kant, the one basis for the
assurance that "God's in his heaven; all's right with the
world."

One is to get the final revelation in terms of decidedly
moral categories. It is "rising and not resting," it is
"seeking the soul's world" and "spurning the worm's,"
it is not passively "knowing," but morally acting, that

is to confirm one's faith. What already tends in the present life towards such confirmation is not "knowing" the outer world, but living "my own life."

Where, among these rather manifold types of mankind, did Paracelsus stand? Was he a mystical quietist, or was he in any fashion a mere positivist? Did Browning conceive him as in substantial agreement with his own views? We need not attribute to Browning, at twenty-two years of age, any very elaborate or articulate philosophy when we conceive him taking sides concerning this ancient and familiar issue with regard to the method and the region of the divine revelation. In "Paracelsus," as in "Asolando," the general view and the terminology of the poet are identical. Paracelsus is no mystical quietist or positivist. He unites experience and intuition. But he does not look in the moral world for the divine revelation. He looks elsewhere. He belongs, then, to another class than Browning or the ethical idealists who follow Kant. What is this class?

There is a type of men whom one might call the Occult Idealists, or in other words the Physical Mystics. Men of this type seem to themselves to possess overwhelmingly clear intuitions of the divinest depth; but these always relate to the spiritual interpretation of particular physical facts. The word of the Lord comes to such men, but in the form of a theoretical revelation as to the meaning of this and this in the world of outer experience. They, therefore, are never content in the "holy inner temples." They dislike purely speculative systems, as well as all inner dreaming. They are very impatient, too, of the limitations of human nature. They deny such limitations. One can know whatever one is deep enough to interpret in the facts of nature. Equally, however, such men despise those mere non-mystical empiricists, who have and who respect no holy intuitions. Our empirical mystics find no facts "hard," as do the positivists, but all facts deep. They do not much believe in a God whom either speculation or meditation finds in the cloistered solitudes of the mind. They want to find him in this or in that physical fact, in this sign or wonder, in that natural symbol, in yonder reported strange cure of a sick man, in weird tales of second sight, in the still unread lore of the far East, in "psychical research," in the "subliminal self," in the stars, in the revelations of trance mediums, in the Ouija board or in Planchette — perhaps in a pack of cards, or in the toss of a coin. Nowadays we are more or less familiar with this type of empiricists, who still rather uncritically trust their intuitions; of collectors of facts, who mean thereby to prove the reality of the universal order and of the spiritual world; they seem never quite sure of the divine omnipresence until they have looked behind this door, or have peered into the cupboard, to see whether God after all is really there.

4. The historical Paracelsus was, on the whole, a man of this type — an empirical mystic who devoted himself to physical studies. For this class we have the rather awkward but almost unavoidable general name, Occultist. By Occultist we do not mean merely one who believes that there are divinely mysterious, *i. e.*, truly occult, things in our world. The Kantian or Ethical Idealist believes in such mysteries, and is in no wise an occultist. But the latter is rather one who believes in a particular method of proving and interpreting the presence of the divinely occult. This method is a sort of restless collection of quaint and varied facts of experience. Quaint these facts must be; for what lies near at hand is never so clearly divine, to such eyes, as the dis-

tant, the uncommon, the foreign. In our own day God is to be found in the far East; here at home we can obtain him only at second hand. The Arabs and the Hindoos are the true adepts. So Browning's Paracelsus sets out on long and indefinite travels. The occultist's facts must be varied. In the Father's house are many mansions, and their furniture is extremely manifold. Astral bodies and palmistry, trances and mental healing, communications from the dead and "phantasms of the living" — such things are for some people today the sole quite unmistakable evidences of the supremacy of the spiritual world. Some of these things were known to the real Paracelsus; others, as varied, he also knew and prized.

The real Paracelsus was a medical man, whose philosophy and occultism were chiefly valuable in his own eyes as laying a foundation for his skill as a healer. This aspect retreats into the background in Browning's poem, for obvious reasons, such as the difficulty of employing forgotten medical lore in verse. The Paracelsus of the poem is at once a dreamer of universal dreams and an ardent empiricist.

> What fairer seal
> Shall I require to my authentic mission
> Than this fierce energy? — this instinct striving
> Because its nature is to strive?

So he tells us in the first act, where the young aspirant for a divine mission bids farewell to his two friends ere he sets out on a long wandering in search of his knowledge. But what this "striving" proves is, he says, the presence of

> God helping, God directing everywhere,
> So that the earth shall yield her secrets up,
> And every object there be charged to strike,
> Teach, gratify, her master God appoints.

In other words Paracelsus is going, in the service of God and man, to scour the earth in the search of numerous lost facts of some vast significance for human welfare.

To this conception of the young dreamer's life mission his friend Festus replies, with a certain wonder, that one so sure of God as Paracelsus at the outset of his great quest appears to be, might as well seek for all this healing truth near by, in

> Some one of Learning's many palaces.

Why should Paracelsus thus look for the truth only "in strange and untried paths"?

> What books are in the desert? Writes the sea
> The secret of her yearning in vast caves
> Where yours will fall the first of human feet?

Festus doubts the very sincerity of his friend's quest for knowledge, since it seems to involve scorn for all the accessible lore of the past ages of learning, and a mere resort to the accidental experiences of the aimless wanderer.

The reply of Paracelsus goes very deep into his own character, and reveals to us a certain scorn of the mediocrity of ordinary men, a scorn often characteristic of dreamers, of every type; a sense of the unique intensity of his own inner life — a sense upon which is founded his love for lonely ways; his assurance of his immediate intuitions of the divine; and finally, a curious and very characteristic belief that this immediate intercourse with God is not of itself enough, and that it points out to him a very hard, a very long, but a very wonderful path along which he must henceforth go — a path that is to lead to the discovery of an endless multitude of special truths, and such a multitude as it almost crazes him to contemplate; this path is the path of the collector of special facts of experience. The passage of the poem contains some of the most frequently quoted and least understood lines of the whole work. Paracelsus tells first about the moment of his discovery of his mission, when he learned the wide contrast between his own powers and calling and those of ordinary men. He then narrates his inner experience of a conversation with the divine voice that spoke in his soul at that great moment, and he closes: —

> I go to prove my soul!
> I see my way as birds their trackless way.
> I shall arrive! What time, what circuit first,
> I ask not: but unless God send his hail
> Or blinding fire-balls, sleet, or stifling snow,
> In some time — his good time — I shall arrive.

This spirited announcement of the youthful undertaking of Paracelsus contains thoughts that many readers too lightly pass over. One is too easily deceived by this young man's ardent words. One forgets that Browning is here but the dramatic poet, who does not mean us to take these tenders for true pay. As a fact Paracelsus is by no means as inspired as he fancies. Let us analyze the situation a little. Paracelsus has already gained, as he thinks, a very deep insight into the world. God is, and Paracelsus communes with him, directly, and in his own heart. Nevertheless, he must go somewhere, for years far away, to find — what? A new religion? No, Paracelsus is no religious reformer. A new revelation of God's "intercourse" with men? This is what he himself says. In fact, however, this "intercourse," from his point of view, concerns the cause and cure of human diseases. This is indeed a grave matter, and one for a long quest. But where would the medical student of that time naturally look for the path to be followed in this quest? The reply of course would be, "some one of Learning's many palaces." One would study the traditional medical art, and would then try to improve upon it as one could. But Paracelsus rejects this way altogether. Why? Because the immediate intuition, this direct revelation from God, shows him that not upon such traditional ways lies the goal. But if one communes thus directly with God, why not learn the secrets of the medical art at first hand, by immediate revelation, at home in solitary meditation, without wandering? This is the well-known way of some modern "mental healers." God speaks in the heart. Why try the desert and the sea caves? Why wander through nature, looking for new remedies? The reply is that Paracelsus is a born empiricist, and cannot rest in his intuitions. They are vast, these intuitions, and immediate, but they are not enough. There is the whole big outer world, this storehouse of specimens of divine truth. One must see, feel, touch, try. In that way only can one learn God's will, and the art of healing.

Still one asks, with Festus, Did not the ancients, whom Paracelsus rejects, collect experiences in their own way? Could not one study facts wherever there are "learning's palaces" and sick men? Why wander off into the vague? If the world of experience concerns you, then, precisely as if you were a mere positivist, you need the coöperation of your fellows in your research. Why not then, like the modern ethical idealist of the Kantian type, accept the inner light as giving you ideals, but obtain also the outer world facts by the aid of public and common labors, researches, traditions? Why despise one's fellows in order to learn God's will?

Nay, our occultist must reply, just there is the rub. One wants the facts, but only as interpreted by the inner light; and the inner light, for an occultist, is not something rationally universal and human, like the insights upon which a Kantian idealist depends, but is the possession only of the favored few. One must, therefore, find out God's will all alone by one's self. One may accept no help from another's eyes, no coöperation from one's meaner fellows. At best the traditions of some far off occult lore, the secrets of unknown Oriental adepts, may be trusted as guides. This inner light of the occultist is something so personal, immediate, and precious, that one cannot believe it common to all mankind in case they only reason. Nor can one regard one's intuitions as concerning only a spiritual order, such as the natural world, being a merely phenomenal expression of man's limitations, fails to embody. One is too ardent an empiricist, and too impatient a mystic, to accept any human limitations at all. Thus, then, the occultist's view gets its definition. We have to take into account all the elements, the vast, immediate, private intuition, and the restless love of facts, in order to get this definition. The hard path before Paracelsus is the path of an endless collection of precisely the most novel and scattered facts of nature. Only such novel and scattered facts can be worthy of the attention of a person whose intuitions are private, immediate, and yet universal. One's intuition is that these facts somehow all belong together, as all the world is one. Therefore, the farther off, the more incoherent, the dimmer, the more "secret" the special facts, the better will they serve, when you find them, as examples of God's will; for God made them all somehow into his one world, to magnify his own power, to display his glory, to heal his suffering children. But how long the "trackless way," where indeed only God is to guide, because the entire search has no principle save the single intuition that God himself is great, and that, therefore, even the remotest things in time and in space are in his eyes one, since He made them, and must somehow secretly have linked them!

Here lies a sick man. What has caused his sickness? Perhaps something astral. The stars are linked to us by a divinely ordained sympathy. Astronomy is one of the "pillars of medicine." We must know the stars well, else we cannot judge about their effect upon diseases. What is best fitted to cure this patient? God of course has provided a remedy, and has left it lying somewhere in the world — that vast world which is all one place for God, but which, alas, is so wearily big and manifold for us. The only way is to look with the eye of a trained intuition for some hidden sign, such as quite escapes the vulgar eye, whereby the remedy of this particular disorder may be recognized when you meet with it in nature. The divine kindliness has provided each of nature's remedies with a sort of sign or label. The flowers, the leaves, the fruits of remedial plants indicate by their colors, forms, textures, the particular diseases that they are fitted to cure. This was the famous doctrine of "signatures," of which the real Paracelsus made so much. But again, only the experienced man, taught at once by the God within and by his own eyes that restlessly look hither and thither without, can learn to recognize these signs, labels, remedies. The divine apothecary (the phrase is borrowed from the real Paracelsus himself) has marked, as it were, all these his natural medicine flasks — flowers, plants, minerals — with a certain sort of occult language, and has then left them scattered about the whole world. Only a wanderer can find them. Only a philosopher, taught of God direct, can read the labels, these cryptograms of nature. Hence this possessor of intuitions must ceaselessly wander; and his wanderer must ceaselessly depend only upon the inner light to guide him. Everything in the universe is connected with everything else. Hence "the mighty range of secret truths that long for birth." Mystic links bind man, the microcosmus, to the whole of nature, the macrocosmus. The physician must know these links in order to heal. Above all must he remember that everything in nature reveals, not so much itself, as something else. The world is all symbolic. God loves, in nature, to express himself darkly by signs, portents, shadows of truth. All these concern the philosophical physician, and they are, alas, so secret, so hard to read. God, who in the heart, speaks so plainly — well, in nature He hides himself in a mystic dumb show, and helplessly gesticulates like an untaught and enthusiastic deaf-mute. Such is the essential creed of any occultist. Here is a kind of doctrine that pretends, above all, to honor God; yet, as a fact, one who pursues this "trackless way" behaves as if the God of nature were a sort of Laura Bridgman, whom the occultist first teaches to talk intelligibly.

5. I have thus thought it right to insist upon certain characteristics of the real Paracelsus, whom Browning unquestionably had in mind as he wrote the passage the close of which has been quoted. I have dwelt long upon these characteristics because here lies the key to the whole poem. Browning has a certain deep personal fondness for the occultists. Their type fascinates him. He reads and portrays them often. Yet, on the other hand, he is never able, either in his youth, when he wrote this poem, or in later life, to share their doctrine. In "Paracelsus" he means to set forth their great defect. He often later returns to the problem. The same theme is treated in "The Strange Experience of Kar-

shish." Karshish and Paracelsus are, to borrow the speech of the occultists, different incarnations of the same spirit. Browning admires the "picker-up of learning's crumbs," the mystic who pursues the occult all through the natural world. The error of the occultist lies in supposing that God is in this way revealed, or to be found. Browning's own opinion, as poet, has a close relation to ethical idealism.

For Browning, God is revealed within, not without, our own human nature. Therefore, and here is the main point of Browning's criticism of occultism, it is in our spiritual communion with one another, it is in our world of human loves, and even of human hates, that one gets in touch with God. When man really meets man, in love, in conflict, in passion, then the knowledge of God gets alive in both men. The true antithesis is not between the pure intellect and the affections; for your occultist is no partisan of the pure intellect. He, too, is in love, in mystical love, but with outer nature. Nor is the antithesis that between the scientific spirit and the spirit of active benevolence. Paracelsus, as one devoted to the art of healing, is from the first abstractly but transcendently benevolent. His is simply not the scientific spirit. The antithesis between "knowledge," as the occultist conceives it, and "love," as the poet views it, is the contrast between looking in the world of outer nature for a symbolic revelation of God, and looking in the moral world, the world of ideals, of volition, of freedom, of hope and of human passion, for the direct incarnation of the loving and the living God. The researches of the occultist are fascinating, capricious—and resultless. It is the student of men who talks with God face to face, as a familiar friend. The occultist, peering about in the dark, sees, like Moses in the cleft of the rock, only God's

back. The truly occult world is that where the lovers
and the warriors meet and part. There alone God is revealed. Search as you will in the far East, in the deserts,
in the sea caves, you will never find any natural object
more verily occult than are his love's eyes to the lover.
Browning's mysticism thus has always an essentially
human object before it. He, therefore, sometimes depicts, with especial fondness, the awakened occultist,
who has just learned where lies the true secret of our relations with God. So it happened with Karshish —

> Why write of trivial matters, things of price
> Calling at every moment for remark?
> I noticed on the margin of a pool
> Blue-flowering borage, the Aleppo sort,
> Aboundeth, very nitrous. It is strange!

Here speaks the true occultist. But now there awakens in him, unrestrainable, the new insight, which the
meeting with the risen Lazarus has suggested: —

> The very God! think, Abib; dost thou think?
> So, the All-Great, were the All-Loving too —
> So, through the thunder comes a human voice
> Saying, "O heart I made, a heart beats here!
> Face, my hands fashioned, see it in myself!
> Thou hast no power, nor mayst conceive of mine,
> But love I gave thee, with myself to love,
> And thou must love me who have died for thee!"
> The madman saith He said so: it is strange.

It is the Christian mystery of the Incarnation that is
here in question. But as we know, Browning was no
literally orthodox believer, and the essential truth of
Christianity was, for him, identical with his own poetical faith that the divine plan is incarnate in humanity,
in human loves and in all deep social relationships,
rather than in outer nature. A similar train of thought

guides the half-conscious inspiration of the young David in the poem "Saul," as the singer of Israel feels after the prophecy of the Incarnation, and reaches it at last through a sort of poetic induction by the "Method of Residues." First, with all the fascination of the occultist, though with all the frank innocence of the untutored shepherd, David ransacks the whole natural world for God. As the youth is an optimist, he meets here indeed with no obstacles to his fancy; he is troubled by none of the natural mysteries that would baffle the more technical occultist; but still the story, even when most rapturously sung, when fullest of the comprehension of nature's symbolism, lacks the really divine note. God is somehow not quite revealed in all this. And hereupon David struggles, toils, pauses, hesitates — and then, with one magnificent bound of the spirit, springs wholly beyond the world of the occultist to grasp at once the most transcendent of mysteries and the most human of commonplaces: —

'T is the weakness in strength that I cry for! my flesh that I
    seek
In the Godhead! I seek it and find it. O Saul, it shall be
A Face like my face that receives thee: a Man like to me
Thou shalt love and be loved by, forever: a Hand like this
    hand
Shall throw open the gates of new life to thee! See the Christ
    stand!

It is by the light of this kind of poetic intuition of the true place of the divine in our world that Browning, in "Paracelsus," lets experience criticize the occultist.

6. As the hero, therefore, of such a critical poem Browning chooses a mystic of the Renaissance. This mystic's creed is, on the whole, that of the real Paracelsus — a neoplatonic philosophy of nature. The first

of its main features, as expounded in the dying speech of Paracelsus, is Monism. God is not merely above all, He is through all nature; He is included in everything. Then there is the symbolism so characteristic of the whole doctrine. Every natural process has a mystic meaning. Everything is alive, and has relations to all other things. Further, man, as microcosm, is a copy in miniature of the whole universe. Hence, in order to understand man, as a physician must do in healing diseases one must look about in all directions, without. Thus arises the need of an endless collection of special experiences, and hence, also the constant need of deep intuitions in order to comprehend the maze of facts. Every speck expands into a star. Such a search means in the end madness and despair. As a fact, for Paracelsus, the stellar world is needed to explain all sorts of phenomena in the lower regions. This view, and the doctrine of "signatures," inspired all his work — and poisoned the very life-blood of it.

Browning, too, had his own sort of mysticism. He also was a monist. But the poet makes his hero confess that he "gazed on power" till he "grew blind." Not that way lies the truth. He who gazes not on power, but on the "weakness in strength" of the human spirit, he alone finds the way to God.

In the course of the poem, Browning brings this occultist face to face with a spiritual opponent, who tries to show him the truth, and in part succeeds. This opponent is a typical, a universally sensitive, a thoroughly humane artist. The "lover" and the "knower" of the poet are thus explicitly the artist and the occultist. The doctrine that Aprile teaches is, first, that God is love, and, secondly, that the meaning of this doctrine is simply that God is the "perfect poet, who in creating acts his own creations." God, then, is related to his world as the true lover is to the desires of his own faithful heart, or as the artist is to his own inspired works. This is, indeed, mysticism, and it is neither for the young Browning nor for his characters any highly articulate theory of the world — any technical philosophy. But it is certainly an intelligible and intuitively asserted doctrine as to how to find the divine in experience. What it asserts is this: If you want to know God, live rather than peer about you; be observant of the moral rather than of the physical world; create as the artist creates rather than collect facts as the occultist collects them; watch men rather than things; consider the secrets of the heart rather than the hopelessly mysterious symbolism of nature; be fond of the most commonplace, so long as it is the commonplace in human life, rather than of the most startling miracles of the physical world; discover new lands in man's heart, and let the deserts and the sea caves alone; call nothing work that is not done in company with your fellowmen, and nothing true insight that does not mean work thus shoulder to shoulder with your comrades. All this, in substance, Aprile teaches; and this, and nothing else, is what he and Browning here mean by "Love." The parallelism with the later poems, "Karshish" and "Saul," is emphasized in a later edition of the "Paracelsus" by the lines added at the end of Aprile's dying speech: —

> Man's weakness is his glory — for the strength
> Which raises him to heaven and near God's self
> Came spite of it: God's strength his glory is,
> For thence came with our weakness sympathy,
> Which brought God down to earth, a man like us!

It is not the power of God as revealed in nature, but the love that in Him, as a being who is alive like us, links his perfect life to our striving, and lives in active and passionate sympathy; it is this alone which makes God comprehensible to us. For only in this attribute is He revealed to us. His other attributes are, in our present state of existence, hopelessly dark to us.

If this is true, then indeed the quest and the method of Paracelsus have been, in Browning's eyes, vain enough. Let us be frank about it. The heroic speech of Paracelsus consists of tenders and not of true pay. It is vainglorious boasting; and must be regarded as such. Or, to speak less bluntly, it is a pathetic fallacy. Paracelsus does *not* see his way as birds their trackless way. On the contrary, his instinct is false, and his way, before one reaches the very moment of his final dying enlightenment and confession, is a blind flight no-whither through the blue. God has no need to waste any hail or fire-balls on the case. Paracelsus is left to himself, and he does not arrive, except, indeed, at that very last moment, at the insight that another man ought to be formed to take his place. All this, from Browning's hopeful point of view, means no absolute failure. Our alchemist, amid all his delusions, remains a worthy tragic hero, devoted, courageous, indomitable, enduring, a soldier at heart. Even the wrath of man praises God, much more his misguided devotion. It is this devotion that to the end we honor even amid all our hero's excesses. But Paracelsus, as he is, is a sincere deceiver of his own soul, and, as far as in him lies, he is a blind guide of his fellows. Here, in the contrast between the truth that lies, after all, so near to his ardent spirit, and the error that is, despite this fact, so hopeless, is the tragedy. Were the truth not so near, the error, indeed, would not be so hopeless. Were the man not so admirably strenuous, he might be converted before his

deathbed. He is no weakling, but a worthy companion
of Faust. Yet just herein lies his earthly ruin.

7. Let us now apply the central idea of the poem to
its action in a brief review. Paracelsus the occultist
aspires, bids farewell to his friends, and then sets out on
his great quest. Years later we find him, older, but
hardly wiser, at the house of the Greek conjurer in
Constantinople, where he seeks magic enlightenment as
to his future. The reply to his request comes in the
shape of the sudden meeting with that mysterious figure,
the dying poet Aprile, who has come to this place upon
a similar errand after a life of failure. The two men
meet, and; in the wondrous scene which follows, Paracelsus learns and, as far as his poor occult wit comprehends it, accepts the ideal of the poet, who "would
love infinitely and be loved." The characters here
brought into tragic conflict, the "lover" and the
"knower," are the Artist and the Occultist. Both are
enthusiasts, both have sought God, both have longed
to find out how to benefit mankind. There is no clash
of reason with sentiment. On the contrary, neither of
these men is in the least capable of ever becoming a
reasoner; both are dreamers; both have failed in what
they set out to do. There is no contrast of "love," as
Christian charity or practical humanitarianism, with
"knowledge" as something more purely contemplative.
Aprile is no reformer. He longed to do good, but as an
artist; he longed to create, but as a maker of the beautiful. His ideal attitude is, in its way, quite as contemplative as is that of Paracelsus. This "knower" is a
physician. This artist, with all his creative ideals, longs
to "love" by apprehending the works of God as shown
forth in the passions of man.

The real contrast lies in the places where the two men

have sought for God, and in the degrees of strenuousness
with which they have pursued the quest. The artist has
sought God in the world of human passion, Paracelsus
in the magical and secret places of outer nature. The
artist has no cause to repent his choice of God's abode;
God is, to his eyes, even too dazzlingly and obviously
there in human hearts, lives, forms, and deeds. The
occultist has been baffled despite his labors. In strenuousness, Paracelsus has had by far the advantage. In
this he is indeed the king. But had Paracelsus combined
Aprile's ideals and powers with his own strenuousness,
what a kingdom might by this time have become his!
Such is the obvious significance of this wonderful scene.

Now, let us attempt an explanation of the vicissitudes
and of the degradation of our hero's later career. The
dying legacy of Aprile to Paracelsus is the counsel not
to wait for perfection, but to c o what the time permits
while life lasts. Accepting this counsel, but very dimly
apprehending the meaning of the artist's ideal of "love,"
    ıd falsely supposing himself to have "attained," where
  e had only vaguely and distantly conceived, the occultist now resolves to show his love for mankind in more
immediate practical relations with them. The artist has
counseled just such closer relations, and this is all that
Paracelsus has been able as yet to comprehend. The
esult is the abortive life in the professorship in Basel.
To Paracelsus the actual spirit of the dead Aprile seems
after all to be unable or unwilling to do anything for him.
One preaches occultism to his students, supposing himself to be acting in the sense of the artist who had counseled him to get nearer to men's hearts. But the words
of these lectures sound hollow even to one's own ears,
and so one is driven to "bombast." The few "crumbs"
of learning, picked up through all those years of wan-

dering, appear now as nothing to the mysteries still un-learned. One had not known, in fact, how small was one's store of collections until after he had burned the books of Galen and the rest, and then had actually begun to teach. One must now resort to boasting, charlatanry, melancholy, self-reproach, and foreboding. The man is too ardent of purpose to admit in public his own defect, but too really noble of soul to tolerate in the least his own charlatanry. God is now indeed far off. The artist said that one found him best and most among living men. But in this lecture-room the poor occultist, peer as he will, can discover with certainty only a mass of fools. The most occult, the darkest, the most fearsome of all the arts turns out to be the art of pedagogy, — the one truly creative art whereby Paracelsus could have hoped to enter Aprile's world.

The inevitable downfall comes, and Paracelsus is driven from Basel. His indomitable temper wins our admiration even after we have learned the utter uselessness of all his magic arts. He now gives us a new version of April's doctrine as he conceives it. In the song, "Over the sea our galleys went," he depicts the hopelessness of trying to come into close relations with men by the devices that are within his own reach. Unlike the real Paracelsus, he can be a poet, but not, like Aprile, an artist comprehending and depicting other men. In his chaos of excitement, in his lamentation over his failure, — yes, in his cups, one must add — he can sing in verse his own tragedy, not the meaning of any life but his own. At length he seems to see the truth. What Aprile really meant must have been that a man must live — a short life and a full one, in loneliness, in chaos, but at any rate in a whirlwind of passion. Thus alone can one learn to know. The occultist shall be joined now with the man of passion. Thus, once again, Paracelsus aspires.

An occultist must finish his days magically. From weary dreams and furious delirium the dying seer miraculously arises, full of seeming vigor and of cool insight, to tell to his friend what knowledge he has attained at this supreme moment. Now at last we do indeed learn the truth. Paracelsus has not "arrived" at what he sought, an earthly mission; but he now sees why he has failed. The old mystical monism was right; but as the seer depicts it before us, a new spirit has come into it. The story of the world is right as of old; but the artist alone had put the true interpretation upon it. Could the Paracelsus of former days but have understood in his time what love meant, could he but have known how all the waves and eddies of human passion, even when they seem farthest from the divine, reveal God as no object in outer nature, however wonderful, can ever do — the occultist would not have aspired in vain! He would have been transformed, as the man of the future shall be, into the artist. This is the final message of Paracelsus, and the meaning of the whole tale.

POPE LEO'S PHILOSOPHICAL MOVE-
MENT AND ITS RELATIONS TO
MODERN THOUGHT

[1903]

ONE of the most notable features of the work of the late Pope Leo was what is usually called his revival of scholastic philosophy. The movement of thought which has received this name is a very complex one. Its consequences have been varied and have not been altogether such as the Pope himself would appear to have foreseen. In any case, they have involved phenomena that have a good deal of interest to the public outside of the Catholic Church. Many students of philosophy, of theology, and even of the natural sciences — students, I mean, who have no direct concern with any of the internal affairs of Leo's own religious body — are still forced, although outsiders, to recognize how important, for the general intellectual progress of our time, the future outcome of the whole Neo-Scholastic movement in the Catholic Church may prove. For if the process which Leo initiated continues to go on unhindered, the positive results for the increase of a wholesome coöperation between Catholic and non-Catholic investigators and teachers will probably be both great and helpful. On the other hand, if this same process is seriously and effectively checked by the forces of conservative officialism within the Roman communion, the consequence will be a return to certain forms of controversy and of mutual misunderstanding amongst some of the principal schools of modern opinion, a return which no lover of reason ought to welcome. The death of the Pope, and the choice of his successor, bring into prominence the distinctly practical issues whose nature is thus suggested. These issues concern, indeed, in the first place, the inner life of the Roman Church. But they also indirectly concern, in a genuine sense, the common interests of modern intellectual progress and of public education.

While I have, of course, neither right nor desire to form any opinion as to the motives and the merits of such partisan divisions and controversies as are present, at this critical moment, within the Catholic Church, I nevertheless feel, as a non-Catholic observer, as a student of philosophy, and also as one who occasionally has reason to consult current Catholic philosophic literature, a good deal of interest in the fortunes of the movement of thought which Leo initiated. I venture to give expression to this interest in the present form, because I suppose that others who, like myself, have no direct concern with the internal life of Catholicism, may still wish to get clearer ideas as to the intellectual relations of modern Catholic thought to modern civilization.

I

THE PLACE OF PHILOSOPHY IN CATHOLIC INTELLECTUAL LIFE

If the so-called Neo-Scholastic movement which the late Pope initiated were indeed only a revival of scholastic metaphysics, and nothing more, it might seem to mean little for mankind at large. But, as a fact, from the very nature of Catholic scholarship, and because of the best established traditions of its educational system, the philosophy of the Catholic schools determines most of what is technically characteristic of the intellectual life of all representative Catholic thinkers. For Catholic theology, in expounding and defending the doctrines of its Church, has an intimate and conscious connection with philosophical opinions such as far surpasses the kind of union of dogma and speculation that other Christian bodies have in recent times been able to retain. In non-Catholic churches, in later periods, the religious life has been emphasized at the expense of dogma, and even doctrinal controversies, when they are recognized as vital, tend on the whole to free themselves as much as possible from philosophical technicalities. The philosophical education of the modern protestant clergyman is consequently, in general, a decidedly uneven and accidental sort of training, whose amount is subject to very arbitrary variations, from man to man, and from school to school. But Catholic tradition has made the relation of theology and philosophy much closer and more uniform; and the most highly equipped and scholarly of the Catholic clergy have been submitted, in the course of their education, to an amount of technical philosophical discipline which one may or may not regard as useful, but which certainly gives to their philosophy a central importance in their minds. Any notable movement in Catholic philosophical training consequently affects the attitude of Catholic scholars towards all sorts of intellectual problems that fall within the range of their interest. Hence, the Neo-Scholasticism which Leo initiated has influenced every aspect of what can be called the distinctively Catholic learning of Europe, and of this country. One must conceive, then, the modern movement of thought in Pope Leo's Church as by no means confined to technical matters of scholastic doctrine.

On the other hand, one, indeed, must not exaggerate the nature of the philosophical reform which the Pope undertook to bring to pass. Like every official act of his Church, Leo's famous instructions regarding the study of philosophy were explicitly the carrying out of a traditional policy in a new instance. Nothing was meant to be novel about the undertaking except the emphasis which the Pope laid upon certain aspects of philosophical education, and the directions which he acordingly gave to teachers and to scholars as to the conduct of their studies. Nothing revolutionary was intended. The new movement was, indeed, quite explicitly a revival. But the intellectual situation in the modern world at the time when this revival was initiated made the undertaking very fruitful, and, as a fact, productive of decidedly unexpected results. A brief explanation may help to indicate, so far as the matter is one of public knowledge at all, both why the Pope's plan was formed and why it proved so effective.

II

THE POSITION OF ST. THOMAS AQUINAS

The classic Catholic philosophy, which has so largely determined the nature of the theological training of the Catholic clergy, received its definite shaping during the thirteenth century. In that century, in fact, a decided revolution was actually effected; not, of course, in the doctrines of the Catholic Church (for these had long since been settled), but in the educational life of the Catholic schools, and especially in the way in which theological teaching came to be related to philosophy. Ever since, in the ninth century, the development of mediæval learning had been fairly begun, the Catholic schools had been seeking for a satisfactory technical guidance for their theological instruction. They had

looked for such guidance not only in the tradition of the
fathers of the Church, so far as that tradition was then
accessible to them, but also in the thought of ancient
philosophy, so far as documents which represented it
were in their hands at all. The resources at the disposal
of their scholarship long remained meager. But at
length a new light began to come to them in the form of
a renewed knowledge of Aristotle, derived, at first quite
indirectly, through Arabic sources. The philosophical
system of Aristotle accordingly began to be of importance for the Catholic schools at the outset of the
thirteenth century. After a period of suspicion and of
hostility, in the course of which Aristotle's doctrine was
even at one time condemned by authority, a reaction
came. Albert the Great, and later his still greater pupil,
Thomas Aquinas, not only studied the relation between
Aristotle's doctrine and that of the Christian church,
but undertook a systematic exposition and defense of
the whole of Catholic theology in terms of the conceptions and of the principal philosophical teachings of
Aristotle, in so far as such a synthesis of Christian theology and Greek thinking proved to be at all possible.
This task was carried to completion by Thomas himself
— the most famous of all the scholastic thinkers.
Thomas very definitely distinguished between the proper office of philosophy (which, as he teaches, expresses
what the unaided human reason can do to find out and
to formulate natural and spiritual truth), and the office
of faith (which enables us, as he holds, to be certain of
revealed truths such as, in a large measure, transcend
what reason can find out). Nevertheless, our scholastic
doctor still assigned a very high rank to philosophy as
an auxiliary to faith, and as an aid in formulating theological truth. He also vindicated for philosophy a cer-

tain limited, but very genuine, freedom of method and of opinion, within its own province. As a result, Thomas stands, from any fair point of view, Catholic or non-Catholic, decidedly high, not only as a theologian, but also as a rational philosophical inquirer. His was an essentially synthetic and harmonizing mind. Not only was his erudition, for his time, enormous; but his reflective working over of his massive and often very heterogeneous materials was marvelously ingenious and thorough-going. While not a great originator of opinions, he was an organizer of thought, and as such was of very high rank. Through him scholastic philosophy attained its most perfect expression. He was especially successful in weaving into an at least plausible unity some of the most contradictory tendencies of Christian theology. Especially in dealing with the extremely difficult doctrine of the Church as to the relation between God and the world, and with the almost equally perplexing theological theory as to the nature of the human soul, and as to its relation with the body and with the natural and spiritual order generally, Thomas showed his skill as a harmonizer of conflicting opinions. Standing, as a philosopher, on the very brink, so to speak, of pantheism, he is still able, as a theologian, so to state the relation of God to the created world as to leave his own orthodoxy unquestionable, and pantheism discredited. Fully aware that a rational explanation of all things as due to God's plan seems to involve a philosophical determinism, Thomas nevertheless, vindicated for man the freedom of the will. Accepting from Aristotle a theory of the soul which at first appears to make the mind quite inseparable from the body, Thomas still defends both the incorporeal nature of the soul and the rational necessity of the doctrine of immortality. And all these dis-

tinctions and unifications of doctrine he states with such
clearness of style, with such subtlety of argument, with
such serenity of manner, and with such gentleness towards all opponents, that both the labors of the thinker
and the cruel tragedies of conflicting opinion involved
seem, as one reads him, to fade into the background, and
the reader remains, with the scholastic doctor himself,
in the light of a very kindly spirit and of a very ingenious intellect. One need not be convinced in order to
admire.

Now Thomas Aquinas has stood, from the first, very
high amongst Catholic teachers. After a comparatively
brief period in which he was the object of somewhat
violent attack on the part of certain of his contempo-
raries and successors amongst scholastic theologians, the
position of Thomas in the first rank of the doctors of his
Church became unquestioned. Most of the teaching
religious orders (as Pope Leo himself points out in his
encyclical upon Thomas's philosophy), have long required, as a matter of rule, that the doctrines of Aquinas
should be the model and guide for all their own instruc-
tors. Thomas has consequently been, for centuries, the
typical scholastic theologian, and his rivals need not here
concern us.

Nevertheless, despite the almost unbroken traditions
of the primacy of St. Thomas amongst the scholastic
teachers of doctrine, various motives have combined to
make the study of his works at first hand somewhat
neglected, at certain periods, by the theologians of his
Church. For even when he was fully recognized as the
model for the teaching given in the various religious
orders, it was possible and easy to substitute briefer
compends for his own works, and the making of textbooks has been, amongst Catholic schools, much what

it too often is elsewhere. One textbook may copy another, more or less unintelligently; tradition degenerates; and Thomas, as we now learn from Catholic sources, often used to be pretty far away and to remain in too large a measure unread, even when one professed to be teaching his opinions. Moreover, the course of contemporary controversy, as well as the ambitions of individual writers and teachers, often led Catholic schools to neglect their more strictly scholastic tradition altogether, for the sake of some other and more modern fashion of thinking. And in any case the voluminous works of the later scholastics, of the sixteenth and seventeenth centuries — men of very much less power than Thomas — were long likely to stand as a sort of barrier in the way of the older master, hindering students from getting a knowledge of his own writings at first hand, however much his primacy might be formally recognized.

It was in order, not so much to restore St. Thomas himself to this formally recognized dignity which, in the minds of Catholic teachers, he had never lost, as to secure for his original works a study, and for his methods as a thinker the prominence which Leo held to be their due, that the late Pope, almost at the outset of his pontificate, in the encyclical of August 4, 1879, directed that the "precious wisdom of St. Thomas" should be restored to its ancient place, should be propagated as widely as possible, should be applied to the defense of the Catholic faith against assailants, should be studied as carefully as possible in its original sources, and should be interpreted as the regular basis for the philosophical instruction in Catholic schools.

III

SIGNIFICANCE OF THE POPE'S ENCYCLICAL

So far the Pope's letter appears, to the external observer, to be concerned with matters that interest his
own clergy and their pupils almost exclusively. But the
encyclical has another aspect, and emphasizes another
purpose that the author had in mind. The philosophy
of St. Thomas, so Leo points out, must, in the Pope's
opinion, prove especially useful in combating the errors
of modern thought, and in stating the case of the Church
to the world of today. Therefore, to the end that the
revival of the study of the greatest of the scholastic
doctors shall prove effective in serving the purposes of
the modern Church, the Pope, towards the close of his
encyclical, emphasizes the importance of studying
modern philosophical and scientific problems in the light
of the Thomistic doctrine. The physical sciences, Leo
insists, "will not only receive no detriment, but will
greatly gain from a restoration of the older philosophy."
There is, he is assured, "no conflict" between the
"philosophical principles" of the school and the "certain and admitted results" of the modern study of nature. Meanwhile, as the Pope adds, it is in no wise his
intention to propose that the present age shall accept
such results — if there are any such results — of the
scholastic philosophy, as are found to be actually opposed to the ascertained truths that have come to light
in later times. It is the *wisdom* of St. Thomas that he
means to emphasize and to bring again to honor; and he
does not plead for the blind acceptance, along with this
wisdom, of any demonstrable errors that the human
fallibility of the scholastic doctors may have left standing in their works. In brief, while nearly the whole of

what the Pope says, in his encyclical concerning St. Thomas, takes the form of the most emphatic and unqualified eulogy of that thinker's doctrine, modern Catholic scholarship is, in this letter, called upon to undertake the task of "increasing and perfecting the old by means of the new," and is required to make the deliberate effort to rethink the results of modern science in terms of the scholastic principles, while the admission is made that, in this process, there may indeed prove to be some results of scholastic philosophical inquiry which will have to be modified in the light of recent research. As for the harmony of modern science and scholasticism, that is expressly declared by the Pope to have to do with the philosophical "principles"; and the Pope tacitly leaves the reader to understand that he is well aware how imperfect was the knowledge of the special laws and facts of the natural world which the scholastic writers were able, in their time, to possess. Thus, however, the task defined by Leo's instructions is not confined to any mere restatement of the letter of the Thomistic doctrine, but extends to a deliberate undertaking to show that Catholic philosophy is adequate to cope, not only with the problems, but with the ascertained results and the positive achievements of modern inquiry. And so, while the invitation to participate in the intellectual work of the modern world, and to vindicate their own philosophy by explicitly applying it to the questions and ideas of today, occupies but a brief place in the closing paragraphs of the Pope's encyclical, there can be no doubt of the prominence of this aspect of his purpose in Leo's mind.

Now it is easy thus to assert that no ascertained result of modern science or philosophy is in conflict with the true principles of scholasticism. That assertion, in one

form or another, may be found in the proper paragraph
of almost any compend of scholastic philosophy. It is
also easy to label any non-Catholic doctrine an error.
That, too, the Catholic textbooks, however brief, had
not failed to do from time immemorial. But the novelty
and the special interest of Leo's letter lies in the fact
that he thus counseled his scholars to make good such
assertions, first through a new and studious restoration
of the classic scholasticism in its integrity, and, secondly
through a deliberate effort to bring it into explicit relation to modern problems, and to make other people see
the matter as the Catholic thinker saw it. When one
adds that the Pope, as it were, in parenthesis, admitted
in two very brief but weighty passages of his encyclical
that this process would inevitably involve certain modifications of the philosophical tradition in order to adjust
scholasticism to the modern world, one begins to see how
momentous for Catholic scholarship might prove to be
the task which the Pope set before his Church.

When you appeal afresh to the verdict, not merely of
tradition, but of a renewed and living philosophy, you
deliberately undertake the task, not merely of asserting
what you believe, but of analyzing, and of making quite
explicitly conscious, the grounds of your assertion.
When you break away from mere compends and textbooks, and require the detailed understanding of the
whole work of so many-sided a thinker as was St.
Thomas, you put yourself in the position of imitating
not so much his mere formulas as his spirit of research.
He lived, in his century, in a plastic age. He was a hero
and a reformer of teaching. You tend to make men today try to be like him. When you undertake to assimilate, in a philosophical spirit, the whole result of modern
inquiry, you inevitably expose yourself to the fate of be-

ing in some measure assimilated yourself during the process. For any man inevitably tends to become what he thinks. When you combine all these undertakings in one, and set the whole world of Catholic scholars to work enthusiastically upon the new task, you are likely to find, after twenty years or more have passed, that St. Thomas's spirit is, indeed, more potent than his letter, that the application of this spirit of inquiry to modern problems has indeed brought you into closer touch with the intellectual issues of the day, but that there is also a tendency to the modification and to the modernization of your own Catholic thinking — a tendency that goes farther than you at first had anticipated. Is this result for the best? That is a question that Catholics must answer for themselves.

As an outsider, I do not, I think, at all exaggerate the degree to which the intellectual life of Catholicism has actually been altered in the course of this process. I recognize how very conservative the great body of Catholic theologians have remained, and I do not imagine that either the dogmas or the political policy of that church will undergo any notable change at any early date in consequence of the movement of which I speak, no matter how far it goes. But what I do see, as I look over the recent literature of discussion, is (1) that there is a distinct increase of active coöperation on the part of Catholic scholars in the relatively neutral tasks of modern science and scholarship. I see also (2) that there is a great increase in the understanding and appreciation of philosophers (such, for instance, as Kant), whom Catholic teachers all used to condemn without reserve or knowledge, but whom some of them, notably in France, have lately been disposed not only to comprehend, but also, in certain respects, openly to follow.

And (3) I also read, occasionally, efforts to show that there is nothing in the "philosophical principles" of scholasticism which is at all hostile to the transformation of species, or to the whole set of doctrines known by the name of evolution, in so far, at least, as these doctrines, are matters of natural science. Nor are such views limited to men like the late unhappy Mivart-men who are at heart only half-way Catholics, and who, any day, may have to break with their church as he did. No, I find such views maintained, with various modifications, by men whose position amongst the faithful seems, at least, when viewed from without, to be quite secure.

The late Pope in 1899 expressed in a letter to the French bishops his deep sorrow over the just mentioned movement amongst French Catholic philosophers in the direction of Kant's philosophy. And it is quite true that this movement is, on its face, opposed to the spirit, as it very certainly is to the letter, of the encyclical of 1879. Yet the links that bind the original effort which Leo initiated to the philosophical movement in France which, in 1899, he deplored, are not hard to trace. Instead of some brief, sharply worded paragraph about the "absurd errors" of Kant, such as the older scholastic compends were likely to contain, Leo's method as he outlined it in his encyclical, once actually applied to the study of philosophy, has now substituted the lengthy, careful, scholarly, sometimes bitter, but also sometimes very dispassionate reviews of modern thinkers, and of Kant among the number — reviews which are now so much more common than they used to be in the works of Catholic philosophers. After all, was not St. Thomas in his century tolerant in dealing with his philosophical adversaries? Was he not scrupulously fair in stating an

opponent's case and almost invariably gentle in tone?
And was he not ready on occasion to learn from the very
Arabian philosophers whom he refuted? In fact, then,
this Thomistic revival has certainly led to a spirit of increased care in expounding, and of increased fairness
and gentleness in characterizing the philosophical and
theological opponents of Catholicism. And, therefore,
is it surprising that, without intending in the least to
sacrifice their faith, certain of the French Catholic
thinkers have been led, in the course of their studies, to
find more truth in Kant than they had anticipated, and
to assimilate him indeed to their own teachings, while
in turn being in some degree assimilated by him. If
some of these thinkers, disregarding the letter of Leo's
original instructions, no longer make the philosophy of
the school at all prominent in their teachings, is that
more than one natural result of encouraging thoughtful
men to attempt afresh the task of bringing the Church
near to the intellectual life of the modern world? A
similar freedom, as we know, has appeared in a good
deal of recent Catholic scholarship regarding questions
of scripture criticism. And other symptoms of a relative
spiritual independence are notable in many regions of
Catholic thought upon which I cannot here enter.

IV

TENDENCIES IN ST. THOMAS WHICH INVITE CHANGE

I have spoken of some of the symptoms, in recent
Catholic scholarship, of the growth of broader and
fairer methods of investigation and of polemic than
formerly prevailed. I am the more disposed to refer
these symptoms, as effects, to the Neo-Scholastic movement as a direct or indirect cause, in view of the fact

that St. Thomas Aquinas himself, typical Catholic thinker as he is, still furnishes in his method and in his system many features that especially seem to invite, yes, almost to require, development, and in the end change, just as soon as you try to use him, in the way contemplated by Leo, as a mediator between modern thinking and the doctrine of his Church. I have already indicated some of these features. To explain in any detail what they are, I should indeed have to enter upon technical philosophical problems. As a fact, Thomas's system is in its very essence an elaborate effort to mediate between opposing theological tendencies. In consequence, St. Thomas in his own day modified ideas even while he harmonized them. In this sense he was progressive. To study the detail of his thinking, in the light of modern inquiry, and then to undertake, in his spirit, still further theological mediations, this is inevitably to arouse into renewed growth the very type of philosophical thinking for which he stood, namely, the type of thinking which modifies former conceptions even in the act of defending them. But the problems of today are infinitely more complex than were those of the thirteenth century. The new mediations will tend in consequence, just in so far as they are pursued in St. Thomas's own spirit of thorough-going conscientiousness, to lead to greater changes in the conceptions of Catholic theology than he in his time brought to pass. If such change was at all to be dreaded by Catholic opinion, it would, therefore, have been safer to leave St. Thomas imprisoned in the old-fashioned scholastic methods and to leave modern thought to be condemned, in the old way, in a few brief paragraphs by these textbooks. Pope Leo, after all, "let loose a thinker" amongst his people — a thinker, to be sure, of unquestioned orthodoxy, but after all a genuine thinker whom the textbooks had long tried, as it were, to keep lifeless, and who, when once revived, proves to be full of the suggestion of new problems, and of an effort towards new solutions.

In three parts of his system St. Thomas, to my mind, especially invites some measure, at least, of critical reconstruction, so soon as you undertake carefully to review his position in the light of modern philosophical inquiry. First, his theory of the nature and limits of human knowledge, a theory derived from Aristotle, especially calls not merely for restatement, but for readjustment, as soon as you try to apply it to the interpretation of our modern consciousness. The historical dignity of this theory is unquestionable. We owe much to Leo and to the Neo-Scholastic movement for calling its problems afresh to our attention. But the very effort to bring this theory face to face with modern thought must result in a change of this traditional doctrine — a change which may be slow, but which will be sure to prove pervasive and momentous for Catholic philosophy. The before-mentioned Kantian movement amongst the French Catholic philosophers is but one symptom of this aspect of the new sort of thinking. The questions involved are technical, but they concern the whole problem of the scope and the office of religious faith, and so, in the end, they tend to modify the whole attitude of the theologians most concerned.

Secondly, the problem of the relations between God and the world, as St. Thomas treats that topic, is one which has only to be reviewed carefully in the light of modern science and of modern philosophy, to secure an alteration of the essentially unstable equilibrium in which Thomas left this heaven-piercing tower of his speculation. Here I, of course, have no space to speak of a philosophical problem to which, as a student of philosophy, I have devoted so much of my own attention — namely, the problem about the conception of God. But when I read, in more than one recent philosophical essay of Catholic origin, expressions that admit the decidedly symbolic and human character of the language in which even the dogmas of the Church have to be expressed, so far as they relate to the nature of God, when stress is also laid, very rightly, upon that aspect of St. Thomas's teaching which emphasizes this very inadequacy of even the traditional formulas to the business of defining divine things, when I meet at the same time with admissions that St. Thomas's positive theory of the divine attributes involves these or these apparent contradictions, which still need philosophical solution — then, indeed, I see not that our more modern thinking is wholly right and Thomas wrong — but that Catholic theology is nowadays in a position where it is bound either to progress, or else to abandon the whole business of reviving the spirit of serious philosophical thinking. I see too, that St. Thomas as a mere authority does not suffice for the purposes even of my Catholic brethren, but that St. Thomas as a thinker has set them afresh to thinking, so that they, like the rest of us, are living in an age of transition. They will no doubt, keep their essential dogmas; but they will tend to conceive the contents of these dogmas in new ways. And that process, in the course of centuries, will go very far, unless they somehow arbitrarily cut it short, by ceasing to philosophize.

In the third place, the before-mentioned doctrine of St. Thomas as to the nature of the human soul, and as to its relation to the body, and as to the sense in which man possesses free will and individuality — all this doctrine is one especially liable to modification and readjustment in the light of modern inquiry. Here chances to be, in fact, one of the favorite regions of study for the Neo-Thomistic authors. Essays and volumes on the relations between Thomism and modern psychology are very numerous in Catholic theological literature. And the other problems about man's evolution, nature, and destiny are very frequently reviewed by writers of the same school. Here, too, the spirit of fairness and of thoroughness seems to be growing. Here, too, the mutual understanding between Catholic and modern thinking tends to increase. And here, indeed, from the nature of the problems at issue, Thomas's Aristotelianism seems to have an especially good chance to show its power to assimilate modern results. But nowhere more than here does the other tendency also inevitably assert itself. The traditional doctrines are in their turn assimilated. They grow nearer to those which they were to overcome. The result tends to a distinct modernizing of Catholic thought upon these as upon other fundamental matters.

V

THE OUTLOOK

Is this process to continue? Where is it to end? Is it likely to have important consequences for modern thinking at large? I have already indicated my views as to these matters. The process here in question is, on the whole, of real importance to the intellectual world at large, because Catholic Scholars are numerous, are often of great ability, and are men whose coöperation in the common interests of human thought is distinctly worth having. Unity of opinion is not so desirable, in this world, as is unity of spirit in the search for truth; and the later movement of Catholic thought has, on the whole, tended to a distinct increase in such unity between their activities and the world of modern inquiry. We who are without have no interest, as ourselves inquirers, in winning controversial victories over Catholics, or in converting them to our peculiar ideas. But we are interested in whatever helps them to take part in the common intellectual life of their time. We think that Leo, as a fact, helped them even more than he originally intended, to do just this thing. And if the process goes on unhindered, the final result must, we believe, prove very important both for Catholic thought, and for spiritual good-will among men. Of course, in this paper I have not attempted to estimate the vast forces that tend to keep Catholic thought conservative, and to crush out all these newer variations of opinion. Everyone knows that those conservative forces are vast, and that what I have here indicated forms only a part — and so far, doubtless, a relatively small part of modern Catholic mental life. But I have meant to indicate the presence of a certain leaven that may, in time, serve to leaven the whole lump.

Of "liberal Catholicism" we have heard a good deal of late. We usually hear of it in connection with the political, or, in general, with the worldly activities of the Church. I confess that, as a political institution, as an organization having worldly interests and ambitions, the Catholic Church never awakens my sympathy and seldom even arouses any considerable interest in my mind. For in respect of these worldly matters I can never fathom its true motives, nor understand its methods, while on the other hand I feel so sure of the ability of the modern world to take care of itself that I have no serious fear of the permanent triumph of what is called "clericalism." I recognize the practical importance of keeping safe the great principles of modern civilization. But I do not feel that these principles, at least in our country, are sufficiently endangered by any plans of clerical politicians to make the matter of our political relations to the Catholic Church one that has at present any great interest for me. On the other hand, the intellectual life of the Catholic Church seems to me something very interesting. The cause of sound thinking and of dispassionate inquiry has suffered so much in the past from dreary and bitter religious controversy that it is a welcome thing to see these symptoms of the coming of a time when the scholars of the Catholic Church may be willing to coöperate in the general progress of science and of philosophical inquiry rather than to condemn in block, as errors, thoughts which the clerical judges have not taken the trouble to understand. Is St. Thomas, the angelic doctor, destined to act as a peacemaker, and to teach his Church to love new light, even as, in his century, he also loved, and used, the new light that Aristotle seemed to him to bring?

If this result is to come about, it will inevitably involve, as I have pointed out, a certain assimilation of traditional Catholic ideas to those of modern thought. But I have, in addition, indicated what I firmly believe, namely, that such processes of assimilation are also inevitably mutual. I do not imagine either that the Catholic Church will ever abandon its characteristic dogmas, or that the modern thought which is now non-Catholic will ever again adopt those dogmas. But I do see that we who study modern philosophy must gain by understanding the point of view which scholasticism represents, and what we shall gain is especially an increase of our sense of the historical continuity of human thinking — a sense which religious controversy has often tended to confuse. St. Thomas and his fellows have something to say to us, as well as to Catholics, and I am glad to have it said. Meanwhile everybody has an interest in the substitution of reasonable mutual toleration, coöperation and understanding, for blind hostility. Hence, one watches with keen concern a process which seems to tend, in this sense, to the organization of a "liberal" form of Catholicism.

But will Catholic officialism — conservative as it is, political as its motives have to be, reactionary as its policy has so often been — will such officialism permit the new Catholic scholarship further liberty to develop on these lines? Will not the new Pope, whoever he may prove to be, undertake to bring to a pause the evolution of these tendencies towards a reform of Catholic philosophy, and towards an era of good feeling between Catholic and non-Catholic science and scholarship? I confess to a good deal of doubt upon this subject. I confess also that I am rather disposed to anticipate a reaction against all this natural, but, as I fancy, officially unexpected growth that has taken place in the world of Catholic scholarship within the last two decades. The Catholic Church is today, as of old, an institution under the control of men to whom scholarship and even wisdom will always be secondary to motives of a decidedly worldly sort. I cannot hope that the officials will, in the long run, tolerate the philosophers, unless the latter show themselves less vital in their inquiries, and less eager in their mental activities, than they have recently been.

But what an admirable opportunity for a genuine spiritual growth will be lost if Leo's revival of Catholic philosophy has even its first fruits cut off, and is not permitted to bear the still richer fruit that, in case it is unhindered, it will some day surely bring forth.